E-GOVERNMENT

ICT PROFESSIONALISM
AND COMPETENCES

SERVICE SCIENCE

T0180746

IFIP – The International Federation for Information Processing

IFIP was founded in 1960 under the auspices of UNESCO, following the First World Computer Congress held in Paris the previous year. An umbrella organization for societies working in information processing, IFIP's aim is two-fold: to support information processing within its member countries and to encourage technology transfer to developing nations. As its mission statement clearly states,

> *IFIP's mission is to be the leading, truly international, apolitical organization which encourages and assists in the development, exploitation and application of information technology for the benefit of all people.*

IFIP is a non-profitmaking organization, run almost solely by 2500 volunteers. It operates through a number of technical committees, which organize events and publications. IFIP's events range from an international congress to local seminars, but the most important are:

• The IFIP World Computer Congress, held every second year;
• Open conferences;
• Working conferences.

The flagship event is the IFIP World Computer Congress, at which both invited and contributed papers are presented. Contributed papers are rigorously refereed and the rejection rate is high.

As with the Congress, participation in the open conferences is open to all and papers may be invited or submitted. Again, submitted papers are stringently refereed.

The working conferences are structured differently. They are usually run by a working group and attendance is small and by invitation only. Their purpose is to create an atmosphere conducive to innovation and development. Refereeing is less rigorous and papers are subjected to extensive group discussion.

Publications arising from IFIP events vary. The papers presented at the IFIP World Computer Congress and at open conferences are published as conference proceedings, while the results of the working conferences are often published as collections of selected and edited papers.

Any national society whose primary activity is in information may apply to become a full member of IFIP, although full membership is restricted to one society per country. Full members are entitled to vote at the annual General Assembly, National societies preferring a less committed involvement may apply for associate or corresponding membership. Associate members enjoy the same benefits as full members, but without voting rights. Corresponding members are not represented in IFIP bodies. Affiliated membership is open to non-national societies, and individual and honorary membership schemes are also offered.

E-GOVERNMENT

ICT PROFESSIONALISM AND COMPETENCES

SERVICE SCIENCE

IFIP 20th World Computer Congress,
Industry-Oriented Conferences,
September 7-10, 2008, Milano, Italy

Edited by

Antonino Mazzeo
University of Naples
Italy

Roberto Bellini
AICA
Italy

Gianmario Motta
University of Pavia
Italy

 Springer

Editors
Antonino Mazzeo
Federico II
University of Naples
Italy

Roberto Bellini
AICA, Milano
Italy

Gianmario Motta
University of Pavia
Italy

p. cm. (IFIP International Federation for Information Processing, a Springer Series in Computer Science)

ISSN: 1571-5736 / 1861-2288 (Internet)
ISBN: 978-1-4419-3522-9   e-ISBN: 978-0-387-09712-1

Printed on acid-free paper

springer.com

IFIP 2008 World Computer Congress (WCC'08)

Message from the Chairs

Every two years, the International Federation for Information Processing hosts a major event which showcases the scientific endeavours of its over one hundred Technical Committees and Working Groups. 2008 sees the 20th World Computer Congress (WCC 2008) take place for the first time in Italy, in Milan from 7-10 September 2008, at the MIC - Milano Convention Centre. The Congress is hosted by the Italian Computer Society, AICA, under the chairmanship of Giulio Occhini.

The Congress runs as a federation of co-located conferences offered by the different IFIP bodies, under the chairmanship of the scientific chair, Judith Bishop. For this Congress, we have a larger than usual number of thirteen conferences, ranging from Theoretical Computer Science, to Open Source Systems, to Entertainment Computing. Some of these are established conferences that run each year and some represent new, breaking areas of computing. Each conference had a call for papers, an International Programme Committee of experts and a thorough peer reviewed process. The Congress received 661 papers for the thirteen conferences, and selected 375 from those representing an acceptance rate of 56% (averaged over all conferences).

An innovative feature of WCC 2008 is the setting aside of two hours each day for cross-sessions relating to the integration of business and research, featuring the use of IT in Italian industry, sport, fashion and so on. This part is organized by Ivo De Lotto. The Congress will be opened by representatives from government bodies and Societies associated with IT in Italy.

This volume is one of fourteen volumes associated with the scientific conferences and the industry sessions. Each covers a specific topic and separately or together they form a valuable record of the state of computing research in the world in 2008. Each volume was prepared for publication in the Springer IFIP Series by the conference's volume editors. The overall Chair for all the volumes published for the Congress is John Impagliazzo.

For full details on the Congress, refer to the webpage http://www.wcc2008.org.

Judith Bishop, South Africa, Co-Chair, International Program Committee
Ivo De Lotto, Italy, Co-Chair, International Program Committee
Giulio Occhini, Italy, Chair, Organizing Committee
John Impagliazzo, United States, Publications Chair

WCC 2008 Scientific Conferences

TC12	**AI**	Artificial Intelligence 2008
TC10	**BICC**	Biologically Inspired Cooperative Computing
WG 5.4	**CAI**	Computer-Aided Innovation (Topical Session)
WG 10.2	**DIPES**	Distributed and Parallel Embedded Systems
TC14	**ECS**	Entertainment Computing Symposium
TC3	**ED_L2L**	Learning to Live in the Knowledge Society
WG 9.7 **TC3**	**HCE3**	History of Computing and Education 3
TC13	**HCI**	Human Computer Interaction
TC8	**ISREP**	Information Systems Research, Education and Practice
WG 12.6	**KMIA**	Knowledge Management in Action
TC2 **WG 2.13**	**OSS**	Open Source Systems
TC11	**IFIP SEC**	Information Security Conference
TC1	**TCS**	Theoretical Computer Science

IFIP
- is the leading multinational, apolitical organization in Information and Communications Technologies and Sciences
- is recognized by United Nations and other world bodies
- represents IT Societies from 56 countries or regions, covering all 5 continents with a total membership of over half a million
- links more than 3500 scientists from Academia and Industry, organized in more than 101 Working Groups reporting to 13 Technical Committees
- sponsors 100 conferences yearly providing unparalleled coverage from theoretical informatics to the relationship between informatics and society including hardware and software technologies, and networked information systems

Details of the IFIP Technical Committees and Working Groups can be found on the website at http://www.ifip.org.

e-Government- Program Committee

Antonino Mazzeo Dip. Informatica e Sistemistica University of Naples Federico II, Italy (Chairman)
Paolo Prinetto, ICT Faculty of the Politecnico di Torino, Italy and University of Illinois at Chicago
Nicola Mazzocca, Dip. Informatica e Sistemistica, University of Naples Federico II, Italy
Gianluigi Benedetti, Ministero delle Riforme e Innovazione nella Pubblica Amministrazione, Italy
Floretta Rolleri, CNIPA Centro Nazionale per l'Informatica nella Pubblica Amministrazione, Italy
Mauro Calise, University of Naples Federico II and International Political Science Association, Italy
Carlo Batini, Dip. Informatica Sistemistica e Comunicazione of Milano Bicocca University, Italy
Mauro Pezzè, Dip. Informatica Sistemistica e Comunicazione of Milano Bicocca University, Italy
Maddalena Sorrentino, Dept. of Economics, Business and Statistics University of Milan, Italy
Derrick de Kerckhove, Dept. of French at the University of Toronto, Canada
Laurence T. Yang, Ph.D.Department of Computer Science, St. Francis Xavier University, Canada
Manish Gupta, Ph.D. CTO, India Systems and Technology Lab, IBM Bangalore, India

ICT Professionalism and Competences - Program Committee

Roberto Bellini, AICA, the Italian Computer Society (Chairman)
Renny Bakke Amundsen, DND, the Norwegian Computer Society
Moira De Roche, IFIP – I3P, International Professional Practice Programme, South Africa
Marco Ferretti, CINI, Consortium of Italian Universities for IT
Juan Garbajosa, Universidad Politecnica de Madrid, Spain
Roger Johnson, BCS, the British Computer Society, UK
Giulio Occhini, AICA, the Italian Computer Society
Franco Patini, Confindustria, Confederation of Italian Industry
Nello Scarabottolo, CRUI, Italian Universities Chancellors Conference
Niko Schlamberger, CEPIS, Council of European Professional Informatics Societies
Stephen Seidman, IEEE Computer Society
Paolo Schgör, AICA, the Italian Computer Society
Pietro Paolo Trimarchi, Ragioneria Generale dello Stato, Italian Ministry of Finance
Peter Weiss, GI, Gesellschaft für Informatik, Germany

Service Science- Program Committee

Contents

Service Science

E-GOVERNMENT

E-GOVERNMENT FOR SMALL LOCAL GOVERNMENT ORGANIZATIONS

Walter Castelnovo

Dipartimento di Scienze della Cultura, Politiche e dell'Informazione, Università dell'Insubria, via Carloni, 78 – 22100 Como (Italy), e-mail: walter.castelnovo@uninsubria.it

The Italian National Centre for Information Technology in Public Administration (CNIPA) introduced the concept of Local Alliances for Innovation (ALI) as the tool for the inclusion of small municipalities in the spread of E-Government in Italy. Based on the CNIPA's definition, the paper discusses the concept of ALI as an organizational model that can be resorted to in order to reduce the administrative fragmentation of the system of Local Government in Italy. By elaborating on the relation between the ALI model and the model of inter-municipal cooperation, the paper considers under what conditions an ALI could evolve into an Integrated System of Local Government, that is a system of Local Government Organizations strictly interoperable. Since it determines a form of virtual integration among the partners, an ISLG allows a simplification of the system of Local Government while preserving the autonomy of its members.

1 The inclusion of small municipalities in then spread of E-Government

Starting from the year 2002, the development of E-Government in Italy has been based mostly on projects funded under the National Action Plan for E-Government (DIT 2002), managed by the Italian National Centre for Information Technology in Public Administration (CNIPA). The National Action Plan has been based on two phases supporting innovation projects on a territorial level. The first phase started in 2002 with an announcement that funded 134 projects with 120 million euros (for an overall value of about 500 million euros).

The second phase, that is still going on, includes the funding of projects specifically devoted to the inclusion of small local government organizations (SLGOs, municipalities with less than 5000 inhabitants, that represent about the 72% of the Italian municipalities) in the spread of E-Government (CNIPA 2007a).

Please use the following format when citing this chapter:

Castelnovo, W., 2008, in IFIP International Federation for Information Processing, Volume 280; *E-Government; ICT Professionalism and Competences; Service Science*; Antonino Mazzeo, Roberto Bellini, Gianmario Motta; (Boston: Springer), pp. 1–10.

The need of such funding arises from the observation that SLGOS often lack the resources necessary for handling innovation projects.

A possible solution to this problem is the sharing of resources and competencies among SLGOs, based on the model of inter-municipal cooperation (Hulst and van Montfort 2007). For this reason CNIPA provides special funding for SLGOs that define cooperation agreements for the activation of Local Alliances for Innovation (ALI), based on the model of inter-municipal cooperation. (CNIPA 2007b).

CNIPA defines ALI as alliances of SLGOs promoting inter-municipal cooperation for the management of Information Systems, technological infrastructures and ICT -based services with the aim of:

- improving the back office activities of the member municipalities through the optimization of the use of human and financial resources;
- improving the quality of the services delivered to citizens and enterprises;
- improving the processes of inter-institutional cooperation among the organizations of the Public Administration;
- achieving economies of scale in the use of ICTs

CNIPA's announcement for the funding of the ALIs specifies some of their competences, which include the definition of cooperation agreements among SLGOs for the management of services, the definition of procedural and organizational standards in order to guarantee the optimal use of the shared resources, the improvement, both quantitative and qualitative, of the services available for citizens and enterprises.

To access the funding ALIs are required to deliver at least four services to the member municipalities, according to one of the following modalities:

1. assuming the responsibility for the management of the technological platform in ASP modality and delivering assistance and training activities;
2. supporting the municipalities in their contractual relations with service providers in case of outsourcing;
3. assuming the responsibility for the management of the whole service.

Whatever the model implemented, ALIs are required to aim at the optimal use of both the instrumental and professional resources available within the municipalities adhering to the aggregation. In fact, by resorting to resources already available (especially the professional competencies) ALIs can reduce the need to acquire new resources, that would imply the increasing of the costs for the functioning of the alliance.

In case the option (3) above had been selected, the optimal use of the professional competencies already available could be achieved either by transferring them to the ALI (which could affect the functioning of the organizations they leave) or by implementing a cooperation model based on the sharing of resources belonging to different organizations. In this case the ALI should guarantee a sharing of resources among partners that could be highly heterogeneous from the organizational point of view.

This paper will describe a process for inter-organizational integration that could be implemented by an ALI in order to evolve an aggregation of SLGOs into a system of partners strictly interoperable, also at the organizational level (which makes the sharing of professional competencies possible). More specifically, in section 2 the concept of Integrated System of Local Government (ISLG) will be introduced and the conditions enabling forms of strict inter-organizational cooperation (up to cooperability) will be considered. Finally, in section 3 a process for the implementation of an ISLG through the virtual integration of the members of an ALI will be described as a possible solution to the problem of the administrative fragmentation of the system of Local Government.

2 Inter-municipal cooperation and cooperability

Interoperability is a fundamental concept for inter-organizational cooperation. However, many different definitions of this concept can be found in literature, focusing on different aspects, as shown by the following definitions (AA.VV. 2007):

1. the ability of two or more systems or components to exchange and use information (IEEE 1990)
2. the ability to exchange data in a prescribed manner and the processing of such data to extract intelligible information that can be used to control/coordinate operations (NCS 1996)
3. the ability of the systems, units, or forces to provide and receive services from other systems, units, or forces and to use the services so interchanged to enable them to operate effectively together;
   the conditions achieved among communications-electronics systems or items of communications-electronics equipment when information or services can be exchanged directly and satisfactorily between them and/or their users;
   the capacity to integrate technology between or among different technical platforms. This form of integration is achieved through information engineering, which translates process requirements into software programs (DoD 2001).

The definitions (1) and (2) focus on systems inter-connectivity and components inter-changeability (Stegwee and Rukanova 2003), whereas the definition (3) adds to the concept of interoperability a different aspect concerning the ability of the partners of the cooperation to operate effectively together. Actually, although systems inter-connectivity and components inter-changeability can be considered as necessary conditions for inter-organizational cooperation, they cannot be considered as sufficient conditions.

Generally, inter-organizational cooperation does not concern simply information exchanges among different organizations; rather it concerns the capability of different organizations to operate together in order to achieve a common goal. In this sense, to enable an inter-organizational cooperation some form of organizational compatibility is needed, besides systems interoperability. This aspect of inter-organizational cooperation has been considered within the ATHENA project (ATHENA 2007) where an interoperability framework has been defined based on four layers of interoperability:

- Applications layer, data and communication components
- Knowledge layer: organizational roles, skills and competencies of employees and knowledge assets
- Business layer: business environment and business processes
- Semantic layer: support mutual understanding on all layers

With reference to E-Government, the multi-dimensionality of interoperability has been underlined also within the European Interoperability Framework for Pan-European E-Government (EIF) that aims at determining the conditions to make public administrations of EU countries interoperable. The framework considers three aspects of interoperability: technical interoperability, semantic interoperability and organisational interoperability (IDABC 2004).

Both ATHENA and the EIF define interoperability in a way that goes beyond the compatibility of systems and applications, recognizing the need to account for a broader concept of organization compatibility.

In a different context, concerning the definition of interoperability as an essential element for the effective formation of Joint, Allied or Coalition task forces, (Clark and Jones 1999) describes an organizational interoperability maturity model in which the organizational elements allowing a full compatibility of the partners are defined by four attributes characterizing inter-organizational cooperation. The attributes are Preparedness, Understanding, Command Style and Ethos. On the base of the different values such attributes can take, different levels of cooperability (Gompert and Nerlich 2002) can be defined as in the table 1 below:

Table 1. Organizational Maturity Model

Levels of coo-perability	Preparedness	Understanding	Command style	Ethos
Unified	Complete, normal day-to-day working	Shared	Homogeneous	Uniform
Combined	Detailed doctrine and experience in using it	Shared communications and shared knowledge	One chain of command and interaction with home organizations	Shared ethos but with influence from home organizations
Collaborative	General doctrine in place and some experience	Shared communications and shared knowledge about specific topics	Separate reporting lines of responsibility overlaid with a single command chain	Shared purpose; goals, value system significantly influenced by home organizations

| Ad hoc | General guidelines | Electronic communications and shared information | Separate reporting lines of responsibility | Shared purpose |
| Independent | No preparedness | Communication via phone, etc. | No interaction | Limited shared purpose |

The organizational interoperability maturity model described in (Clark, Jones 1999) exclusively considers the non-technical aspects of interoperability (Stewart, et al. 2004). As such, the organizational interoperability maturity model can be integrated with a description of the levels of Information Systems interoperability, for instance the one introduced in (AA.VV. 1998).

The correspondence among the levels of cooperability and the levels of Information Systems interoperability can be summarized as in table 2:

Table 2. Relation between the Organizational Maturity Model and the Levels of Information Systems Interoperability model.

Levels of cooperability	Levels of Information Systems Interoperability (LISI)
Unified	Enterprise (Universal): Interactive manipulation; Shared Data and applications
Combined	Domain (Integrated): Shared data; "Separate" applications
Collaborative	Functional (Distributed): Minimal common Functions; Separate data and applications
Ad hoc	Connected (Peer-to-Peer): Electronic connection; Separate data and applications
Independent	Isolated (Manual): Non-connected, use of manual gateways (diskettes, etc.)

The correspondences in Table 2 point out how the achievement of a certain level of cooperability (i.e. organizational interoperability) requires at least the achievement of the corresponding level of integration of the information systems; yet, without this implying that a close integration at the technological level can also determine a close integration at the organizational level.

The conditions characterizing the different levels of cooperability combined with the conditions characterizing the corresponding levels of information systems interoperability can be used to define the properties of a cooperation environment that can be implemented to support an inter-municipal cooperation. Depending on their more or less restrictive character, the conditions defining the cooperation environment can lead to more or less strict forms of partnership among SLGOs, up to the definition of an Integrated System of Local Government (ISLG), as described in (Castelnovo and Simonetta 2005, 2006).

An Integrated System of Local Government is made up of SLGOs that, on the basis of a preliminary sharing of interests (e.g. increasing both the efficiency and effectiveness of the administration, realization of economies of scale and of scope, management of technological and organizational innovation, etc.), jointly define systematic forms of cooperation based on the appropriate cooperation environment.

The conditions defining the cooperation environment concern both technological, operative, organizational and regulative conditions, as summarized in the table 3 below:

Table 3. Conditions for interoperability

	conditions concerning the sharing of infrastructures (virtual or physical) for the network communication
Technological interoperability	conditions defining the standards for communication and for systems interoperability
	conditions for the definition and the sharing of security policies for the access to information resources and for their use
	conditions concerning the standardization of the processes
	conditions concerning the definition of the operational standards
Operational interoperability	conditions for the sharing of the resources (physical resources, information and knowledge) within the network
	conditions for the monitoring of the activity of the members of the association
	conditions concerning the creation of shared managerial styles
Organizational interoperability	conditions for the creation of a shared organizational culture
	conditions concerning the definition of a shared system of values
	conditions for the definition of shared strategies and policies
Regulative interoperability	conditions concerning the adoption of a uniform and standardized language for process description;
	conditions concerning the definition of a shared organizational ontology and a shared terminology;
	conditions concerning the definition of a shared enterprise model

Within an ISLG, sharing a cooperative environment makes the partner strongly interoperable, not only on the technological level, but on the organizational level as well, up to the achievement of levels of full cooperability among the partners. In this sense, the setting up of an ISLG can be considered as the result of a process of joint technological and organizational innovation.

3 From Local Alliances for Innovation to Integrated Systems of Local Government

Although an integrated system is sometimes considered to be more tightly coupled than a system of interoperable components, it is useful to stress that the distinction between systems integration and systems interoperability (up to cooperability) is a question of perspective. What is seen from outside as the result of the integration of different organizations, from the point of view of the partners can simply be a system of independent and strictly cooperable organizations.

ISLG members are not, strictly speaking, integrated in the system, as that would imply an overcoming of their autonomy and individuality; actually, the implementation of an ISLG simply amounts to the sharing of the appropriate technological and organizational platform, which makes interorganizational cooperation easier. In this sense, the activation of an ISLG could also be considered as the result of the transformation of an aggregation of SLGOs, that could have been set up in order to achieve immediate results, in a long-term, well-structured cooperation.

The integration among the partners within an ISLG is only virtual and it is determined by the strengthening of the conditions of interoperability (up to cooperability) rather than by a real organizational integration. This has some particularly important consequences:

- each member of the ISLG keeps its autonomy, though it agrees to coordinate its activity with that of its partners and to systematically share resources (of various sorts) with them;
- as the integration is exclusively determined by the adoption of a shared cooperation environment, the activation of an ISLG:
  - could simply be the result of the transformation of an aggregation of SLGOs in a stable and strategic cooperation;
  - does not necessarily require the definition of new levels of government (as it happens in the case of institutionalized forms of integration.

Thanks to these characteristics, an ISLG can represent a solution to the need to overcome administrative fragmentation, in order to achieve the rationalization, the simplification and the reduction of the costs of the system of Local Government.

As defined by CNIPA, ALIs are simply aggregations of municipalities that define cooperation agreements for the implementation of various forms of inter-municipal cooperation. In broad terms, inter-municipal cooperation may be defined as an arrangement between two or more government organizations for accomplishing common goals, providing a service, or solving a mutual problem (Council of Europe 2007). In this sense, a municipality could resort to inter-municipal cooperation also for opportunistic reasons; for instance, taking advantage of favourable conditions (such as funding exclusively devoted to aggregations of municipalities) or solving an immediate problem. In case of an opportunistic cooperation, the same municipality can join different aggregations, even without territorial contiguity constraints; moreover, the cooperation could be episodic since it is not based on a long tem commitment to the partners.

However, in order to achieve the rationalization, the simplification and the reduction of the costs of the system of Local Government through inter-municipal cooperation, the aggregations that set up must necessarily be stable in time and respond to a strategic commitment of the partners towards the cooperation. By defining a cooperation agreement for the activation of an ALI, the members of an aggregation of municipality make such a commitment. However, the adhesion to an ALI by itself does not guarantee the stability of the cooperation. Actually, such a result could be achieved more easily through the sharing of a cooperative environment. In fact, sharing a cooperation environment means to adhere to the conditions of technical interoperability and, above all, to the cooperability constraints that define it. This can mitigate the opportunistic behaviour of the partners (which is one of the main causes of aggregation instability) and, therefore, can force the stability of an aggregation that turns into an ISLG.

From this point of view, an ALI can evolve into an ISLG as a result of an organizational innovation process that aims at the strengthening of the conditions for the cooperation. Such a process should be focused on the development and the subsequent adoption of a shared cooperation environment, mostly based on the non technical aspects of interoperability, as those considered in section 2 above.

As it has been defined, an ISLG simply determines a virtual integration among the partners and, as such, it does not depend on the geographical collocation of its members. However, since an ALI is defined on a territorial basis, an ALI that evolves into an ISLG keeps its territorial basis. This allows an ISLG to provide answers to the specific needs of a local community, both by delivering particular services required by the socio-economic local environment and by preserving the peculiar characteristics of the local system of Government.

The territorial basis of an ISLG does not preclude the possibility that, through the coordination of a higher institutional level authority, different ISLGs can be made cooperable. This could determine a further process of (virtual) integration on a larger territorial scale, allowing the systematic cooperation among different ISLGs defined at the local level.

From this point of view, it is possible to define a process for the reduction of the administrative fragmentation at the Local Government level that, starting from the activation of an ALI, could lead to a system of Local Government (virtually) integrated, for instance, at Regional level. Such a process could be based on the strengthening of the conditions for the inter-institutional cooperation among municipalities at the lowest level, and among ISLGs at a higher level.

This integration process, that can be considered as a process for the simplification of the system of Local Government, can be described also in terms of the maturity model for inter-municipal cooperation summarized in table 4:

Table 4. Maturity model for inter-municipal cooperation

Administrative fragmentation	Presence of completely independent organizations that have not defined any form of cooperation.
Episodic cooperations	Presence of different forms of inter-municipal cooperation, due to the necessity of taking advantage of favourable situations (such as funding exclusively devoted to aggregations of municipalities). The cooperation is opportunistic; the same municipality can join different aggregations,

	even without territorial contiguity constraints.
Stable aggregations (ALI)	Setting up of stable and multi-functional aggregations, which implement long-term sharing of different kinds of resources. The cooperation is no more opportunistic: joining an aggregation is a strategic decision.
Integrated Systems of Local Government	Stable aggregations involved in an integration process (in terms of co-operability conditions), setting up an integrated system. The inter-municipal cooperation turns into systematic sharing of information, technological and human resources.
Cooperation among ISLGs	The cooperation is not anymore restrained to a territorial area; different interoperable ISLGs can cooperate within a wider context defined by regional bounds.

4 Conclusions

Inter-municipal cooperation represents a well-known organizational model SLGOs can resort to in order to share resources that they individually lack. By assuming the Local Alliances for Innovation as the model for the inclusion of small municipalities in the spread of E-Government, the Italian National Centre for Information Technology in Public Administration acknowledges inter-municipal cooperation as a tool for the rationalization, the simplification and the reduction of the costs of the system of Local Government.

In the paper the achievement of these objectives has been related to the implementation of systematic forms of cooperation among municipalities belonging to stable aggregations. The stability of the aggregations can be forced by the adoption of a cooperation environment that, depending on the conditions characterizing it, can determine a form of virtual integration among the partners.

Such a virtual integration, achieved through the strengthening of the interoperability conditions (up to cooperability) allows a reduction of the administrative fragmentation, even in those contexts in which the simplification of the system of Local Government cannot be achieved by means of a forced merger of municipalities.

References

AA.VV. (2007), *Current Perspectives on Interoperability*, Technical Report, CMU/SEI-2004-TR-009 - ESC-TR-2004-009, Carnegie Mellon Software Engineering Institute.

AA.VV. (1998), *Levels of Information Systems Interoperability (LISI)*, C4ISR – Architecture Working Group"; online: www.dod.mil/nii/org/cio/i3/AWG_Digital_Library/pdfdocs/lisi.pdf.

ATHENA (2007), *Advanced Technologies for interoperability of Heterogeneous Enterprise Networks and their Applications* - an Integrated Project sponsored by the European Commission - www.athena-ip.org.

Castelnovo, W., Simonetta, M. (2005), "Organizing E-Government for Small Local Government Organizations", *Proceedings of the 5th European Conference on E-Government*, Antwerpen.

Castelnovo, W. and Simonetta, M. (2006), "Networks of SLGOs: from systems interoperability to organizational cooperability", *Proceedings of The 6th European Conference on E-Government*, Marburg.

Clark, T., Jones, R. (1999), "Organisational Interoperability Maturity Model for C2", *Poceedings of the Command and Control Research and Tecnology Symposium*, Newport.

CNIPA (2007a), *Linee di azione (II fase)*; online: http://www.cnipa.gov.it

CNIPA (2007b), *Avviso per il cofinanziamento di progetti proposti dalle Alleanze Locali per l'Innovazione (ALI)*; online: http://www.cnipa.gov.it

Council of Europe (2007), *Draft Report on Inter-Municipal Cooperation*, Directorate General I - Legal Affairs, Directorate of Cooperation for Local and Regional Democracy, Council of Europe, 2007.

DIT (2002), "Avviso per la selezione di progetti proposti dalle Regioni e dagli Enti locali per l'attuazione dell'e-Government", *Gazzetta Ufficiale*, n. 78, 3 April 2002.

DoD (2001), *Department of Defense Dictionary of Military and Associated Terms*, Operational Plans and Joint Force Development Directorate, Washington DC., online: http://www.dtic.mil/doctrine/jel/new_pubs/jp1_02.pdf.

Gompert, D. C., Nerlich, U. (2002), *Shoulder to Shoulder - The Road to U.S. European Military Cooperability. A German American Analysis*, RAND Corporation, on-line:http://www.rand.org/.

Hulst, R. and van Montfort, A.. (2007), *Inter-municipal Cooperation in Europe*, Springer, Dordrecht.

IDABC (2004), *European Interoperability Framework for Pan-European E-Government Services*. Version 1.0; online: europa.eu/idabc/.

IEEE (1990), *IEEE Standard Glossary of Software Engineering Terminology (IEEE Std 610.12-1990)*, The Institute of Electrical and Electronics Engineers, New York.

NCS (1996), *Telecommunications: Glossary of Telecommunication Terms (Federal Standard 1037C)*, National Communications System; online: http://www.its.bldrdoc.gov/fs-1037/.

Stegwee, R. A., Rukanova, B.D. (2003), Identification of different types of standards for domain-specific interoperability, Standard Making: A Critical Research Frontier for Information Systems, MISQ Special Issue Workshop.

Stewart, K., Clarke, H., Goillau, P., Verrall, N., Widdowson, M. (2004), *Non - technical Interoperability in Multinational Forces*, Command and Control Research and Technology Symposium - The Power of Information Age Concepts and Technologies, QinetiQ Ltd.

Why is *True* eGovernment still difficult to be achieved?

Fugini Mariagrazia[1], Maggiolini Piercarlo[2], Nanini Krysnaia[2]
[1]Department of Electronics and Information
[2]Department of Management Engineering
Politecnico di Milano
{mariagrazia.fugini,piercarlo.maggiolini}@polimi.it, k.nanini@hotmail.it
Boselli Roberto[3], Cesarini Mirko[3], Mezzanzanica Mario[3]
[3] Department of Statistics, Università degli Studi di Milano Bicocca,
{mirko.cesarini, mario.mezzanzanica}@unimib.it

Abstract The objective of this paper is to present a framework to understand the complex and ambiguous phenomenon of Electronic Government (eGovernment) and the several existing models that allow to understand it. Then, the paper discusses the main difficulties in achieving true eGovernment and a way to overcome them. In fact, the eGovernment label has been often given for granted by simply using ICT, e.g. exploiting interoperability frameworks or automatizing services in the Public Administrations. This gave the impression, or even the illusion, of an authentic quality improvement (in efficiency and effectiveness) in the exercise of government functions by different public entities. Actually, in most cases, what happened was only an enhancement in the provisioning of public services, rather than a true improvement of government activities. The paper discusses this misunderstanding and gives hints to achieve true eGovernment functions.

1. Introduction

Public Organizations essentially carry out two tasks, often in a mixed way, depending on the single Organization: 1) they provide **public services** to citizens; 2) they **govern** the collectivity (defined on a territorial basis), promoting and granting common interests (such as health, education, safety, housing, environment, and so on), according to the ways citizens have agreed upon such tasks (through participation – in various forms – to politics).

The two tasks are related. In particular, the first one acts as a tool for the second one, but still the government task does not reach its goal only by delivering public services. Reducing the **government tasks** to public services *provisioning* would mean reducing **citizens** as *consumers* of those services.

Nowadays, Information and Communication Technologies (ICTs) have been massively introduced in PAs (Public Administrations). Recently, the use, especially when innovative, of ICT in Public Sectors has been called *eGovernment (Electronic Government)*, giving the idea -or the illusion- of an improvement in

Please use the following format when citing this chapter:

Mariagrazia, F., et al., 2008, in IFIP International Federation for Information Processing, Volume 280; *E-Government; ICT Professionalism and Competences; Service Science*; Antonino Mazzeo, Roberto Bellini, Gianmario Motta; (Boston: Springer), pp. 11–20.

quality (in terms of efficiency and effectiveness) in government functions by Public Organizations.

By the way, in most cases up to now, what has happened -and is still happening- is more similar to an empowerment and improvement in the use and the provisioning of public services than a real technological support to government activities (including democratic participation).

Furthermore, it is wise questioning whether we are facing a pure terminological misunderstanding (in that case, it would be sufficient to substitute *eGovernment* with *e-Administration*), or rather a cultural change (transforming citizens from public services *consumers* to individuals who choose politicians really promoting the creation of infrastructures, even technological, supporting the community interests overcoming the idea –dated back to Aristotle– that individual wellness derives, first of all, from the "city" wellness).

The thesis we are intended to present, in order to give a contribution in terms of a theoretical and a methodological framework, is that ICTs (especially the one related to organizational innovations in PAs) can truly be a tool for e-Government, in the full meaning of this term.

The paper is organized as follows. Section 2 classifies PA functions, Information Systems supporting PA activities, and Social Systems. Section 3 illustrates PAs and models of employing ICT. Section 4 discusses on eGovernment as a tool for Government to improve political participation and what in our opinion are the difficulties in achieving true eGovernment.

2. Classifications of PA Functions, of PA Information Systems and of Social Systems

In order to understand the logics underlying the use of ICT and to identify the prevalent models in ICT adoption and diffusion, administrative functions can be classified as follows:

1. **Internal administration**, for example: human resources and financial management.
2. **Service delivery**, for any administered entity (citizens and socio-economic agents), such as water services, street cleaning and garbage removal services, healthcare and education, and so on.
3. **Government** (of collectivity and of her territory), through tools ranging from urban plans to laws on the job marketplace.

On the basis of such classification, we are presenting a taxonomy of PA Information Systems in the following paragraph.

2.1. A Classification of PA Information Systems

The trend in Information System development goes into two directions: Administrative and Statistical Information Systems.

a) **Administrative Information Systems:** These systems are devoted to *public administration management,* which is a well-defined and precise task. The systems are fed by *documents,* as sub-products of administrative acts, which represent the *Information sources.* This kind of systems have a well defined role for *who* uses information and the reasons *why* such information is used, evidencing the reasons of information creation.

Population registries, land registries, car registries, or company registries are examples of Administrative Information Systems.

b) **Statistical Information Systems:** Statistical Information Systems have no specific users, but they can rather be classified as *generic decision makers.* In these systems, information collection is typically based on census, polls, markets and registries analysis, inquiries, and so on.

Administrative and Statistical Information System often are inter-related, since their data sources can be used to feed them in one direction or vice versa. Actually, administrative information retrieval is used for statistical purposes: for example, acts related to building concessions can flow into Statistical Information Systems regarding the overall urban activities of a Municipality.

2.2. A Classification of Social Systems

A classification of the social systems affected by PA Information Systems is now given, focusing on the kind of integration and organization present among the social system components.

In our approach, Social Systems can be classified as follows: *a) Hyper-integrated Systems, b) Meso-integrated Systems,* and *c) Hypo-integrated Systems.*

a) Hyper-integrated Systems

These are, for instance, a family, a group, or a clan. They do not need formal and structured Information Systems to exchange information, due to the nature of the links among their members. Political parties (on - but not limited to - a local scale), where client-type relationships exist between administrators and citizens, are social phenomena that can be classified as hyper-integrated systems.

Even the related Information System does not need to be formally structured because both information exchanges and communications are informal (since they occur in a context where the transmission of traditions, moral values and norms, and a strong personalization of inter-individual relationships are the most relevant aspects). In this kind of systems, traditions represent the memory of the hyper-integrated organization, which becomes accessible only after a long apprenticeship (sometimes, a true initiation). The clan organization is not totally extraneous to PA systems, meant as a political system. In fact, such systems are based on trust, values, and norms through relationship sharing.

b) Meso-integrated Systems

Such systems are "Organizations" in their full meaning. E.g., the systems called *bureaucracies* are *meso-integrated* social systems. An industrial company is typically meso-integrated: each department aims at producing specific parts for the final assembly of the whole product. The whole company aims at achieving both revenues and profit, related to unit production and sale. Analogously, a Municipality conforms to a meso-integrated system: each councillorship provides services to the administered population, and favors its social and economic development.

c) Hypo-integrated Systems

A territorial collectivity (a Municipality or a Region) is Hypo-*integrated*. Each socio-economic unit (agricultural, industrial, commercial, etc.) produces goods or services, which are not *per se* oriented to the interest of the whole collectivity, but rather to the unit survival and development. Other samples of Hypo-integrated systems are the collectivities such as people, an ethnic group, or a Nation.

2.3. Comparison between meso- and hypo-integrated systems

In our approach, Municipalities and Regions (hence -*latu sensu*- Organizations) can be classified both as meso-integrated systems and (in the sense of territorial collectivities) as hypo-integrated systems. Therefore, it is worth detailing the differences between meso- and hyper-integrated systems (Tab.1).

In *meso-integrated systems* (which are social artifacts, that is, social systems specifically built for a purpose), the organizational structure ruling the subsystems is well identified, and the autonomy degree of the sub-systems is formally defined. Such systems can be easily represented by organizational workflow charts. The system dynamics is observable: a clearly located memory exists in the organization, and it is constituted by procedures and work methods more or less accessible and controllable. This means that in a meso-integrated system institutional and organizational tools can be exploited to *pilot* the system from one state to another: e.g., a manager can order an employee to perform a task.

Tab. 1: Features of meso- and hypo-integrated systems

MESO-INTREGRATED SYSTEMS
1. Each subsystem is clearly oriented to the common task
2. The structure is defined
3. The degree of autonomy of subsystems is formally defined
4. The system dynamics is sufficiently observable and controllable
5. The knowledge (memory) is localized
HYPO-INTEGRATED SYSTEMS
1. Each subsystem   per se is not targeted to the interest of the whole system
2. The structure is not evident
3. Subsystems have a high degree of autonomy
4. The system dynamics is scarcely observable and controllable
5. The knowledge (memory) is fragmented

Instead, hypo-integrated systems create *observation problems*, since memory is very fragmented: in fact, there are several operators inside who have a high degree of autonomy both in operative and decisional situations. The *structure* is clear in a hypo-integrated system (although being fluid, dynamic a d very fuzzy) but control *problems* occur. Municipality or Region administrators are not *owners* of their citizens: they cannot order to a farmer what should be planted or to a company what should be produced or purchased.

During the development of a Public Organization Information System, the Organization is often regarded as a bureaucratic structure, isolated from the territorial context, and operating to achieve only institutional purposes, following well-defined procedures on the basis of laws and norms. In other words, the trend is to limit the Public Organization as a meso-integrated system, while, in a more extended vision, the Municipality and the Region (to resume the above mentioned examples) are a territorial collectivity, and hence, hypo-integrated systems The bureaucratic structure is only a subset of a wider system, where the elective political entities, the administered community, and the whole territory of competence have to be considered according to a holistic view.

3. PA Organizations and Models Employing ICT

Basing upon the above proposed way of intending Public Organizations, we identify now four typologies of PA and the related models of Information Systems, according to the information exchange needs and use.

3.1. Bureaucratic Model

The Bureaucratic Model conceives a Public Organization as an entity whose task is to emit rules and to control their application: the PAs are in charge of legitimating public-interest matters. A strong separation between politicians and managers undergoes this model. In the bureaucratic model, the Administration is structured around the principle of the *conformity of acts,* that is, what is relevant for an action undergoes a predefined juridical function. Consequently, all the data generated by PA, are constituted by formal acts registering events (both internal and external), as referencing juridical acts.

Hence, ICT applications mainly take account of registry activities, taxation, certifications, and official acts management (deliberations, regulations, licenses, etc.).

3.2. Social Model

The social model regards the Administration as an organization, providing (directly or indirectly) services to the administered citizens. ICTs are used to provide services in a more effective way and the great part of interventions focuses on service automation. The implementation of new information services based on ICT adheres to this view: Public Organizations create special services to inform the community about service availability, about economic, cultural, or sport initiatives taking place in the territory of competence. Up to now, this model of PA and the related use of ICT, is what people call eGovernment.

3.3. Using ICT to Support the Social Model: e-Administration

As discussed previously, *eGovernment* has often been associated to: "PA supported by ICT". Initially, such support has been exploited to improve back-office activities: ICT infrastructure have been built meting the specific requirements of the administrative offices (supporting mainly the bureaucratic view, according to our scheme). ICT has played the role of bureaucratic activities supporter for a long time, before it began to overcome the boundaries and became a powerful means to foster interaction with citizens and enterprises on the territory. For several PAs, Internet has immediately resulted in an improvement in terms of availability – web sites are open 24/7 – and of information retrieval - web sites easily retrieve information with a good degree of interaction from home/office. The further step has been to enable on-line form filling: in fact, previously, the forms were downloadable via network but they had to be filled in manually. What became clear soon was that the global rethinking of the procedures, in order to better exploit the Internet and its related technologies.

Such an evolution is nowadays a reality in Europe, but still its development speed varies from Country to Country. Relevant differences can be observerd not only among different Countries, but also –and this is interesting– among population subsets. E.g., services specifically targeted to the enterprises are more developed than those offered to the private citizens.

From various surveys, the emerging idea is that *eGovernment,* is, till now, essentially limited to the stage of *e-Administration.*

In recent years, ICT has been contributing to make services more and more simple and integrated into a network perspective. Anyway, there are already many problems to solve, due to *organizational barriers* (opposition to change, obsolete norms) and to *technical barriers* (e.g., interoperability matters due to obsolete technologies, security and safety, multi-channel devices, and so on).

The great expectation in a significant cost reduction has been the primary goal, leading the development of eGovernment. Actually, such an expectation has turned out to be illusory. The reason is that differently from private organizations (that can select their customers) PA can not refuse to interact with "costly customers", especially since these are users who mostly have to relay on public services (e.g., elderly, handicapped, sick or poor people). Actually, e-Services are added on top of existing services, rather than refactorying them. It is important to understand that eGovernment services can't be regarded as separate from the existing channels of off-line provisioning, i.e., traditional channels based on personal contacts, which often need to be maintained or empowered to grant or improve the quality of service.

3.4. "Inclusive" eGovernment

EGovernment (even when limited to e-Administration) should be targeted to provide public services accessible and relevant for *each* citizen or enterprise (Liikanen, 2003). This means that eGovernment should provide not only efficiency (typical to the enterprises), but also equity, i.e., equal rights and participation opportunities for all, and should actuate practically what Liikanen calls *inclusion*.

Equity is the most important topic for social justice but inclusion is relevant from an economic viewpoint, too: exclusion represents a cost in terms of underutilization of human capital. EGovernment will have its maximum completion when all citizens will be enabled to use technological devices, even though they have low competences, or live in remote regions, or have low incomes, or, in addition, have specific psychological or physical needs.

We have already underlined that Government differs from an enterprise in that it cannot choose its customers, but, instead, it has to serve anybody's needs. If enterprises can focus on efficiency, PA must pursuit both efficiency and equity. From the technological point of view, the devices have to be accurately chosen in order to reach all the population in an equity perspective. For this reason, promoting on-line services only by means of PC would mean excluding a great part of people who are "digitally divided". The number of accesses to Internet via a PC is growing every day; nevertheless, the same on-line services delivered though the Internet could be also delivered by means of, say, interactive TV technology, as TV surely reaches almost all the families. Moreover, other digital devices able to connect to the Internet are rapidly spreading, (e.g., mobile phones, Pocket Digital Assistants and so on), especially among young people.

In summary, a *multi-channel* approach to information provisioning is needed. However, managing efficiently public service delivery through a multi-channel platform is still a hard challenge and calls for a lot of effort, both in terms of money, technologies and human resources. Furthermore, the risk to aggravate the already existing and heavy *"Digital Divide"* is behind the corner.

3.5. Political Model

According to the Political Model, PA are organizations of political *governance*, that is, the center of *socio-economical* and *territorial planning*. The specific nature of the PA as a public entity for political governance emerges straightly. We are now focusing on Municipalities, Provinces or Regions in terms of *Organizations*, to rather privilege them as *Collectivities and Territorial Areas*.

PA are well organized and defined entities with juridical orientations and regulations; they have workforce, organizational structures, customers and users. But, beside this, they represent a small part of complex social and territorial systems where people and socio-economic units are integral elements of the administered collectivity. ICT, in this framework, is helpful for:

- governing and controlling political and socio-economic phenomena, creating a qualified information-based network supporting the government activity and planning (in this view, sometimes the term eGovernance is appropriate);
- favoring the relationships between the "Government" (and its institutions) and citizens (single and in associations), allowing their participation and control in the government activities. In this case, it is more appropriate to talk about e-Democracy).

3.6. Clan Model

Finally, the view of the Administration as a "clan" coexists with the other visions, but the "clan" dimension is very important when a relationship (based upon trust) links electors and elected, in the sense of representatives and represented.

Often, the word "clan" assumes a negative connotation. We go over this limited perspective since we simply intend to put into evidence a specific mode of exchanging information in a social system, as the clan organization is.

"Party-cracy" (the occupation of PA by parties) and "lobbing", together with "favoritism groups", represent the degenerated aspects of such an organizational model. However, every time we face a democratic relationship based on trust, involving citizens and representatives, we are in presence of clan logic.

Such a form of clan-based operation is present in most social systems. Anyway, where such organizational form is privileged, it impacts also on the way Information Systems are interpreted and created. Information exchange and personal relationships are going to be informal, as they involve elective organizations. The information exchange is also informal between these entities and the bureaucratic structure, between public administrators and citizens (electors), organized in parties, associations, pressing groups, etc.

If this clan model is ignored, the risk is to disregard a notable (and important) part of the information flow, which is relevant also for the government of the collectivity. In this context, the fundamental role of *Civic Networks* should be analyzed deeply.

4. eGovernment as a Tool for Government and Political Participation

Going back to Liikanen's work, eGovernment, first should allow citizens to know how their central, regional and local Administrations operate. Moreover, it should enable people to participate in the decisional processes from the beginning, allowing them also to monitor the expenses of public money.

EGovernment, in this sense, could be a tool to realize **Open Government**: *"eGovernment should help democracy to function better"*. This means to increase population's involvement and participation in social and political initiatives. Every step of the decisional process should be clear. Open Government, hence, means also increased transparency and responsibility, since they represent a necessity to fight corruption and fraud.

4.1. Why Is It So Difficult to Achieve True eGovernmet?

Taking into account the models of PA and their related needs for adequate Information Systems, what is going to be considered now is the

This section is focusing on the reason why ICT is so rarely used to support government activities, taking into account the models of PA previously introduced and their related Information System requirements. Some objective difficulties can be identified, besides the lack of political wills on these themes.

Information belongs to the whole in a scattered way, since

The main difficulty in the realization of *hypo-integrated Information Systems* -and real eGovernment- (e.g. territorial and socio-economic Information Systems) stands in that information describing the several elements of a community (socio-economic and institutional actors) is minimally owned by Public Organizations, since it is disseminated and distributed on the territory: consequently, knowledge is fragmented and is hold by single social units. Under which conditions is it then possible that single social units share their knowledge within the PA context? In our opinion, this is possible only if *information suppliers* are, directly or indirectly, involved in the information flow either as users or as simple beneficiaries of its exchange. In other words, single social units (families, enterprises, associations, etc.) would rather exchange their personal knowledge only if aware of the advantages they could gain back. Furthermore, knowledge sharing will be more easily set up if collaboration occurs within the exchange process: an *information agreement* is needed in order to set up and maintain the system (Ciborra et al. 1987). A further reason in adopting a *contractual approach* to Information Systems relies on the observation of social systems: political ones can be described as *negotiated exchange networks*. Then, the same Information Systems become a support to negotiation and exchange regulation processes.

Governance and its supporting decisional and Information Systems can be interpreted similarly. According to this approach, public programs and planning are not conceived only as tools of corrective intervention of spontaneous initiatives on the territory, but rather as negotiation and intermediation tools among the different elements playing in the hypo-integrated territorial systems (political parties, trade-unions, economic groups, other PA, etc.). Defining socio-economic targets is not an unilateral act of PAs, but rather the result of a negotiation process carried out by numerous institutional actors, having political, social, and economic nature. Moreover, the negotiation process (both explicit or implicit) does not take into account only the process goals, but also of the *indicators* to be adopted to outline needs and requirements, or to define standards. The target of the negotiations are the same *data* that move and feed the government activities as well. Otherwise, it would be hard to understand, for example, the great efforts (often successful, unfortunately), operated by groups of constituted interests and by the same Governments to condition mass media.

Only after understanding the need for the redefinition of government activity, we could achieve a real eGovernment and then move from actual *e-Administration* to *eGovernance* and *e-Democracy* (Lenihan, 2002). Table 2 helps to articulate and understand what is included in the different acceptations of eGovernment.

Tab. 2 Correspondence between models of PA and types of eGovernment

Public Administration Models	eGovernment Types
Bureaucratic Model	eAdministration
Social Model	EAdministration (ePublic Services)
Political Model	Actual eGovernment (eGovernance; eDemocracy)
"Clan" Model	eDemocracy; Civic Networks

5. Acknowledgments.

This paper has been partially supported by the Italian TEKNE Project.

References

- Ciborra, C., and Gasbarri, G., and Maggiolini P. "System design for local authorities: Participation based on 'Information Contracts'", in *System design for human development and productivity: Participation and beyond,* P. Docherty, and Fuchs-Kittowski K., and Kolm P., and Mathiassen L. (eds), North-Holland, Amsterdam, 1987

- Lenihan, D.G. "Realigning Governance: From EGovernment to E-Democracy", *Centre for Collaborative Government*, Ottawa, April 2002

- Liikanen, E. "EGovernment and the European Union", *UPGrade*, Vol. IV, No. 2, April 2003

A normative approach to democracy in the electronic government framework

Andrea Maggipinto
C.I.R.S.F.I.D., University of Bologna
andrea.maggipinto@unibo.it

Ezio Visconti
Osservatorio "Centro Studi Informatica Giuridica" - Milan
osservatorio.mi@csig.it

Abstract. The process of modernization in the public administrations is considered to be the result of the implementation of computer science applications and digital technologies in the Public Administration (PA) for achieving institutional functions. The so called "electronic government" is one of the key objectives laid out in DG Information Society's i2010 Action plan, in which Europe aims to bring administrations closer to citizens, for example by providing on line public services. In this scenario of changing of means and goals, the electronic dialogue between agents – i.e. Public Administrations, citizens and enterprises – represents the key element for the development of the public sector. But e-government is neither a simple tool to provide better services in a better way by PA. to citizens nor a simple question of downsizing the administration (the back office) and up-sizing services (the front-office) – i.e. a rebalancing from administration to services on a planned and sensible basis. Modern democracies are facing new challenges through the communication and information technology. The expression "electronic democracy" is characterized by the modality of citizens direct participation in the political life. In truth, this expression evokes wider and universal values.

1 Introduction

The process of modernization in the public administrations is often considered to be the result of the implementation of computer science applications and digital technologies in the Public Administration (PA) for achieving institutional functions, i.e. increasing the legitimacy, accountability and transparency of the decision-making process and involving them citizens directly in the policy process.

In particular, the European Community has recognized the importance of introducing technologies in public administrations to improve the organization, the effectiveness of the system and its transparency. In fact, the so called "electronic government" is one of the key objectives laid out in DG Information Society's i2010 Action plan [1], in which Europe aims to bring administrations closer to citizens, for example by providing on line public services. New digital technolo-

Please use the following format when citing this chapter:

Maggipinto, A. and Visconti, E., 2008, in IFIP International Federation for Information Processing, Volume 280; *E-Government; ICT Professionalism and Competences; Service Science*; Antonino Mazzeo, Roberto Bellini, Gianmario Motta; (Boston: Springer), pp. 21–29.

gies, supporting transparency and participation, represent a way for good governance and to exercise civil and political rights.

Like in every sector of the social organization, the so called "public digital
revolution" is based on what normally is called "Information and Communication
Technology" (ICT), the technology for the elaboration and the transmission of
electronic information.

2 Framework: e-government and the electronic dialogue

New instruments and objects have emerged from this technological scenario
which arose for instance in Italy in a historical moment when the Italian Public
Administration had just begun a process of organizational and procedural modernization with Laws nn. 142 and 241 in 1990. This technology impact is only
relevant if it accomplishes the primary objective of the modernization process,
namely simplification, transparency and social equality – into effect.

The "electronic government", or e-government, is a complex and multidimen-
sional issue.

The European Commission defines it "as the use of information and communication technologies in public administrations combined with organisational change
and new skills in order to improve public services and democratic processes and
strenghthen support to public policies" [2].

The electronic government is not just ICTs: it also includes rules and procedures, because the public administration cannot innovate without a normative
drive.

Electronic government also includes organization and processes. It starts with a
deep analysis and a re-engineering of internal and external processes within an organization. Activities are subjected to a profound redesign and restructuring from
a procedural, an organizational, and a regulative point of view. Processes, organization, rules and best practices are identified because they are considered sources
of knowledge for e-government plan.

But electronic government also involves communication, interface methods and
metaphors. For example, public services are planned and grouped in "life events",
according to the flows of events in everyday life; the same goes for the enterprises. Moreover, multi-channel accesses should be guaranteed: the web, mobile
phones, call centres, one-stop shops, earth digital television.

In this scenario of changing of means and goals, the electronic dialogue between agents – i.e. Public Administrations (PPAA), citizens and enterprises -
represents the key element for the development of the public sector. This interactive communication – not a mere unidirectional flow of information from Institutions to the citizen through often over informative websites – is able to carry out a
sharing of information and knowledge that is both an instrument and the main task
for the public administrations in the relationship with the citizens.

3 European action plan

As the use of ICT grows, so does its impact on society, also in the relationships between Institutions and citizens.

E-government is expected to improve and accelerate administrative efficiency in order to reach the EU's Lisbon targets of sustainable economic growth and competitiveness. The Commission is encouraging member states' actions by financing projects and securing the technical interoperability of e-government services across Europe.

In particular, the Member States have to achieve an Inclusive European Information Society, as we can see in the third priority of i2010 Action plan: "achieving an Inclusive European Information Society that promotes growth and jobs in a manner that is consistent with sustainable development and that prioritises better public services and quality of life".

"Electronic inclusion" aims to prevent the risks of digital exclusion, that is to ensure that disadvantaged people are not left behind and to avoid new forms of exclusion due to lack of digital literacy or of Internet access. At the same time e-inclusion also means tapping new digital opportunities for the inclusion of socially disadvantaged people and less-favoured areas. The Information Society has the potential to distribute more equally knowledge resources, to offer new job opportunities, also by overcoming the traditional barriers to mobility and geographic distance, and to make the Institutions closer to the citizens.

"Inclusive eGovernment" is the use of ICT to provide public services that enrich citizen's lives, stimulate public participation in the community, strengthen democracy and reach out to people at risk of social, economic or digital exclusion.

4 Participation and transparency

Internet represents a great instrument for sharing and meeting ideas, also political. That's the reason why is undeniable that the Network has a social function. So it has a direct effect also on the relationships between Citizens and Institutions.

Quite often the expression "electronic democracy" (or e-democracy) is characterized by the modality of citizens direct participation in the political life. In truth, this expression evokes wider and universal values.

It is not possible to define the unique model of democratic State. There are many reasons (above all, extra-legal) on which the choice towards a particular kind of state and system of government are made, and these reasons surely cannot be conditioned by the introduction of new technologies. The before mentioned instead facilitates the Institutions to more efficiently manage the procedures in which the State functions, also if these technological instruments are used by direct, deliberative or representative democracy.

The governance of technological innovation represents a way to fuel the continuous renewal towards more efficient democratic models. The collaboration between citizens and Institutions is only a positive aspect if it's well planned and constructed. However, there are two reasons for which the instruments of direct participation do not represent the main aspect of the technological innovation in the digital era.

Firstly, in the so called "advance democracies" it seems clear that the recognition of individual rights lessens the citizens political involvement and their interest in Institutional activities. Whereas, in developing countries, where there's a lack of individual rights, there seems to be more political involvement from the citizens through direct participation mechanisms.

Secondly, the real obstacles of the direct citizen participation in the law making process and decision making should be considered. They are not surely technological, but organizational, cultural and also constitutional. So, before planning technological instruments for direct participation, it would be opportune to consider all the aspects and the questions related to the direct participation mechanisms.

The pluralistic theory underlines nowadays the crisis of the representative democracy, so maybe it would be logical that the associations and the interest groups should get more involved into political life.

The technological society shows the problem of the democratic society: the necessity to reduce the complexity of the problems, so these can be achieved by the democratic processes.

The interdependence of the social sectors makes worse the complexity of the political decisions. In this technical-scientific and highly organized society, there is the risk of the discrepancy between social needs and decisional competences.

It isn't by chance that in Italy mechanisms – like the public consultations – have been introduced to achieve the goal of involving the social organizations and to better satisfy the social needs.

In connection with the instruments of participation, it will be decisive the way in which in Italy the principle of the Article 9 of the D.Lgs. 82/2005 (the "Code of the Digital Administration") will be achieved: "The State favours every use of new technologies in order to promote a greater participation of the citizens, also living abroad, to the democratic process and in order to facilitate the exercise of the political and civil rights, both individual and general rights".

The participation of the citizens to the political life will be possible through mechanisms that involve the communities and the political groups, based on the principle of liberty and equality. These mechanisms of "structured participation" represent a big incentive for the promotion of the associations: the communities – local or global ones – have today the possibility to create discussions and cooperation through the Internet.

This way of organized collaboration would be useful to mediate between individual interests and political power, a method for developing democracy and the e-government plans. The functional efficiency of the Institutions and the public administrations will depend on this mediations.

But transparency is also an important principle, one of the main elements of democracy, because describe the visibility of all institutions actions to the "world out there". It's the essential condition for the control of governments and parliaments; it's a "democratic imperative".

Each government process has to be made trackable and all documents, messages and work flow steps have to be made identifiable at the moment of querying itself and backwards to earlier moments.

Transparency of government indicates the willingness to take responsibility and provide legitimacy of all governmental actions to citizens and even pressure groups. The public value of transparency is the support it provides for the legitimacy of any given government, enabling criticism and proof of equal treatment before the law.

But openness therefore helps to ensure that the citizen, who, being made aware of both the internal functioning of the government and of the information on which decisions are based, is equipped to actively participate in the decision making process.

4 Technologies and preconditions of democracy

Modern democracies are facing new challenges through the communication and information technology.

First of all, the risk of divergence between universal constitutional principles and principles that regulate Governments action. The formal acknowledgment of individual rights does not assure a coherent exercise of the political and the administrative power. It is necessary to overcome the compromise determined by the social usefulness and political necessity. This compromise could make individual rights less effective.

In the "Information Society", equal conditions of access to the information must be guaranteed to put the equality principle into effect.

The governments have to write up preconditions on which the self-determination of the citizens is based, in order to avoid the otherwise unavoidable social divide (both generational and territorial).

The divide between rich and poor has also other deep roots, but we believe that the access to the information represents one of the conditions for the equality of the citizens in the free exercise of the political and civil rights.

The Public Institutions have the task of assuring intellectual formation of the citizens and the employees in computer science according to articles 8 and 13 of the Code of the Digital Administration. This intellectual formation is indispensable for the effective employment of new technologies in the relationships with Public Administration. The governments must assure an efficient scholastic system, to achieve an adequate level of knowledge of technologies that is necessary for the socialization and the intellectual and cultural formation of citizens.

But this formation is only useful in a scenario in which people are allowed to use technological instruments. In fact the so called "digital divide" represents the inequality of citizens both in their abilities to use new technologies and in the conditions of access to them.

In a recent opinion adopted by the Committee of the Regions [3], two kind of digital divide are stressed:

1. the first one is the "infrastructural digital divide", whereby the gap between those living in areas where advanced infrastructure and services are available and those living in areas with permanent geographical and natural handicaps where such infrastructure is lacking. This is a substantial barrier to the participation of all in the Information Society and to the possibility to follow innovative ways of interacting with Institutions and local administrations. The Committee calls it "a very real and substantial democratic deficit";

2. the second one is the "cultural digital divide", a gap in the knowledge needed to become a user of ICT Services between new and old Member States, between one Member State and another, between urban and rural areas and between the different generations and social classes that make up European society.

The Commission has made a communication [4] focused on the territorial divide regarding broadband access. It aims to make governments and institutions at all levels aware of the importance of this divide and of the concerns about the lack of adequate broadband services in the less developed areas of the Union. The Communication implements one of the priorities of the i2010 initiative – a European Initiative for growth and employment.

In the Communication, the Commission says: "Governments at all levels have recognised the impact that broadband may have on everyday lives and are committed to ensuring that its benefits are made available to all". And in particular on the e-government: "Broadband improves the capability of eGovernment services and allows a better interaction between governments, easing access to government for citizens and businesses. It facilitates the development of high-quality services and may increase organisational performance resulting in efficiency gains for the public administrations".

As new technologies have a strong impact on the social structure and create the conditions of its emancipation, the digital divide instead frustrates the any democratic development. In a technologically advanced society a "real citizenship" could be only if there are all the social and cultural preconditions.

Once these preconditions of democracy are created, the demand for electronic interaction and the ability of the PPAA to satisfy this demand will initiate a virtuous process that will carry the public sector to the complete innovation.

It's obvious that technologically neutral choices must be undertaken which mustn't lead to a specific "tecno-dependency".

We believe technology is not an independent entity that produces social effects. In the analysis of the relationships between society and technology, it's therefore necessary to reconsider the thesis on the social changes caused by technology. The exact contrary is also true: the society influences the technology and it governs (or should govern) the technological progress in accordance with the social needs.

As already emerged in others fields (for example the protection of environment as a common good), the Government should make political choices keeping in mind the rights of the citizens of tomorrow, also in relation to the technological progress.

The rights of the future generations will also depend upon the choices that Countries make in the modernization process of public sector.

5 Governance?

E-government is neither a simple tool to provide better services in a better way by P.A. to citizens nor a simple question of down-sizing the administration (the back office) and up-sizing services (the front-office) – i.e. a rebalancing from administration to services on a planned and sensible basis.

Indeed according to Erkki Liikanen, member of the European Commission, it "should help to make democracy function better ... increasing democratic participation and involvement" [5].

To put briefly: E-government is a tool that promise to fulfill the conditions of good governance (not simply governance!), i.e "a method/mechanism for dealing with a broad range of problem/conflicts in which actors regularly arrive at mutually satisfactory and binding decisions by negotiating with each other and cooperating in the implementation of these decisions" [6], a method/mechanism having, as stated by the Commission of the European Communities [7], a set of five major characteristics, namely openness, participation, accountability, effectiveness and coherence.

Now, although there has been a god deal of thinking and writing about governance, the term remains largely descriptive rather than explanatory, ranging from a state-centric approach, in which government is the most important actor and steers society through authority (governance with government) to a network approach, stressing social systems autopoietic and self organizing structure (governance without government).

In between the two extremes of governance we find other more moderate approaches considering governance as a socio-political and linguistic process, such the so called "Duch School" where governance "is cooperative rather than adversarial, with policy outcomes resulting from overcoming the decisional and coordination problems inherent in large complex policy arena" [8].

It is not the aim of our paper to discuss deeply this huge amount of different conceptions of governance and the even more understandings of different modes of governance. We simply argue that any governance model is an idealised-normative model strangely oblivious of the contradictory tensions in which any form of governing is inevitably embedded [9].

What is missing in the governance literature are - let apart the very complicated question relating to the actual meaning of terms such state and civil society and their relationship, i.e. is ontological, epistemological and methodological value - "the relations of domination or subordination within governance, between levels of governance and in the context of wider political-economic transformations" [9].

In other words and to conclude this short overview of the governance theme: what governance theorist fails to take into account is what Michel Foucault calls "governmentality", i.e the dramatic expansion in the scope of government, featuring an increase in the number and size of the governmental calculation mechanisms in order to produce the citizen best suited to fulfil governments' policies, through the elaboration and implementation of specific technologies of power (mentalities, rationalities, and techniques) aiming at governing subjects [10, 11].

In this perspective, democracy is not mainly elections, laws, and institutions but a society, a lived cultural experience, "not just out there in the public sphere," as Barbara Cruikshank [12] has put it, "but in here, at the very soul of subjectivity." Government is best conceived not as prime mover but as catalyst and resource of citizens, neither the problem nor the solution.

Democracy is, in fact, an "ideal form of life" (Karl Polanyi). It occurs in multiple sites, enlists multiple talents in addressing public problems, and results in multiple forms of strategic relationships of power and, at the same time, in strategies and conducts of common wealth. Resistance – positive resistance – is no longer merely reversal, but consists in a subject's becoming-autonomous within a structured set of institutions and practices through immanent critique.

Someone of you, we hope many, probably remember the famous dialogue between Alice and Humpty Dumpty in Lewis Carroll's famous novel, Through the Looking-Glass; a dialogue in which the two characters are discussing about semantic and pragmatic.

"When we use a word," Humpty Dumpty say, "it means just what we choose it to mean - neither more nor less". To this troublesome statement Alice objects the following: "The question is whether you can make words mean so many different things". And that is the answer by Humpty Dumpty: "The question is which is to be master - that's all".

Is the governance literature a form of humptydumptyan theory?

References

1. i2010 - A European Information Society for growth and employment. Communication from the Commission to the Council, the European Parliament, the European economic and social committee and the committee of the regions. Brussels, 1.06.2005 COM (2005) 229 final.

2. The Role of eGovernment for Europe's Future. Communication from the Commission to the Council, the European Parliament, the European economic and social committee and the committee of the regions. Brussels, 26.9.2003 COM (2003) 567 final.

3. Opinion of the Committee of the Regions on Bridging the Broadband Gap and i2010 eGovernment Action Plan. 02.13.2007, 2007/C - 146/09.

4. Bridging the Broadband Gap. Communication from the Commission to the Council, the European Parliament, the European economic and social committee and the committee of the regions. Brussels, 20.3.2006, COM (2006) 129 final.

5. E. Liikanen, "e-Government and the European Union", speech at The Internet and the City Conference 'Local Government in the Information Society'. Barcelona, 21.3.2003. UPGRADE - The European Journal for the Informatics Professionals, vol. IV, no 2, April 2003, p. 7.

6. P.C. Schmitter, Participation in governance arrangements: is there any reason to expect it will achieve 'sustainable and innovative policies in a multi-level context'?, in J.R. Grote, B. Gbikpi (eds.) Participatory Governance. Political and Societal Implications, Opladen: Leske and Budrich, 2002, pp. 51-69.

7. Commission of the European Communities, European Governance. A white paper (COM 2001) 428 final, Brussels: CEC.

8. B.G. Peters, Governance: A Garbage Can Perspective, in Rehie Politikwissenschaft / Political Science Studies, Wien, 2002.

9. E. Swyngedouw, Let the People Govern? Civil Society, Governmentality and Governance-Beyond –the –State, available at www.ru.nl/socgeo/colloquium/humboldt.pdf

10. M. Foucault, Il faut défendre la société. Cours au Collège de France 1976, Paris: Gallimard/Seuil, 1997.

11. M. Foucault, The Subject and the Power, in H. Dreyfus, P. Rabinow, Michel Foucault: Beyond Structuralism and Hermeneutics, Brighton: Harvester, 1982.

12. B. Cruikshank, The Will to Empower: Democratic Citizens and other Subjects, Ithaca, N.Y., Cornell Un. Press, 1999.

Knowledge Representation and Management for E-Government Documents

Flora Amato, Antonino Mazzeo, Antonio Penta and Antonio Picariello
Universitá di Napoli "Federico II", Italy
Dipartimento di Informatica e Sistemistica, via Claudio 21, 80125, Naples
{*flora.amato, mazzeo, a.penta, picus*}@unina.it

Abstract In the last few years bureaucratic procedures didn't show a significant reduction in the volume of paper documents created. In order to reduce the huge amount of space for archiving and preserving documents and to speed up the secarh process, a semantic-based dematerialization process should be performed. In this paper we describe a novel system that manages several kind of bureaucratic documents in the e-gov domain, automatically extracts several interesting information and produces a suitable semantic representation that may be considered as the first step towards a full automated document management system.

1 Introduction

The presence of a great amount of information is typical for bureaucratic processes, such as the ones related to public administrations. Such information is often recorded on papers, or in a digital but not unique format, and the related management process is not well-structured and very expensive, both in terms of space used for storing documents, and in terms of time spent for searching documents in archives.

In addition, the manual management of these documents is absolutely not error-free. The aims of this paper is the definition and the design of methodologies and techniques for synctatic-semantic documents management, and in particular, for information retrieval aims. Text processing is very interesting for e-government related activities: public or private government structures, in general, might be very interested in this kind of processes.

The dematerialization activity uses different techniques from interdisciplinary fields: in particular, several efforts have been done regarding legal ontologies, both from a theoretical – in order to define legal lexical dictionaries – and for the application point of view, as for instance can be evidenced from the large number of e-gov initiatives in Europe – putting a great emphasis on the study of the struc-

Please use the following format when citing this chapter:

Amato, F., et al., 2008, in IFIP International Federation for Information Processing, Volume 280; *E-Government; ICT Professionalism and Competences; Service Science*; Antonino Mazzeo, Roberto Bellini, Gianmario Motta; (Boston: Springer), pp. 31–40.

ture and *properties* of legal information, as well on organization, storage, retrieval, and dissemination within the context of the legal environments. We notice that several works to represent legal knowledge has been proposed, such as: Valente's Functional Ontology of Law [1], Frame-based Ontology of Visser [2], McCarty's Language of Legal Discourse (LLD) [3] and Stamper's Norma [4]. As a consequence of such theories, several ontologies are now available, such as: ON-LINE (Ontology-based Legal Information Environment), DUBA (Dutch Unemployment Benefits Act), CLIME (Cooperative Legal Information Management and Explanation): Maritime Information and Legal Explanation (MILE) and Knowledge Desktop Environment (KDE) [3]. Several approaches based on the wordNet project have been also done: in particular in Italy, JurWordNet [5] is the first Italian legal semantic knowledge base [1].

It is worth noticing that, despite the vast amount of efforts, several challenging problems still remain opened, especially related to the *automatic ontology building process*. The use of Pattern Recognition techniques on the sentence level for the identification of concepts and document classification for automatic document description is described in several works, as SCISOR[6] and FASTUS [7]. In the system BREVIDOC, documents are automatically structured and important sentences are extracted. These sentences are classified according to their relative importance [8]. From the Natural Language Processing (NLP) point of views, legal research concentrates on the automatic description of documents. In particular, the main focuses are: development of thesauri, machine learning for features recognition, disambiguation of polysems, automatic clustering and neural networks. The most important systems are FLEXICON, KONTERM, ILAM, RUBRIC, SPIRE, the HYPO extension [9] and SALOMON. In order to describe the peculiarities of our work, throughout the paper we will use a running example, as discussed in the following.

Example 1 *(Notary Documents)*. Let us consider the Italian juridic domain, and in particular the notary one: a notary is someone legally empowered to certify the legal validity of a document. Let us suppose to analyze a *buying act*. In real estate market, in Italy and also in some other european countries, when someone has the intention of buying or selling a property, such as houses, pieces of lands and so on, a notary document, certifying the property transaction from an individual to another one, is signed. Such document is generally composed by an *introduction part* containing the caption, a part containing the *biographical data* of the individuals involved in the buying act, a section containing *data about the property* and a sequence containing several rules regulating the sales contract. Consider for example the Italian sales contract fragment, proposed in figure 1; an Italian reader can easily detect the areas concerning the caption, the personal data and the property attributes. In a similar

---

[1] We gratefully acknowledge ITTIG - CNR, Italy, and particularly dott.Tiscornia, for the use of JurWordNet in this work

way, we propose a system that: i) detects the several sections containing relevant information (segmentation), and ii) transforms the unstructured information within the retrieved section into a structured document, by means of iii) structural, lexical and domain ontologies.

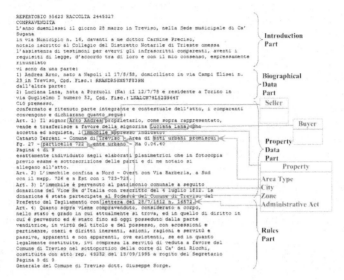

Fig. 1 An example of Notary Documents

The paper is organized as follows: in section 2, the general system architecture is outlined; section 3 describes the theory underlying our work, in particular the onto-logical levels for legal information management; the *RDF* document building strat-egy is described in section 4 and, eventually, some conclusions are discussed in section 5.

2 System Overview

In order to describe the main functionalities and characteristic of the proposed work, figure 2 shows at a glance the architecture of system. In the following we will briefly discuss the main parts of the system. *Text Extractor*: this module extracts the plain text from the source file, preserving the document format. The input of the module is a digitalized file, such as a pdf file, and the output is formatted textual data[2] *Structural Analysis*: this module performs the preprocessing of digital semi-structured text. It identifies the textual macro-structures which allow the recognition of text sections, according to the information provided by the structural ontology, that rep-resents the organization of the documents in the legal domain. This module contains

---

[2] in ASCII format

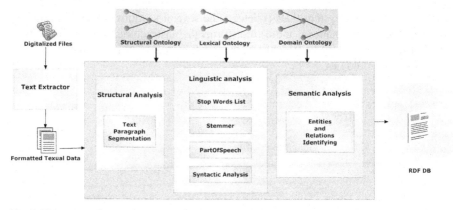

Fig. 2 The proposed system

a *Text Segmentation*, able to cut the document into a set of elements (i.e. paragraphs) on which further processing will be performed. The subdivision of the document into segments of text makes more accurate the further syntactic and semantic analysis.

Lexical Analysis: this module performs a syntactic-semantic annotation of text, by means of a labeling strategy; in particular, each text element is associated to a grammatical category (*verb, noun, adjective, and so on*) and to a syntactic role (*subject, predicate, complement, etc*). In order to do that, several traditional *NLP* components are then used, i.e. a *Stop Word List*, in order to eliminate un-relevant words in the sentence, such as pronoums, articles and so on; a *Stemmer*, for removing the commoner morphological and inflexional forms from words in Italian language [10]; a *Part of Speech Tagger*, for detecting the several grammatical part of a sentence; and a *Syntactic Analyzer*, for recognizing the logic-syntactic relation existing between "sintagms". To these aims, we use ontologies based on the Ital-Wordnet[11] lexical database.

Semantic Analysis: This core module performs novel information extraction techniques. By means of structural, legal domain and lexical ontologies, this module detects concepts and relations among concepts. Our proposed semantic analyzer produces a proper semantic annotation, codified in *RDF* triples. In particular, it associates an appropriate concept to each discovered single entity.

3 Document Representation

In the legal domain, almost all the documents is still written using natural languages on hard papers. Even though, the unstructured form of document follows a well determined sequence: in a notary act, for example, the notaries use a use a certain pre-defined structure, that is codified by laws or normative rules.

For these reasons, we say that our legal realm manages semi-structured documents written in a simplified natural language.

Let us introduce some preliminary symbol: a *Structure-UnarySet* ($\mathscr{S}\mathscr{U}$) over a domain $\mathscr{D}^S$ is the set of unary predicates, called *structure-concepts* (*sc*), a *Document-Structure-UnarySet* ($\mathscr{D}\mathscr{S}$) is a non empty subset of $\mathscr{S}\mathscr{U}$ containing all the necessary concepts for defining the structure of a given document according to a regular description; the *Structure-BinarySet* ($\mathscr{S}\mathscr{B}$) over domain $\mathscr{D}^S$ is the set of binary predicates, called *structure-relations* (*sr*).

According with the introduced notation, we can describe the legal document at different levels, such as the *Base-Document* ($\mathscr{D}^B$) that is the set of textual lines inside a document, called *Paragraphs-Sections* (S^P) : these lines specify a text-areas that can be overlapped; note that we can have different $\mathscr{D}^B$, depending on the different set of partition criteria used. We use a *Tbox* defined as a *Structure-TBox* composed by a finite set of axioms, made up by the elements of $\mathscr{S}\mathscr{B}$ and $\mathscr{S}\mathscr{U}$, expressed in form of $\mathscr{S}\mathscr{H}\mathscr{O}\mathscr{I}\mathscr{Q}$ (D_n) description logic, for capturing the knowledge about the structure of the documents. In order to characterize a fragment of our TBox $\mathscr{T}$ associated to a particular section, we use *TBox-Module* ($\mathscr{T}\mathscr{M}$) defined as restriction of the initial set of axioms χ.

Example 2 (Structure-TBox). Considering example 1, a *Structure-TBox*, may be formed by several axioms selected by an expert for the "biographical-section", containing "name" and "surname" of "person", "address", "security social number", i.e.:

$buying\_act \equiv = 4has\_section.section,$
$biographical\_section \subseteq section,$
$biographical\_section \equiv 2has.person,$
$person \equiv \exists\ hasName \cap \exists\ hasSurname \cap \exists\ hasSSN \cap \exists\ is\ born\ in.city$.

In other words, this is the set of axioms of the *Structure-TBox* that are the *TBox-Module* related to the biographical _section.

Each *TBox-Module* is characterized by means of a proper key, used to find what is the best fragment according to a given score; we thus use the following invertible function, *KnowledgeKey-Function* (ψ):

$$\psi: \mathscr{T}\mathscr{M} \ \rightarrow \ k \in \mathscr{K}$$

k being a unique key used to identify $\mathscr{T}\mathscr{M}$ and $\mathscr{K}$ the set of these keys.The $\mathscr{T}\mathscr{M}$ in example 2, is identified by a key $k=\{CODICE\backslash s *FISCALE\backslash s *[A- Z0- 9\backslash s], nat\ [o,a]\}$; in this case, the key is a mixture of a regular expressions. The patterns in the keys can be selected taking into account also the features extracted from standard natural language process on the text.

We are now in a position to introduce what we mean for a structured document related to the document D. A *Structured-Document* $\mathscr{S}\mathscr{D}$ is a set of 2-tuples:

$$\mathscr{S}\mathscr{D} =\{?S^P_1, k_1?, .. ?S^P_h, k_\mathrm{h}?\}.$$

S_i^P, and $k_i \in K$, $i \in \{1..h\}$ being *Paragraphs-Sections* and a knowledge key (obtained by applying the ψ function to a $\mathscr{D}\mathscr{M}$) respectively. Note that different $\mathscr{D}\mathscr{M}$ (domains, structure, or lexical) may point to the same *Paragraphs-Sections*,then we could have in $\mathscr{SD}$ some tuples with the same Paragraphs -Sections but differnt keys.

Given these tree different kinds of knowledge, i.e. structural, domain and lexical knowledge, we use the first one for text segmentation aims, the second and third ones are also used to infer more specific concepts related to the semantic content of the document: in particular, the individuals and the keywords extracted from a section are interpreted as concepts and the relative relations are then inferred using both domain and lexical ontology modules.

Eventually, we define the knowledge associated to the documents, in terms of Knowledge-Chunk,kc.(kc) is an triple defined according with the *Model and Syntax of Resource Description Framework (RDF) Specification*. The final description of the legal document, *KnowledgeChunk-Document*, is :

$$\mathscr{KC}^{D} \in \{D, kc_1....kc_l\}$$

kc_i, $i \in \{1..l\}$ being the previous Knowledge-Chunks and D their related document.

Example 3 (Knowledge-Chunk). For example for the "buyingAct", called *ID-Do-01*, we should have three Knowledge-Chunk:
$kc_1 = \langle myxmlns:ID\text{-}Do\text{-}01, buyingAct:asset, "Immobile" \rangle$,
$kc_2 = \langle myxmlns:ID\text{-}Pe\text{-}01, foaf:name, "Ludovico" \rangle$,
$kc_3 = \langle myxmlnsID\text{-}Pe\text{-}01, buyingAct:seller, myxmlns:ID\text{-}Do\text{-}01 \rangle$, and
$\mathscr{KC}^{D} = \{ID\text{-}Do\text{-}01, kc_1, kc_2, kc_3\}$
where myxmlns foaf and buyingAct are predefined xml name space.

4 Information Extraction from burocratic document

In this section we describe the several algorithms that are used in our system. The first algorithm we discuss is the text segmentation algorithm.

In our model, text segmentation is the problem of assigning the several extracted fragments to a structured document, according to a the knowledge characterizing the legal document itself.

The first step we propose is that of extracting simple fragments of the text, using some partition rules that are dependent from: i) normative prescriptions; ii) tradition of single notary schools; iii) common use of the single notary. A variety of rules may thus be detected, using several criteria. In the following we give an example of several possible criteria that we have retrieved by real notaries expertise. In particular, we use the following criteria

1. starting from the beginning of the document, or from the word following the end of the previous section, every section is ended by a punctuation character;

2. starting from the beginning of the document, or from the word following the end of the previous section, every section ends before the keywords 'art.'or 'articolo'(law articles in english).

3. to identify each section, we use particular tokens, as "notaio", "vend", "acqui", "compravend", "rep", "repertorio", (in english: notary, sell, buy, article and son on): a section is a portion of text containing one of these tokens. To detect a section, we need to identify the starting and the ending word of it; we thus use the following procedure: let us give three tokens in the document: T_{i-1}, T_i, T_{i+1}, in order to identify the starting word of the section relative to T_i, we consider the interval $[T_{i-1}, T_i]$ built using the sequence of words appearing in the document between T_{i-1} and T_i; we individuate the word w_{middle} located in the middle of this interval. Now we try to find punctuation mark ':'closer to w_{middle}; if such mark doesn't appear in the interval, we look for '.', else for ';'or,even, ',', and consider the first word after this. If the interval doesn't contain any punctuation mark, we simply use as the w_{middle} word for the section related to T_i. Similar reasoning, on the interval $[T_i, T_{i+1}]$ is done to determinate the ending word of the section.

In figure 3 we show an example of applying three initial partition criteria on the same act fragment. Once extracted several partitions from a given text, the following definition describe a suitable general function for text segmentation purposes.

Fig. 3 Application of tree on the same Act fragment

A Segm-Function (ϱ) is a function that associates an element of Base-Document to a $\mathscr{SD}$:

$$\varrho : \mathscr{D}^B \rightarrow \mathscr{SD}$$

Note that a Segm-Function may be implemented in a variety of way; in this paper, we propose an association between an S^P and a k according to a minimum score computed comparing the patterns extracted from text and those represented by the key. A possible implementation of ϱ function is given by algorithm 1.

A possible implementation of ϱ function is given by algorithm 1.

Algorithm 1 : Segm-Function algorithm

Input : $\mathscr{D}, \mathscr{K}_{\mathscr{SL}}, \mathscr{K}_{\mathscr{DO}}, \mathscr{K}_{\mathscr{LO}}, N_C$
D is the document,
$\mathscr{K}_{\mathscr{SL}}, \mathscr{K}_{\mathscr{DO}}, \mathscr{K}_{\mathscr{LO}}$ is the range of KnowledgeKey-Function for the structure Tbox and domain, lexical ontology respectively,
N_C is the enumeration of the partion criteria,
Output: $\mathscr{SD}$,
$\mathscr{SD}$ is the Structured-Document
begin
   $\mathscr{SD}^* = \{\emptyset\}$
   foreach $i \in N_C$ **do**
      $scoreVec[i] = 0$;
      $\mathscr{SD} = \{\emptyset\}$;
      $\mathscr{D}^B = getParagraphsSections (D,i)$;
      foreach $S^P_j \in \mathscr{D}^B$ **do**
         $\langle\mathscr{SD},i\rangle scoreVec = structureFunction(S^P_j, \mathscr{K}_{\mathscr{SL}}, \mathscr{K}_{\mathscr{DO}}, \mathscr{K}_{\mathscr{LO}}, \mathscr{SD}, scoreVec)$
      end
      $\mathscr{SD}^* = \mathscr{SD}^* \cup \{\langle\mathscr{SD},i\rangle\}$;
   end
   $\mathscr{SD} = getStructuredDocument(\mathscr{SD}^?, scoreVec)$;
end

In algorithm 1, *scoreVec* is an array of scores; *getParagraphsSections* takes in input a given Document together with a partition criteria, and returns a *Base-Document*; *structureFunction* is a function that has the role of matching a *Paragraphs-Section* with one of *TBox-Module* in input and and of retrieving a the tuple having the best score together with the score itself; *getStructuredDocument* computes the best *Structured-Document* dinamycally built considering those sections having the best sum of the scores previously computed.

The segmentation algorithm is followed by an RDF extraction, as described in algorithm 2.

In this algorithm, the *InferenceProcedure* extracts *knowledge-chunks* from texts using a mix of inference mechanism, concepts and relations extraction. For example, we can use generic rules that are a combination of token patterns and/or syntactic patterns, in order to derive the instances of some concepts or relations, and eventually using subsumption on *TBox-Module* for deriving more specific concepts.

Example 4 (Putting all together: RDF triples extraction). In this subsection we present an example in order to show how the system works. Starting from the run-

---

Algorithm 2 : *RDF-Extractor* (*RDFex*) algorithm

Input: *DS*
DS is the Structured-Document.
Output: $\mathcal{KC}^{D}$,
$\mathcal{KC}^{D}$ is the *KnowledgeChunk-Document*
begin

  $\mathcal{KC}^{D} = \{D\}$
  foreach $\langle S_i^P, k_j \rangle \in \mathscr{SD}$ **do**
    $\mathcal{SM} = \psi^{-1}(k_j)$,
    $kc = InferenceProcedure(\text{S M}, S_i^P)$
    $\mathcal{KC}^{D} = \mathcal{KC}^{D} \cup kc$
  end

end

---

ning example document, the system extracts the relevant information and, the results are presented in a *RDF* triples containing the attributes identified into the buying-selling document. As shown in the figure 4, the system has extracted from one hand,

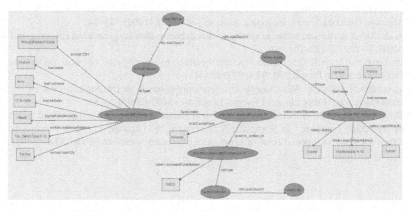

Fig. 4 A section of *RDF* graph extracted from a Notary Act in fig 1

several triples from notary act between the notary and the people involved into the buying-selling process with their generalities and in particular who is the seller and who is the buyer and, on the other hand, the related relationship property.

5 Conclusion and future works

In this paper we have presented a general system as the core of an e-gov information system in the notary domain. In particular, we propose the use of different levels of ontology and of NLP techniques in order to transform semi-strucutured documents into structured *RDF* triples and we described suitable algorithms that are able to segmentate and to extract relevant information from notary documents. The experimental section has shown very encouraging results. Future works will be devoted in developing index methodologies for semantic retrieval purposes.

References

1. Valente, A., Breuker, J.: A functional ontology of law (1994)
2. Visser, P.: The formal specification of a legal ontology (1996)
3. McCarty, L.T.: A language for legal discourse i. basic features. In: ICAIL '89: Proceedings of the 2nd international conference on Artificial intelligence and law, New York, NY, USA, ACM (1989) 180–189
4. Stamper, R.: The role of semantics in legal expert systems and legal reasoning. Ratio Juris 4(2) (1991) 219–244
5. Tiscornia, D.: Some ontological tools to support legal regulatory compliance, with a case study. Workshop on Regulatory Ontologies and the Modeling of Complaint Regulations (WORM CoRe 2003) Springer LNCS (November 2003)
6. Jacobs P S, R.L.F.: Scisor: Extracting information from on-line news. Comm ACM 33(11) (1990) 88–97
7. et al, H.J.R.: Sri international: Description of the fastus system used for muc-4. Fourth Message Understanding Conference, Morgan Kaufmann (1992) 143–147
8. et all, M.S.: A full-text retrieval system with a dynamic abstract generation function. in Proc SIGIR 94 (1994) 152–161
9. Bruninghaus St, A.K.D.: Finding factors: Learning to classify case opinions under abstract fact categories. in Proc ICAIL'97 (1997) 123–131
10. Zanchetta, E., Baroni, M.: Morph-it! a free corpus-based morphological resource for the italian language. Proceedings of Corpus Linguistics 2005 (2005) 23–32
11. Roventini, A.: Italwordnet: Building a large semantic database for the automatic treatment of the italian language. In Zampolli, A., Calzolari, N., Cignoni, L. (eds.), Computational Linguistics in Pisa, Special Issue of Linguistica Computazionale Vol. XVIII-XIX (2003)

The Accounting System of Central State Administrations

Francesco Cancellaro[1]

[1] Ministry of Economy and Finance – Department for National General Accounting (RGS), Italy, francesco.cancellaro@tesoro.it

Abstract: The many important innovations and reforms that over the years have involved Public Administration in a change and growth process have resulted in the dissemination of new analytical technologies aimed at exploring cost structures and the correlations between costs and achieved results, so as to support Government decision-makers with dependable and verified data.

The achievement of this goal has been facilitated by the legislation introduced in this area over the years and by ICT's continued evolution.

More specifically, IT evolution has brought about the use and dissemination of information systems related to the State Budget and the management of the public expenditure of central State administrations through the standardization not only of its criteria, but also of the tools employed, ensuring an efficient and timely execution of operations.

The Ministry of the Economy and Finance (MEF) and the State General Accounting Department (RGS) are today a crucial pivot of a complete system that supports central State Administrations in the implementation of all their accounting, economic and financial activities and that is going through further evolution, both in the use of new technologies and in the extension of the functional reach of correlated processes.

Keywords: information technology mandate, digital signature, substitutive conservation system

1. The situation prior to the introduction of the information technology mandate

General State Accounting (RGS) was born as a set of technical and auditing criteria regulating State Budget management operations. Gradually, these accounting operations have been inserted into the legislative system, thus creating a homogenous body of regulations.

Please use the following format when citing this chapter:

Cancellaro, F., 2008, in IFIP International Federation for Information Processing, Volume 280; *E-Government; ICT Professionalism and Competences; Service Science*; Antonino Mazzeo, Roberto Bellini, Gianmario Motta; (Boston: Springer), pp. 41–46.

More specifically, Law No. 468 of 1978 has pursued the goal of ensuring a stricter abidance to the rule of mandatory financial backing and has introduced the legislative tool of the Budget Law.

In abidance with this piece of legislation, some MEF-RGS administrative processes related to the Budget and the management of expenditure have been automated, the system for the creation and the management of the State Budget has been put into place in order to support the drafting of the Budget Law and the Central Budget Offices have drawn up procedures for the elaboration of the expenditure paperwork sent by Administrations.

2. The Use of Innovative Tools: The Information Technology Mandate

In 1994, with the adoption of Presidential Decree 367, began a new phase characterized by a marked change and innovation in the expenditure management administrative process. Information technology for the management of expenditure was introduced in order to substitute paperwork and to ensure verified information, efficient controls and speedy payments.

Furthermore, the liquidation of expenditure chapters was allowed through every accreditation or payment methods available in the banking and postal circuits.

The implementation of the Decree was achieved in 1999 by the introduction of the "Information Technology Mandate", an electronic expenditure order that, once digitally signed by MEF-RGS bureaus, is sent to the Bank of Italy through specific electronic channels, thus initiating a process of de-materialization of paperwork.

3. The SIPA – Integrated System for Administrative Payments

The creation and complete implementation of the Information Technology Mandate within all users (Central Budget Offices, General State Accounting Department, Bank of Italy), with its significant advantages in terms of payments effected, led to the decision to proceed with the extension of IT processes to the activity implemented by Central Administrations in the elaboration of their expenditure chapters and their delivery to the RGS.

The year 2000 witnesses the creation of the SIPA, Integrated System for Administrative Payments, an eGovernment project aimed at Public Administrations, citizens and enterprises.

The SIPA has as its main goal the substitution of paperwork with electronic documents in all that relates to variations in Budget chapters, to documents subject to legal verification on the part of the RGS, to documentation entailing a direct relation between expenditure managers and the Bank of Italy and to fixed expenditure chapters.

The pursuit of these goals led to the following advantages for Administrations:
- The elimination of paperwork in dealings with RGS and Bank of Italy bureaus.
- The timely knowledge of the accounting situation of individual expenditure chapters.
- The availability of periodic accounting in automated form.
- The rationalization of processes related to the financial accounting of Administrations.
- The acceleration of payments through their integration with banking and postal services.
- The reduction of costs (both in terms of time and money) related to payment management.

In order to implement and manage the SIPA a dedicated **Coordinating Committee** was put into place bringing together the RGS, the Court of Audits, the Bank of Italy and the CNIPA, in order to:
- Elaborate programs aimed at promoting the participation of Administrations.
- Issue technical regulations on SIPA's infrastructure.
- Decide on requests to join the SIPA.

4. The Spreading of Innovation: The Management Accounting System (SICOGE)

The first step taken by the SIPA was the implementation of the connection of individual Administrations to the R.U.P.A (Public Administration Unitary Grid) and the interconnection between the networks of the R.U.P.A. and the R.N.I (National Inter-bank Grid), thus creating a data transmission system that guaranteed maximum security requirements on a par with those used by Italy's banks. This interconnection proved crucial to enable the digitalization of the expenditure management process of Administrations.
In 2001, MEF-RGS implemented the SICOGE (Financial Accounting Management Information System), totally integrating it with the RGS Information System (SIRGS). Through this system, every Administration could manage its budget and its complete expenditure process through the RUPA/RNI channel as a secure vehicle for data transmission to the RGS. This also allowed for the elimination of paperwork in the transmission of a significant amount of accounting documents. The process in fact currently involves 150,000 accreditation orders, 600,000 information technology mandates and 18 million IT operations regarding payments and pensions. Thus, the IT management of the administrative procedures of accounting activities allows to reach the following goals:
- Promoting the monitoring of Public Administration expenditure, improving the efficiency of the national system as a whole.

- Accelerating payments through their integration with banking and postal services.
- Strengthening the IT capabilities of Administrations and allowing for the development of monitoring and decision-making support systems.
- Promoting the circulation of accounting information between all interested actors (Central Administrations, Local Authorities and Public Institutions).
- Communicating information to enterprises and State creditors regarding the administrative procedures of relevant activities, thus concretely contributing to improving the transparency of administrative activity.
- Simplifying expenditure management processes through the elimination from the administrative process of every step related to the production and transmission of accounting paperwork.

The use of SICOGE on the part of almost every single Administration brings significant benefits to administrative activity insofar as it:
- Allows for the certification of information and a greater speed in accounting operations.
- Promotes an easy integration between central and peripheral administrative offices.
- Allows the use of the digital signature and the elimination of paperwork
- Paves the way for an efficient management control and monitoring of expenditure.
- Optimizes, among other things, the operational costs of the State.

5. The Evolution of the SICOGE

In the meantime, the reform of the State Budget enacted with Law No. 94 of April 3 1997 and implemented with Legislative Decree No. 279 of August 7 1997 introduced Analytical Economic Accounting for the cost centers of Central State Administrations. This significant innovation in accounting standards highlighted the political will to create a budget for "parliamentary decision" and an "administrative-management" budget that would be interconnected and supported by efficient accounting tools capable of constantly informing the budget decision-making process. The Analytical Economic Accounting system for Central State Administrations aimed at the identification, analysis, verification and monitoring of costs, revenues and results of administrative activity allows for an economic qualification of public policies and of the final services that are provided, as well as for a verification of the way resources are employed, defined as an economic value of effective consumption, classified by their nature and allotted to the organization and goals pursued.

The new accounting model, its criteria and rules were defined by MEF-RGS and disseminated throughout all central Administrations. Furthermore, in order to facilitate the delivery of the economic budget documentation to be presented to Parliament, RGS made available to the Administrations a portal for the transmission of their pertinent data. Clearly, individual administrations would then needed a support system to manage all the information needed to draft an economic budget.

This naturally led to the integration of economic budget functions within the SICOGE, whose use had in the meantime been extended to all central administrations.

This system completely integrates economic-patrimonial-analytical data with financial data, thus allowing for monitoring of both the organization's real management costs and related expenses.

This way, every management action becomes visible through both its financial and economic aspects and can be evaluated in monetary terms. These are complementary aspects of the same reality, both significant in the evaluation of administrative activity and of the management performance of individual administration.

The development of this system for the integrated management of economic and financial accounting was conducted by RGS, through Consip, in accord with the CNIPA. It allows administrations to manage all the information they need to represent the use of resources in an economic, patrimonial and analytical way, to support their economic and financial planning activity and to feed in a homogenous, dependable and timely fashion the Analytical Economic Accounting system of Central State Administrations, as well as their own management control systems.

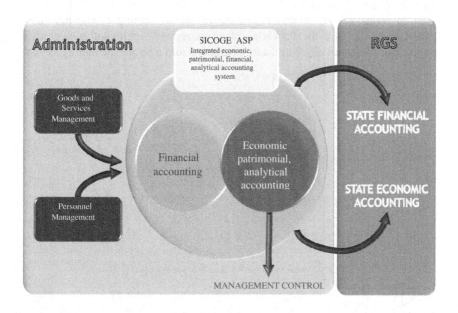

The ever more frequent use of the SICOGE on the part of all administrations, along with the technological evolution of the ICT market, have led RGS and CNIPA to sign an agreement in order to supply SICOGE in ASP (Application Service Provider) modality. This way, RGS acts as service provider, freeing administrations from activities related to the management, maintenance and upgrading of the infrastructure technology, which are delegated to the ASP manager (RGS).

The advantages that are provided through this delivery modality can be summarized in the following points:
- ? Rationalization of operational processes.
- ? Centralized management of the technical infrastructure.
- ? Greater back-office efficiency and total control of the service.
- ? Simplification of the system's functional and technical evolution.
- ? Central control of dialogue with other RGS information systems.

Furthermore, the centralized management of the service on the part of RGS allows administrations to use other services provided by RGS, foremost among them the substitutive conservation system which, in abidance with the legislative requirements dictated by the CNIPA, manages the entire conservation process (conservation, maintenance and search/visualization) in an open, scalable and integrated solution.

The ASP delivery, the digital signature and the substitutive conservation implemented through SICOGE allow the State to pursue the goals it has set for itself in terms of the de-materialization of all accounting flows, but -more importantly- they are the backbone of an extremely significant eGovernment project that integrates all central administrations into a single accounting system.

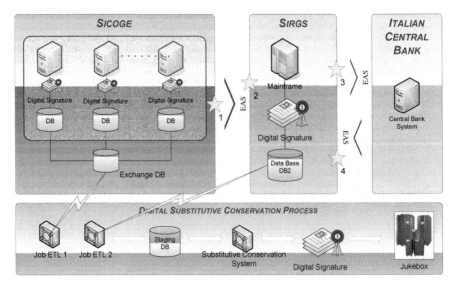

The Italian Public Administration Electronic Market: Scenario, Operation, Trends

Danilo Broggi[1]

[1] Consip - Chief Executive Officer, Italy, danilo.broggi@tesoro.it

Abstract: A critical element that has been generally recognized is that the Italian Public Administration provides services and operates emphasizing the formal abidance to administrative regulations and procedures, having in part lost sight of its institutional goal of providing quality and timely services to citizens and -so crucial in our digital age- the goal of "system creation". The opportunity that Italy is given through eGovernment lies in fact in the possibility of promoting a change management of public services towards a culture aimed at the satisfaction of the final user. From this point of view, eProcurement can become the "Trojan Horse" (or the killer application) capable of promoting change within Public Administration. This is true, first of all, because it synthesizes all the critical aspects of typical change management processes: Structure reorganization, integration and interoperability of functions/service, process re-engineering, professional training and growth of human resources, legislative revision, technology introduction, the monitoring of public expenditure and its monitoring (while maintaining the decentralization of expenditure decisions), as well as quality control. Secondly, because it is an issue that covers horizontally all Public Administrations, whose boundaries and procedures are well known and whose achievable results are therefore highly visible and economically valuable. Thirdly, the contracting sector appears more conducive than others to the promotion of this change process because it has the necessary critical mass in terms of expenditure volume to support innovation. Public contracts account for more than 16% of GNP. Lastly, through a growth in the efficiency of public contracts it is possible to achieve results that are substantial and permanent in the areas of process savings, good and services cost savings and of positive externalities in terms of tool innovation that will promote market innovation

Keywords: eGovernment, eProcurement, Public Administration Electronic Market (MEPA)

Please use the following format when citing this chapter:

Broggi, D., 2008, in IFIP International Federation for Information Processing, Volume 280; *E-Government; ICT Professionalism and Competences; Service Science*; Antonino Mazzeo, Roberto Bellini, Gianmario Motta; (Boston: Springer), pp. 47–56.

1. Defining eProcurement

Considering the entire supply value chain, eProcurement tools, those employed in electronic search-selection-purchase, may be implemented from the requirement manifestation phase to the invoicing and payment management phase. More specifically, if one considers the electronic tools employed by public authorities to select their contractors, one may employ the term ePublicProcurement.

Public eProcurement may be defined as the set of technologies, procedures, operations and organizational modalities that allow for the on-line selection and provisioning of goods and services through the opportunities offered by the development of the Internet and electronic commerce. Public eProcurement is obviously influenced by the different structure that characterizes the contract categories related to the specific role played by Public Administration within the legislative system as a whole.

Consequently, the areas of intervention where the introduction of eProcurement within a public entity may have a significant impact are essentially four: Organization, processes, technology and public expenditure.

At the international organization level, the past ten years have witnessed the emergence of a strong interest in themes related to eGovernment and electronic purchasing tools. More specifically, at the EU level there is a strong interest in eProcurement and there have been at least three relevant initiatives on the part of the Directorates General of the European Commission (Internal Market, Information Society and media IDABC, Enterprise and Industry European eBusiness Support Network).

Regarding the Italian scenario, the electronic purchasing tools that are most common in both the Central Public Administration (all managed exclusively by Consip) and at the regional and local levels (managed by ad hoc purchasing agencies or by administrative departments), essentially deal with the search, comparison and supplier and product selection phases. We are talking about electronic shops, electronic tenders and electronic marketplaces.

Compared to electronic tenders and auctions (on-line contractor selection procedures that allow for different sorts of tenders, among them the sealed envelope with the most economically convenient offer), and electronic shops (eShops - "static" eProcurement tools that publish on-line pre-negotiated catalogues where one may shop selecting quantities, with only a limited offer of different options), eMarketplaces are undoubtedly eProcurement's most innovative, flexible and complete tool.

Apart from these tools, the Directive n. 2004/18 and the Legislative Decree n. 163/06 have introduced in Italy the Dynamic Purchasing System, a tool which has yet to be employed that may be described as a totally electronic acquisition process for normal everyday purchases (goods/services with characteristics that are generally available in the market). Always accessible by suppliers, but limited in time (maximum four years), with indicative offers (through on-line catalogues) that may be dynamically improved. This tool is also employable in purchases that are above the community threshold.

In general terms, it is clear that the benefits of the use of eProcurement are more interesting if it is backed by is a strategic approach, in which the commitment and the goals are well defined, where there has been an investment in training and change management of the purchases function and where there has been adequate communication with suppliers.

Regarding specifically transparency, direct empirical experience shows that the use of electronic purchasing procedures leads to a growth trend due to various elements. Briefly, these are: 1) A general and uniform access to information without discriminations. 2) The standardization of procedures. 3) The tracking and monitoring of all contacts, interactions and document exchanges between parties. 4) The minimizing of discretional action in the evaluation phases .

As far as public authorities are concerned, the advantages of eProcurement are directly related to the on-line tools themselves, as well as to the operational framework of eProcurement in the wider sense of the term.

Among the other advantages, which must in any case be interpreted in a systematic approach, one may mention the acceleration of procedures, the reduction of the time spent in purchasing processes, the reduction of the cost of managing tenders, the simplification of processes, the direct and constant monitoring of public expenditure, the professional growth of the personnel in charge of the processes, the increase in the potential pool of suppliers, the savings in prices, the de-materialization of documentation and the possibility to implement digital document management projects.

Both from a first-hand field experience and from a sample-based analysis, what emerges is a number of critical factors that represent real obstacles to the adoption of eProcurement on the part of Italy's PA , as well as a number of false truths.

Among the critical factors, it is important to underline the fact that, apart from the technological obstacles, there are also the typical problems related to an incomplete and ineffective change management program within the Public Administration. More specifically:

– The absence of a clear strategic vision for public eProcurement that is clearly and effectively communicated, that does not raise concerns over long-term strategies and that does not encourage the creation of legislative hiccups that lead to confusion both in the area of demand and in the area of supply.
– The absence of implementing regulations.
– The absence of both an adequate level of training and of a recognition of new professional qualifications among civil servants (e.g., the eBuyer).
– The absence of a monitoring and evaluation activity, as well as of a rewarding system for the Public Administrations and managers that make use of these tools.
– The existence of the digital divide non only as a concept, but also as a real technological barrier (not all Public Administrations have even basic electronic mail and very few use digital signatures).

- The fact that eProcurement platforms sometimes are not stable and often are not all that simple and clear-cut to use.
- The fact that the supply side is hesitant to join in, especially at the local level, fearing a greater competition, if it does not understand that eProcurement is a mandatory path to take in the long run in order to sell one's products to the PA.

Remaining within the organizational and technological framework, it must be recognized that the adoption of eProcurement platforms, especially if they are not open source, is costly and what is even more so is the management of the backoffice (databases and on-line supplier catalogues). The solutions offered by the public central purchasing bodies overcome this problem through their free delivery of solutions to all Public Administrations. It would obviously be helpful if it were possible to share organizational and technological standards in order to promote the interoperability of data and to avoid creating digital barriers in the local markets.

2. The Public Administration Electronic Market (MEPA)

The Public Administration Electronic Market (MEPA) is a public eProcurement tool managed by Consip on behalf of the Ministry of the Economy and Finance. It is a dynamic tool (in that it allows suppliers to register, post and change their wares, services and prices at any moment in time) in which products and services are presented in structured catalogues and described according to standard formats. The purchasers are registered Authorities that, after a search and comparison of the products being offered, may implement purchases directly through orders from the catalogues, or by requesting preliminary offers. An identical product/service may be sold by various suppliers at different conditions (as in the real market) and there is no pre-negotiation on the part of Consip.

The MEPA is part of the wider Program for the Rationalization of Public Expenditure that was launched in 2000 by the Ministry of the Economy and Finance in the wake of the introduction of a new model for the optimization of public provisioning in Italy.

As mentioned, the MEPA is an electronic market where the Ordering Points (OPs) represented by the individuals that have purchasing authority within their respective Public Administrations may search for, compare between and purchase the goods and services offered by the supplier enterprises that are authorized to display their catalogues on the system, within the constraints set in specific tenders published by Consip for the different product categories. It is therefore a market that is:

- Selective, in that its access and use is reserved to users that have passed a qualification process that is based on the verification of the possession of specific requirements.

- Specialized, in that it is aimed at meeting the procedural and administrative requirements that are specific to the provisioning function of Public Administrations and of the companies that interact with them as suppliers (document characteristics, filing procedures, use of digital signatures, etc...).
- Based on a catalogue of authorized products, in that all the commercial transactions that take place in the market deal with goods/services offered by suppliers in catalogue form and displayed on the system following an authorization process that is managed by Consip.
- Usable only for purchases of quantities of goods and services that are valued below the community threshold.

Suppliers may decide where to sell, starting either from a local dimension (their Province), or aiming for a regional range of action, to the option of offering their products/services in the whole of Italy. In this aspect, the system is flexible in that it allows for choices among different operational dimensions (that can be dynamically modified) and between different user characteristics (Public Administrations and Suppliers), that may generate personalized "geographical visits" (ranging from the individual Province to the whole national territory) on the basis of their requirements and capabilities.

Even though it is a highly innovative tool, the MEPA does not change the legislative and commercial regulations that characterize the purchasing processes of the Public Administration, specifically safeguarding the importance of purchaser-supplier relations, especially where the "localization" of the service is a significant component.

The authorization of suppliers aiming to join the MEPA takes place through specific authorization Tenders that are published for all the product and service categories that are sold on the Electronic Market.

The authorization procedure deals both with the suppliers and the products and services that they would like to offer to Public Administrations. In order to offer Public Administrations a qualified list of suppliers and wares, enterprises must have the minimal requirements necessary to prove that they have the professional, economic and financial capacity that is required in the authorization tender and may offer in the system only the goods/services that meet the requirements that are set in the relevant Technical Specifications. The permanence of a supplier in the MEPA guarantees Public Administrations that its statements have been verified and approved by an ad hoc Technical Committee every six months.

Apart from a products and services search engine and an electronic filing system, the Electronic Market offers registered authorities the possibility to process contracts through two different purchasing procedures:

- Direct Order: The Administration may purchase goods and services directly through the catalogues of the suppliers that are registered in the Electronic Market. The publication of a catalogue on the part of the supplier amounts to a public offer reserved to the Administrations that are registered in the Electronic Market.

- Offer Request: This allows the Administration to request from registered suppliers various and diverse offers related to the products and services registered in the Electronic Market, thus allowing them to meet more specific requirements. In simpler terms, this procedure may be used to request more than one preliminary offer from various suppliers on the same product/service, thus putting them in competition and trying to obtain conditions that are more favourable than those offered in the catalogue.

The advantages brought by the use of the MEPA, apart from the general benefits of eProcurement, may include not only cost and time savings in the provisioning cycle, but also changes that the use of the tool might bring within an organization.

As far as the price savings obtained by the Public Administrations are concerned, MEPA's characteristics make for a very complex evaluation.

The heterogeneous and diversified nature of the products and services offered on the MEPA and the different selection modalities that are available (through direct catalogue order, or through offer requests) make it very difficult to identify a general compared analysis model between the purchasing prices obtained by the electronic tool and those obtained by Public Administrations with other methods. Nonetheless, a number of perception polls (seminars, conferences, interviews, etc...) of many Public Administrations that have so far used the MEPA tend to confirm the existence of an economic advantage in terms of price reduction, related especially to a more open market and, consequentially, to greater competition and transparency. As has emerged in analyses made on private business to business eMarketplaces, the decision to introduce these tools is aimed ad producing process savings, even though the average cost savings on the prices of goods/services is estimated to be around 8 per cent.

The full deployment of the benefits that have been mentioned above requires a medium to long-period timeframe, both because the results and the benefits of the use of the Electronic Market are often not immediately felt by the users, but rather manifest themselves in the long run as the user becomes more proficient with the tool, and because there are still some high hurdles to overcome in terms of culture, technology, legislation and administrative structure before one can achieve a complete dissemination of the tool.

It is important to underline the fact that the Public Administration Electronic Market –MEPA- provides a stimulus towards innovation not only for Public Administrations, but also for enterprises, especially the small and medium-sized companies. In these years of dissemination of the MEPA, it has become clear how the use of the tool has brought about benefits in terms of transparency, change management and process savings not only for Public Administrations, but also for the enterprises participating in the program.

Undoubtedly, the participation in the MEPA amounts to the activation of a new channel of commercial relations with the Public Administration –at a limited cost, given that participation in the Electronic Market is free of charge- as well as the extension of the potential market in the context of Public Administrations, both at a national and at a local level. For many companies, the tool guarantees a nation-wide visibility of their offer as well as a greater penetration in their local territory, without requiring further commercial investments.

For the companies that operate locally, the MEPA provides a greater competitiveness related to the localization and/or specialization of their offer that allows to highlight the added value and services provided by local small and medium-sized enterprises. Furthermore, the presence of the MEPA provides a better knowledge of the offer available within the product category of interest and an optimization of one's positioning with regards to the competition.

One must also not forget that the pre-set rules and procedures that are shared by all actors involved in the Electronic Market amount to a guarantee of greater transparency in tender procedures. Through the workings of the market, the presence of suppliers in the MEPA has the collateral effect of generating a spontaneous self-regulation of the system of supply in which "all see and compare themselves to all", making for a greater fairness in competition through transparent procedures.

A further benefit for companies is represented by the possibility of a continuous updating of their offer due to the dynamic nature of the catalogues. This allows suppliers to implement specific commercial strategies that may be aimed at reducing overstocking or at saturating productive capacity. Compared to more traditional supply modalities, the dynamism of catalogues allows to constantly update the supply and to offer in real time promotions in terms of both prices and new product lines. This opportunity is especially taken advantage of in markets that are characterized by products with a high rate of obsolescence.

Another benefit of the use of this technology is given by the lower sales costs brought about by the reduction of the cost of intermediation and of managing the entire sales process. Many companies have made accurate analyses of the costs and savings obtained through their participation in the sales procedures processed through the MEPA.

A last point that should be made is that which relates to the sharing of documentation and know-how. The "packaging" of commercial, administrative and category-related competences provided by the MEPA through its on-line catalogues and the documentation on tenders and technical specification models represents one of principal benefits introduced by the MEPA, both for enterprises and Public Administrations. The documentation's characteristics of completeness and clarity support suppliers in the definition of their offer and makes programming and reporting on the service easier, strongly impacting on the quality of the service that is offered. Furthermore, the possibility given to Public Administrations to use technical specifications and supply conditions that may be personalized according to specific requirements focalizes a greater attention on higher supply standards and a greater guarantee of the quality of supply.

That said, companies, especially the smaller ones, have to overcome some "difficulties", ranging from technical hurdles, to cultural obstacles to organizational ones.

From the point of view of the product category, meaning the nature of the products and services that are negotiable on the system, the MEPA is characterized as a general spending tool.

The selection of the product categories on offer is aimed at meeting the most common goods and services purchasing requirements of Public Administrations and offers a balance between range (the variety of goods/services categories) and depth (the assortment of goods/services in the same category) of choice.

The main characteristics that make a product category appropriate for its activation on the MEPA are a medium-high comprehensive frequency of purchase, a low complexity of its specifications, a "strategic" relevance of the demand/supply, its complementarity with other public administration purchasing tools (e.g,, the framework contracts), a prevalence of orders below the community threshold and a wide-ranging supply in terms of numbers of suppliers.

The growth and consolidation of an electronic market requires the so-called "crossed-network effect", meaning the creation of a population level of both the supply and demand sides that is capable of fostering further participation and interest on the part of other companies, and consequently also other Public Administrations.

In these years of dissemination of the tool, it has clearly emerged that the growth in demand is the one dominant factor determining the expansion of the Electronic Market. Companies are in fact very reactive to the perception of the level of dissemination and acceptation of the tool on the part of the Public Administration.

3. Conclusions

Both at a European and international level, whether within the wider context of eGovernment programs or the more narrow framework of public expenditure rationalization, eProcurement nowadays has taken on a key role in the efforts aimed at the modernization and increased efficiency of Public Administration, as well as at the monitoring of public accounts. The significance and impact that electronic purchasing tools can have derives not only from the fact that public contracts account for 16 per cent of GNP (EU average), but also from the advantages that they bring to Public Administration change management programs.

The Public Administration Electronic Market (MEPA) is undoubtedly one of the most advanced B2G tools around and is recognized as a best practice at the European level.

As is common with many innovative and relatively new projects, apart from the benefits it provides, the MEPA also has a number of critical elements that slow its dissemination.

Specifically, these have been highlighted as a) from the demand side, the problem of digital divide (tied to the inadequate spread of the Internet and of the digital signature) and the inertia of users from the point of view or organizational and cultural change management, and b) from the supply side, a reluctance, especially at the local level, to join the game and play by rules that are more competitive, with the risk of losing some traditional "market niches", as well as the aversion to investing in eCommerce without a clear vision of its long-term returns.

Among the advantages provided by the MEPA, apart from those typical of all eProcurement tools (foremost among them a greater transparency), one should highlight process savings in terms of man/hours compared to traditional contracting methods and the possibility of a detailed and constant monitoring of public expenditure (with the added possibility of a compared analysis of expenditure between different Public Administrations).

Among the theoretical issues that the project has evidenced one should not forget the positive reciprocal externalities between demand and supply and the risks of a digital segmentation of markets brought about by a lack of interoperability between different eProcurement systems.

From what has been detailed so far, it is clear that eProcurement tools like the MEPA may act as a catalyst for an organizational and procedural change within the PA that could impact and offer new opportunities on both the public demand and supply sides.

The scenario that has been traced highlights the strategic role that the Public Administration Electronic Market has acquired in the area of below-threshold purchases for the Public Administration at large. This role is further enhanced by the introduction and development of new purchasing tools, such as the Framework Agreements and the Dynamic Purchasing System.

More specifically, the Dynamic Purchasing System may expand the offer of the MEPA in some product categories, allowing the Public Administrations to take advantage of this expansion whenever the adjudication of contracts has to take place according to open procedures (both below and above the community threshold). Furthermore, the Dynamic Purchasing System presents a working model and some critical success factors that are very similar to those that characterize the MEPA, such as the need to guarantee adequate service levels of the purchasing system in organizational and technological terms, the "tertiarity" of its manager with regards to the negotiating activity of operators of the system and the overall efficiency of the new tool in terms of costs and benefits.

The know-how and the experience that have been acquired on the MEPA by all involved actors – Public Administrations, enterprises, industrial associations and Consip- will facilitate the introduction and use of the new tools.

These developments may call for an evolution of Consip's role from that of a contracting body to that of market maker, because -similarly to what happens within the MEPA- Consip would not be playing the role of a "pure" and simple contracting body (as it does in the context of Framework Contracts), but rather, with variations according to the tools being used (MEPA, Framework

Agreements, Framework Contracts, Dynamic Purchasing Systems), that of manager of a market whose actors operate, from a negotiating point of view, with various degrees of autonomy and thus with variable levels of personalization of provisioning with regards to their needs.

Within this role and on the back of its experience in the planning, management and implementation of new purchasing tools and modalities, the National Purchasing Agency could take on, within the context of the network system to be set up with the regional and local purchasing bodies, a service and "facilitator" role in the promotion of an efficient model in which the purchasing entities and the individual Public Administrations may implement their own electronic purchasing procedures, both above and below the threshold, in a simplified and structured fashion.

ICT PROFESSIONALISM AND COMPETENCES

The Emergence of Software Engineering Professionalism

The Role of Professional Societies in the Emergence of Software Engineering Professionalism in the United States and Canada

Stephen B. Seidman

University of Central Arkansas, USA, sseidman@uca.edu

Abstract: The term "software engineering" was coined forty years ago as a metaphor for the processes involved in designing and constructing large-scale software systems. Since that time, the term has gradually come to refer to a professional engineering discipline. This paper will describe the role played by professional societies in the creation of the professional discipline of software engineering in the United States and Canada.

Keywords: software engineering, professionalism, professional societies, United States, Canada

1. Software Engineering as an Engineering Profession

The first recorded use of the term "software engineering" was at a NATO conference in 1968. According to the conference organizers [1], the term was chosen "was deliberately chosen as being provocative, in implying the need for software manufacture to be [based] on the types of theoretical foundations and practical disciplines[,] that are traditional in the established branches of engineering". This concern arose out of a growing realization that the software development practices used at that time were hampering the development of industrial software systems and applications [2].

In 1968, the "engineering" label was used metaphorically; it was applied to software in the hope that engineering principles could be applied to software design and development. At one level, the success of the label is clear; "software engineering" quickly came to refer to the processes associated with software development. For example, the most prestigious conference in the software engineering discipline is the International Conference on Software Engineering,

Please use the following format when citing this chapter:

Seidman, S.B., 2008, in IFIP International Federation for Information Processing, Volume 280; *E-Government; ICT Professionalism and Competences; Service Science*; Antonino Mazzeo, Roberto Bellini, Gianmario Motta; (Boston: Springer), pp. 59–67.

which traces its roots to a US conference held in 1975. However, it is less clear that applying the "engineering" label to software has led to the transfer of the attributes that characterize the engineering disciplines. Mahoney [2] argues that those who coined the phrase "software engineering" were not completely clear on the specific principles that they thought should be adopted by software developers. Engineering principles mentioned in the early days of software engineering include assembly of systems from components and Taylor-style industrial engineering.

However, engineering is more than a collection of principles. Just as medicine, law, and architecture are professions, engineering is also a profession, and an engineer is therefore a professional. The concept of "professionalism" cuts across all professions. According to Sandra Day O'Connor, retired Associate Justice of the US Supreme Court, "... the essence of professionalism is a commitment to develop one's skills to the fullest and to apply that responsibly to the problems at hand. Professionalism requires adherence to the highest ethical standards of conduct and a willingness to subordinate narrow self-interest in pursuit of the more fundamental goal of public service" [3].

What are the characteristics of a profession? First, the community of practicing professionals must have responsibility for governance of the profession. For this purpose, the professional community is typically represented by one or more self-governing professional bodies. The community is also responsible for controlling entrance to the profession and establishing and enforcing standards of professional behavior.

How does this apply to engineering? Professional engineering bodies can be organized in two ways. First, a society may be responsible for a specific engineering specialty. A typical example is the Institute of Electrical and Electronic Engineers (IEEE). Specialty societies are often organized into an umbrella body, such as the Engineering Institute of Canada. A second form of organization derives from the federal political structure of some countries. In the United States and Canada, for example, individual states and provinces have engineering societies that cut across specialties, such as the Texas Society of Professional Engineers and Professional Engineers Ontario. These local societies are also organized into umbrella bodies: the National Society of Professional Engineers in the US, and the Canadian Council of Professional Engineers (also known as Engineers Canada) in that country.

These professional engineering bodies exercise control over the profession in cross-cutting ways. For example, in the United States, access to the engineering profession is controlled in two distinct ways. First, the 50 states award professional licenses to engineers; licensure is analogous to "chartered status" in the United Kingdom. The criteria for licensure include passing examinations written and administered by the National Society of Professional Engineers. Another dimension relates to the educational credentials of engineers; licensure requirements are lower for holders of bachelor's degrees from accredited university programs. Engineering accreditation in the US is administered by

ABET (formerly known as the Accreditation Board for Engineering and Technology); the members of ABET are the specialty societies mentioned above.

The specialty societies have a major influence on the professional conduct of their members. One key element of professionalism is the ethical component of professional behavior. In order to foster this component, each specialty engineering society has developed a code of ethics that is incumbent on its members. For example, the first of ten points in the IEEE code [4] requires IEEE members to "accept responsibility in making decisions consistent with the safety, health and welfare of the public, and to disclose promptly factors that might endanger the public or the environment".

How does software engineering fit into this professional engineering paradigm? This question can be answered in two ways. First, has software engineering moved beyond its metaphorical roots and come to resemble the other engineering disciplines? Second, has software engineering developed the organizational characteristics of an engineering profession?

Mary Shaw [5] has addressed the first question. She argues that engineering practice is characterized by phrases like "creating cost-effective solutions", "to practical problems", and "by applying scientific knowledge. Shaw describes the emergence of civil and chemical engineering in the nineteenth century, and uses this history to discuss the position of software engineering on the "path toward engineering". Another perspective on the emergence of software engineering as a profession is given by Adams [6]; this paper compares the emergence of this profession in Canada, the US, and the UK.

The second question can be divided into several: How is entrance to software engineering controlled by professional bodies? What about professional licensure and program accreditation? Is there a body of knowledge for software engineering? Is there a code of professional ethics for software engineers? The following sections of this paper will discuss the ways in which professional bodies have addressed these issues in the North American context.

2. Software Engineering and Professional Bodies in the US and Canada

2.1 Professional Bodies and Academic Programs

The United States is the home of two major professional computing societies: the IEEE Computer Society (IEEE-CS) and the Association for Computing Machinery (ACM). Each society has more than 50,000 members; although both societies regard themselves as international, most of their members are in North America. The primary professional computing society in Canada is the Canadian Information Processing Society (CIPS).

For many years, IEEE-CS and ACM have worked together to develop recommendations for computing curricula. Recommendations have been produced for computer science, computer engineering, and information systems. In 2004, the two societies produced curriculum recommendations for software engineering (SE2004) [7].

In the United States, accreditation of university engineering programs was introduced by the Accreditation Board for Engineering and Technology in the 1930s. Computer science programs arrived on the academic stage much more recently, They were first accredited in the 1980s by the Computer Science Accreditation Board. The initial members of this board were the two computing professional societies: ACM and IEEE-CS. In the late 1990s, the engineering and computing accreditation bodies were renamed as their acronyms (ABET, CSAB). CSAB then joined ABET as a professional society, thus giving ABET responsibility for computing accreditation. ABET now accredits programs in a wide range of computing disciplines: computer science, computer engineering, information systems, information technology, and software engineering.

By contrast, the Canadian engineering and computing accreditation bodies are still separate. The Canadian Engineering Accreditation Board (CEAB) has responsibility for engineering accreditation, and CIPS has established the Computer Science Accreditation Council, with responsibility for accreditation of computing programs. While in the US, ABET and CSAB share responsibility for software engineering accreditation, CEAB claims that it has sole responsibility for accreditation of software engineering programs in Canada. This distinction is underscored by the fact that Engineers Canada has used the fact that it has registered the terms "engineer" and "engineering" as its trademarks as a basis for legal action to restrict academic programs in software engineering to departments and colleges of engineering. In this context, it has proved difficult for CEAB and CIPS to work together on software engineering accreditation, and both organizations now independently accredit software engineering programs [8].

2.2 Professional Societies and Engineering Licensure

In the United States and Canada, engineering licensure is a government-recognized professional status analogous to "chartered engineer" status in the United Kingdom and Australia. In North America, practicing the profession of engineering requires a license. However, "practicing the profession of engineering" has come to refer to the responsibilities typically associated with managing major projects. Such licenses are awarded locally, by states in the United States, and by provinces in Canada. In the US, each state has established its own regulations and requirements for engineering licensure, although the educational and experience requirements are similar. In all US states, candidates must pass two examinations common to all states: Fundamentals of Engineering (FE), and Principles and Practice (PE). The first examination covers knowledge common to the traditional engineering disciplines (e.g., statics, mechanics, thermodynamics), while the second examination deals with advanced material specific to a particular engineering discipline (e.g. civil engineering, electrical engineering). In Canada, the educational requirements for licensing are met by graduation from an accredited engineering program.

If software engineering is an engineering discipline alongside other engineering disciplines, it would be reasonable to license software engineers, especially those working on systems that have critical health or safety implications. This has already happened in Canada, where the provinces of Ontario, Alberta, and British Columbia license software engineers. Progress has been much slower In the United States, where Texas is the only state that licenses software engineers. The primary reason for slow adoption in the US is the need to extend the licensure examination to correspond to the education of software engineers. Bagert [9] gives the context and history of software engineering licensing in the United States.

The role of professional societies is also relevant to the emergence of software engineering licensing. In the United States, the two professional computing societies have taken different positions on this issue. In general, IEEE-CS has taken a "watchful waiting" attitude. Since the parent organization IEEE is an international professional society, US-specific issues are the province of a subsidiary organization, called IEEE-USA. This latter organization has recently taken up the issue of software engineering licensing, and IEEE-CS is playing a cooperative but not a leading role in these discussions.

By contrast, ACM's leadership body (ACM Council) adopted a position in 2000 that expressed strong opposition to software engineering licensing. This opposition was based on the contention that the software engineering discipline was not yet sufficiently mature [10]. One consequence of this decision was ACM's withdrawal from cooperation with IEEE-CS on matters relating to software engineering professionalism.

2.3 Professional Societies and Certification

It is important to distinguish between broad-based certifications and product-specific certifications. Broad-based certifications are based on bodies of knowledge that cover an entire professional discipline or a subspecialty within such a discipline. These certifications are generally awarded by professional societies. Examples of broad-based certifications include financial certifications and specialty certifications in medicine or law. In the computing domain, broad-based certifications are available for software engineers and security experts. By contrast, product-specific certifications are based on a specific product or product line, such as a medical device or an operating system. The manufacturers of the products or product lines usually award certifications tied to their products.

Candidates applying for a broad-based certification must meet specific education and experience requirements. A candidate's familiarity with a body of knowledge is generally assessed by examination, although some certification schemes use peer review to assess knowledge and/or professional experience. Most certification schemes require that a certificate holder demonstrate professional activity, commitment to a code of ethics, and continuing education in order to maintain certification. Broad-based certification schemes are governed by national and international standards.

The IEEE Computer Society's Certified Software Development Professional (CSDP) certification scheme is an example of a broad-based software engineering certification. It is targeted to professionals with four years of professional software engineering experience. The origin of the CSDP scheme can be traced back for almost a decade. In 1998, the IEEE Computer Society began to consider the feasibility of certifying software engineering professionals. The CSDP examination was developed over the following three years, with its first offering in 2002. It consists of 180 questions to be completed in 3.5 hours. The examination is offered at testing centers in many countries. There are currently more than 600 CSDP certificate holders, who reside in many countries in all parts of the world. The IEEE Computer Society's Professional Practices Committee (PPC) is currently revising the examination to bring its body of knowledge into conformance with the revision of the SWEBOK body of knowledge (see below). At the same time, the PPC is developing a new examination targeting recent university graduates. This certification will be called the Certified Software Development Associate (CSDA).

An international standard for software engineering certification schemes is currently under development by an ISO/IEC JTC1 working group. An extended discussion of professional certification in software engineering is given in [11].

2.4 Professional Societies and Standards

Another aspect of professionalism is the establishment of standards for professional practice. One way of assessing the state of software engineering professionalism and the role played by professional societies is to examine the world of software engineering standards. In general, technology standards are developed and managed at many levels: by professional and industry organizations, by national standards bodies, and by international organizations.

IEEE is an excellent example of a professional organization with a responsibility for standards development across a wide range of technical specialties (see www.standards.ieee.org). Within this sphere of activity, the IEEE Computer Society has been actively involved in developing software and systems engineering standards for more than 20 years, through its Software and Systems Engineering Standards Committee (S2ESC). An overview of the universe of IEEE software engineering standards can be found in [12]. These standards cover the entire spectrum of the software engineering discipline. Currently, there are 27 active IEEE-CS working groups developing additional software engineering standards. A listing of these groups can be found at the website of the Society's

Standards Activities Board [13]. The topics of the working groups include test documentation, unit testing, and verification and validation.

Software engineering standards are also being developed on the international level. Here, the locus of development is a joint technical committee of the International Organization for Standardization (ISO) and the International Electrotechnical Commission (IEC). ISO is a network of national standards bodies that coordinates national and private-sector standards in many different technology domains, and IEC is responsible for standards in electrical, electronic, and related technologies. In 1987, ISO and IEC established a joint technical committee (JTC1) to develop and manage standards in the rapidly emerging area of information technology. JTC1 has seventeen subcommittees dealing with standards in specific areas of information technology, ranging from coded character sets to biometrics. One of these subcommittees (SC7) is responsible for systems and software engineering standards. SC7 is in turn composed of many working groups that are responsible for developing standards on such topics as software process assessment and software systems documentation. Information about SC7 and its activities can be found at the SC7 website [14]. The IEEE Computer Society has Category A liaison status with ISO/IEC JTC1 SC7, and the S2ESC committee has sent many representatives to SC7 who are actively participating in SC7 working groups. Furthermore, S2ESC has been working to harmonize its software engineering standards with the international standards developed by SC7.

The rapidly growing collection of international standards for software engineering is consistent with the increasing professionalism of the software engineering discipline. The role played by the IEEE Computer Society in developing and promulgating these standards further reinforces this professionalism.

2.5 Professional Societies and Bodies of Knowledge

Professional practice relies on a commonly accepted body of knowledge. This is the case for traditional professions, such as medicine and law, and it is equally the case for emerging professions. For example the profession of project management rests on a body of knowledge that is codified in [15].

In 1999, two professional societies, the IEEE Computer Society and the Association for Computing Machinery (ACM), recognized that the evolution of software engineering as a profession called for the development of a body of knowledge, and initiated an effort to develop a Software Engineering Body of Knowledge [16] (Bourque 1999). This effort was crowned by the release of the SWEBOK Guide in 2004 [17].

However, it is important to note that the Association for Computing Machinery withdrew from the SWEBOK effort in 2000 [10]. This decision was based on ACM's conclusion that the body of knowledge was a step on the path to licensing software engineers, and that such licensing was premature.

Any body of knowledge must be subject to ongoing revision as a profession continues to evolve, and software engineering is no exception. The SWEBOK revision process is underway, and the next revision is scheduled for publication in 2009. The Software Engineering Body of Knowledge has received international recognition, and it has been published as a ISO/IEC technical report [18]. It serves as the technical foundation for the IEEE Computer Society's CSDP certification scheme.

2.6 Professional Societies and Codes of Ethics

As retired US Supreme Court Justice Sandra Day O'Connor said, "Professionalism requires adherence to the highest ethical standards of conduct …" [3]. Consistent with this observation, professional disciplines have developed explicit codes of ethics, and such codes are commonly developed by professional societies. For example a rather generic IEEE code of ethics can be found at [IEEE code]. For software engineering, IEEE-CS and ACM have collaborated to produce an ethics code [19]. The Software Engineering Code of Ethics and Professional Practice [20] has been widely cited as providing an ethical foundation for software engineering practice [21]. Other codes of ethics produced by professional societies refer more generally to engineering or computing practice. An overview of codes of ethics for computer professionals and literature about such codes can be found in [22].

3. Conclusion

The emergence of a professional discipline can be measured along several dimensions: governance, entrance control, preparation, body of knowledge, and ethical behavior. While the initial usage of the term "software engineering" may have been metaphorical, the ensuing 40 years have seen the creation of milestones along all of the dimensions mentioned above. It is therefore reasonable to conclude that software engineering has been moving toward internal and external recognition as a professional discipline, and that this progress can be expected to continue.

References

1. Randell, B., Software engineering in 1968, In: Proceedings of the 4th International Conference on Software Engineering, pp. 1-10, IEEE Press, Piscataway, NJ, USA (1979).
2. Mahoney, M., The roots of software engineering, CWI Quarterly Vol. 3, pp. 325-334 (1990).

3. O'Connor, S. Court of Appeals of Maryland Professionalism Course for New Admittees to the Maryland Bar, In: Professionalism Above and Beyond Ethics vol. 15 (1992). Downloaded from http://ilsccp.org/guidelines#ethics, 17 Apr 2008.
4. Institute of Electrical and Electronic Engineers Code of Ethics (2006), downloaded from www.ieee.org/portal/pages/iportals/aboutus/ethics/code.html, 17 April 2008.
5. Shaw, M., Prospects for an engineering discipline of software, IEEE Software vol. 7, pp. 15-24 (1990).
6. Adams, T. Software engineering in Canada, the US, and the UK: inter-professional relations and the emergence of a new profession. Working Paper #9, Center for Workforce Aging in the New Economy, University of Western Ontario London, Ontario, Canada (2004).
7. IEEE Computer Society. Software Engineering 2004: Curriculum Guidelines for Undergraduate Degree Programs in Software Engineering. Downloaded from sites.computer.org/ccse/SE2004Volume.pdf, 17 Apr 2008.
8. Canadian Information Processing Society, Position Paper on Software Engineering (2000) downloaded from http://www.cips.ca/it/position/softeng, 18 Apr 2008.
9. Bagert, D., Licensing and certification of computer professionals. Advances in Computers, Vol. 60, pp. 1-34 (2004).
10. Association for Computing Machinery, A summary of the ACM position on software engineering as a licensed engineering profession (2000), downloaded from www.cs.wm.edu/~coppit/csci690-spring2004/papers/selep_main.pdf.
11. Seidman, S., An international perspective on professional software engineering credentials, in: Software Engineering: Effective Teaching and Learning Approaches and Practices, IGI Global, Hershey, PA, USA (2008).
12. Moore, J., The Road Map to Software Engineering: A Standards-Based Guide, John Wiley and Sons, Hoboken, NJ, USA (2006).
13. IEEE Computer Society Standards Activities Board website, at standards.computer.org/sesc/s2esc_wkgroups/wkgndex.htm.
14. ISO/IEC JTC1 SC7 website, at www.jtc1-sc7.org.
15. Project Management Institute, A Guide to the Project Management Body of Knowledge, 3rd edition, Project Management Institute, Newtown Square, PA, USA (2004).
16. Bourque, P., Dupuis, R., Abran, A., Moore, J., Tripp, L., The guide to the software engineering body of knowledge, IEEE Software, vol. 16, pp. 35-44 (1999).
17. SWEBOK, The Guide to the Software Engineering Body of Knowledge, downloaded from www.swebok.org, 18 April 2008.
18. International Standardization Organization, ISO/IEC TR 19759:2005: Software Engineering -- Guide to the Software Engineering Body of Knowledge (SWEBOK), ISO, Geneva, Switzerland (2005).
19. IEEE Code of Ethics. Downloaded from http://www.ieee.org/web/membership/ethics/code_ethics.html, 18 Apr 2008.
20. Association for Computing Machinery, Software Engineering Code of Ethics and Professional Practice, version 5.2, downloaded from www.acm.org/about/se-code, 18 Apr 2008.
21. Anderson, R. The ACM code of ethics: history, process, and implications, in: C. Huff and T. Finholt, eds. Social Issues in Computing. McGraw Hill, New York, NY, USA, pp. 48-71 (1994).
22. Tavani, H., (1996), Professional ethics and codes of conduct for computer professionals (1996), downloaded from cyberethics.cbi.msstate.edu/biblio/section03/chap01, 18 Apr 2008.

IT Professional role today and tomorrow

Colin Thompson

(BCS, UK)

Abstract: As IT professionals we live in exciting times. The IT profession is coming of age and the role of the IT professional is changing rapidly.   The traditional IT Department, as a support function dedicated to providing technical solutions to problems defined by *'the busness'*, is set to disappear. The reality today is that IT doesn't just support business, it powers business and the future for the IT profession is all about the development of business-focussed professionals with a much wider range of skills and capabilities than in the past.

Information technology can, and in many instances does, deliver very substantial business and social benefits. It enables organisations to make dramatic leaps in productivity and governments to deliver greatly enhanced service levels that their citizens now expect. But successful IT enabled business change often remains elusive. If we are to realise the full potential of IT the function must move from being viewed as a technical solution provider to be seen as a full transformation partner.

This article draws on UK experience over the past 5 years to outline what all this will mean for IT professionals, for the IT profession and for the institutions that support the profession.

Background

Few things are more critical to the well-being, wealth and welfare of the citizens of the 21st century than the quality of our information and communication systems.   Healthcare, the security of savings, the ability of our companies to compete and the overall health of our national economies; every facet of our personal and business lives, from the mundane to the life-critical, is heavily dependent on computer-based systems and, in consequence, on the competence and professionalism of those who design, build, implement and manage those systems.

Over the past few years there has been rapidly growing recognition of the need to improve consistency in the way new IT systems are developed and complex IT-enabled change programmes are managed. That recognition is driven not just by the need to reduce the risk and cost of failure but increasingly by the need to maximize the dividends of successful IT enabled innovation. Business managers are now acutely aware that exploiting the full potential of IT is fundamental to their ability to compete and to meet customer expectations. Governments too have recognised that effective IT systems are critical to their ability to deliver improved

Please use the following format when citing this chapter:

Thompson, C., 2008, in IFIP International Federation for Information Processing, Volume 280; *E-Government; ICT Professionalism and Competences; Service Science*; Antonino Mazzeo, Roberto Bellini, Gianmario Motta; (Boston: Springer), pp. 69–80.

service to their citizens and, in the UK, the drive towards a more professional approach has been led to some extent by the pressure government has exerted on IT service suppliers.

It was against this background, in early 2005, that the British Computer Society set up a major programme designed to improve both capability and performance in the effective exploitation of IT. The programme has had the active support of other professional institutions and trade bodies and of leading members of the IT and business communities drawn from both the public and private sectors. Significantly, the key objectives [1] for the programme are aimed not at improving the traditional technical performance of IT practitioners but on improving the ability of organisations to exploit the full benefits that IT has to offer:

- *To improve the ability of business and other organisations to exploit the potential of information technology effectively and consistently by increasing professionalism*
- *To build an IT profession that is respected and valued by its stakeholders - government, business leaders, IT employers, IT users and customers - for the contribution that it makes to a more professional approach to the exploitation and application of IT*

These objectives reflect the recognition that a fundamentally new vision is required if the IT profession is to command fully the respect and commitment of its various stakeholders and to play its full part in improving capability and performance. The existing vision, built round a narrow image of activity focussed essentially on technical and engineering issues, will not provide a base for securing the necessary commitment or for driving the required changes. The need now is for an IT profession that has a much greater business focus and which has appropriate business and other non-technical competences to play a full part in all stages of IT exploitation. It must also be a profession that demands much greater personal responsibility and accountability of its practitioners and which requires regular re-accreditation to ensure that its qualifications provide evidence of current, rather than historic, competence. Crucially, it must also be a profession which covers both the *'I'* and the *'T'* of IT – it must be as much about *Information* as about *Technology*.

The need for a more business-focussed IT profession to meet the changing needs and expectations of customers was underlined by a global survey of senior IT and business leaders undertaken by the Economist Intelligence Unit in 2006.[2] 69% of those surveyed – and 83% of the CEOs and Board members surveyed – were convinced that the primary role of IT must shift rapidly from driving cost efficiency to enabling revenue growth.

---

[1] The Professional © 2008 The British Computer Society

[2] Great Expectations: The changing role of IT in business. Economist Intelligence Unit September 2006.

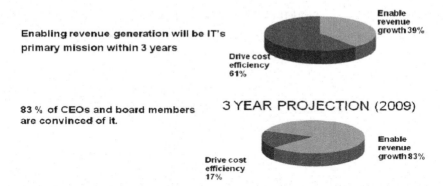

ASSESSMENT NOW (2006)

Enabling revenue generation will be IT's primary mission within 3 years

Enable revenue growth 39%

Drive cost efficiency 61%

83 % of CEOs and board members are convinced of it.

3 YEAR PROJECTION (2009)

Enable revenue growth 83%

Drive cost efficiency 17%

Whether things will have moved this dramatically by 2009 is doubtful but the survey is significant more for the underlying shift in attitude which it reflects than for the quality of its prediction.

This shift in focus represents a considerable challenge for the IT profession and for IT professionals, not least in terms of the new competences and capabilities that will be required. Few would claim that the profession is currently equipped for the new role but it must clearly become so if it is to support both business and wider society in securing the full benefit from IT.

The importance of the traditional technical skills and competences should not be underestimated or undervalued but, as we move further into the 21st century, it will be the ability to exploit both the information and the technology to deliver business and public benefit rather than technical excellence in itself that will distinguish the most successful businesses and national economies. In short, the IT profession has to move from its traditional role of technical solution provider to become a full transformation partner with the business organisations that it serves.

The IT profession

The UK Professionalism programme has included extensive research led by BCS and supported by major organisations in the industry. One of the main aims of that research has been to define the essential characteristics of the IT profession of the future. What, for example, will be the scope of the new profession in terms of practitioner competences, and how do we build a mature profession that will stand comparison with the older professions such as law, medicine and accountancy?

The ambition is to shape and create a mature IT profession with clearly defined professional standards. This will involve putting in place the necessary infrastructure and ensuring that the principles of professionalism are firmly embedded in standard practice. Some idea of the complexity can be gained from the diagram below.

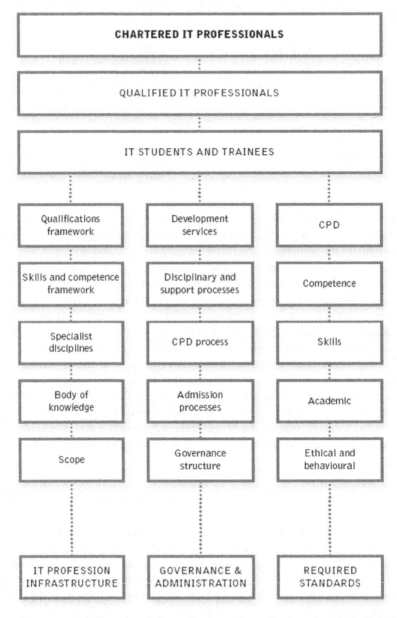

Figure 2: Building the fully effective IT profession © 2008 The British Computer Society

Professional institutions must take the lead here by defining standards, making the governance and administration arrangements and contributing to the professional infrastructure through products and services.

Scope of the Profession

With the spread of the use of IT into every part of our lives the roles undertaken by IT practioners have expanded. There are groups of practitioners who now operate in areas focussed on business change and transformation which can feel far removed from the traditional technological base of the IT profession. These practitioners cannot rely solely on their technical skills but also require skills more atuned to business leadership and management.

There is growing evidence of fluid boundaries between the competence sets of IT professionals and the competence sets of those in other professions such as finance, personnel, training and procurement. The scope of the IT profession is expanding and can be illustrated as follows:

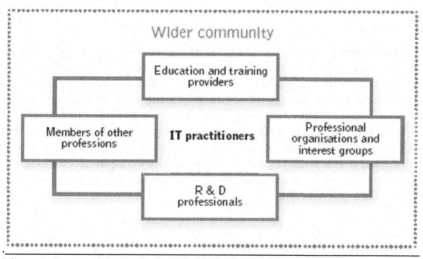

Figure 3: Scope of the profession © 2008 The British Computer Society

The work on practitioner scope within the UK has been led by the IT Sector Skills Council, e-skills UK[3] and has involved extensive consultation with the IT employer community. The result of that work is summarised in the following diagram which provides the basis for the essential segmentation of the new profession into recognised disciplines and specialisms:

---

[3] www.e-skills.com

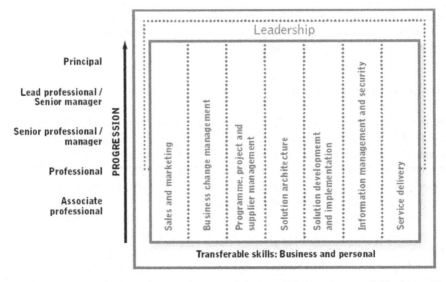

Figure 4: Professional Competency Model © e-skills UK Sector Skills Council ltd 2000-2007

Complementing this model the **SFIA**[4] (Skills for the Information Age) framework provides a common reference model for the identification of the skills needed to develop effective Information Systems (IS) making use of Information & Communications Technology (ICT) and enables employers of IT professionals to carry out a range of HR activities against a common framework of reference.

SFIAplus™ created by BCS to provide a more comprehensive tool, enables benchmarking of both individuals and jobs, whilst providing detailed pointers to training and development resources. This model also underpins an extensive range of BCS professional development products supporting both practitioners and organisations.

Competencies for senior roles

Further research carried out under the BCS Professionalism programme looked at the competencies and capabilities of the most successful Chief Information Officers (CIOs), and others in senior positions. The results[5] suggest that whilst foundation technical and managerial competencies are still important these are not the competencies that drive distinctive performance by those in senior positions. Those foundation competencies will typically be developed and applied by

---

[4] Skills for the Information Age: www.sfia.org.uk

[5] A Competency Framework for Chief Information Officers and Senior Leadership Positions © 2008 The British Computer Society

individuals as they progress through their careers but the defining competencies when they reach senior positions are likely to be those associated with leadership rather than any technical capability.

Building a mature IT profession

Establishing a mature professional infrastructure will be critical if IT professionals are to be supported through the required changes in roles and responsibilities. Clearly, if the ambition is to reach maturity, we need to understand just where we are on that journey at the present time and just what full maturity will look like when we get there. This aspect of the BCS research involved consultation with a wide range of established professional institutions covering other disciplines such as accountancy and medicine and more modern ones such as human resources and purchasing. The following diagrammatic representation provides an indication of the task facing us as we move the profession towards maturity.

The current level of maturity of the IT profession is estimated at between level 1 and 2; to meet the ambition for parity with other established professions we have to rise to at least level 4.[6]

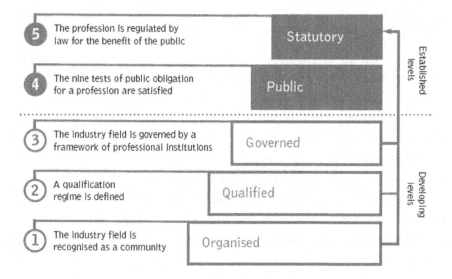

Figure 5: Profession maturity model derived from the Carnegie Mellon University Capability Maturity Model®   © 2008 The British Computer Society

---

[6] Establishing IT as a Profession © 2008 The British Computer Society

Benefits and Opportunities

One of the early lessons from the UK Professionalism Programme was that nobody ever votes against professionalism; no one ever argues that it is not a good thing. But it is also very clear that few are prepared to make a positive commitment to implement the principles of professionalism until they can see some clear business benefit sufficient to justify the investment required. It is also apparent that many people do not recognise the full scope and ramifications of professionalism, often mistakenly equating it solely with the attainment of a technical qualification or a relevant degree.

In the longer run we believe that the case for professionalisation will be self evident. The business world in which the IT profession operates is changing rapidly and those who do not recognise the need for change, or do not respond to that need, are likely to be left behind. In the meantime the business case for a more mature IT profession, working within a professionalised IT industry and business environment is strong and evidenced by the following quotes:

"*Annual cost of IT failure in Europe is $140.5 billion*" – **Gartner**

"*Effectively managed people assets have the potential to increase shareholder value by 30%.*" - **Aberdeen Group**

"*Competent suppliers working with competent customers are 8 times more likely to deliver successful projects*" - **UK Office of Government Commerce**

A report from the Royal Academy of Engineering and the BCS[7] noted "*There is an exceptionally large discrepancy between best practice and common practice in IT*".

Benefits for all stakeholders could be substantial, including significant improvements in:

- Project and programme success
- IT enabled business transformation capability
- Governance and compliance
- Business returns from IT investment
- Competitive edge for both IT suppliers and their customers
- Service delivery for both public and commercial organisations
- IT staff recruitment and retention
- Exploitation of information assets
- Career challenge and development for IT professionals

Customers for the services of the IT industry can expect improved project success rates with stronger innovation capability carried out by more effective and motivated staff.

---

[7] The Challenges of Complex IT Projects © The Royal Academy of Engineering.

Suppliers of IT services will benefit from a competitive edge in bidding for new business, improved consistency of development and delivery and improved relationships with customers. These benefits will in turn lead to enhanced business reputation.

For the IT practitioner there is an ambition that a mature IT profession with clearly defined professional standards will attract high quality people, inspire high performance and represent a career aspiration and opportunity for a wide spectrum of people. These practitioners will benefit from higher rewards, improved career opportunities, more varied job opportunities and increased recognition and respect.

What makes a Practitioner Professional?

So what is it that distinguishes *'a professional'?* And just what does *'professionalism' really* mean? These were two of the question which the BCS programme needed to answer at an early stage. In response to the first question it produced the following definition.

A fully established professional is a practitioner who has specific skills rooted in a broad base and appropriate qualifications, belongs to a regulated body, undergoes continuous development, operates to a code of conduct and recognises personal accountability.[8]

This definition is illustrated by the following diagram

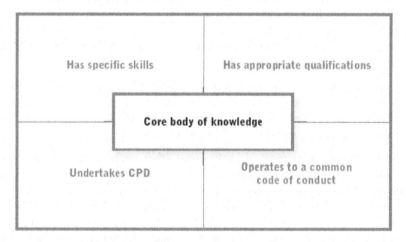

Figure 6: A Professional Practitioner © 2008 The British Computer Society

The essential elements of professionalism are three-fold – competence, integrity and public obligation. Competence is the demonstration of relevant, up-

---

[8] The Professional © 2008 The British Computer Society

to-date skills and capabilities appropriate to the particular task or role with practical experience to complement theoretical knowledge. These capabilities must be combined with a range of non-technical competences including communication and inter-personal skills, domain or business knowledge and, for many, the ability to lead or manage. These competences need to be underpinned by a broader foundation of experience, knowledge and understanding, backed by relevant qualifications and maintained by continuing professional development.

The second element encompasses Integrity, Responsibility and Accountability. A commitment to a published code of conduct, including ethical standards, which ideally is recognised and administered by the professional community, is essential. In parallel with the ethical considerations, and equally vital, is recognition that professionals have a set of obligations and responsibilities to the profession which sit alongside those to their employer or contract of employment. There is a matching professional accountability – justification for their actions and decisions lies firmly with the individual professional. Excuses such as "I was only following instructions" or "I did what the contract stated" are unacceptable to justify a course of action and in many countries are not acceptable in a court of law.

The final element of professionalism is the recognition that professionals have a public obligation. A professional is required to work in the best interest of society and to use their knowledge, skills, attributes and experience to apply IT diligently and carefully for the public good. This requirement, combined with that of personal accountability, places an onerous responsibility on the practitioner not only to make balanced and thoughtful decisions but to understand and be willing to explain the ramifications and consequences of those decisions and the impacts they will have on others.

Justice Sandra Day O'Connor, recently retired from the US Supreme Court summed up the essence of professionalism as:

"*A commitment to develop one's skills to the fullest and apply them responsibly to the problems at hand. Professionalism requires adherence to the highest ethical standards of conduct and a willingness to subordinate narrow self-interest in pursuit of the more fundamental goal of public service*".

The progressive attainment of professional ethos necessitates a hierarchy of standards and qualifications to acknowledge progress and achievement and to set public expectations. Such systems have been, and are continuing to be, developed in Australia, Canada, UK, the USA and elsewhere. In the UK the BCS has introduced Chartered IT Professional (CITP) as the gold standard to recognise professional IT practitioners. There are more than 17,000 registered CITPs and the number is growing rapidly as individuals and employers recognise the importance of defining and acknowledging the achievement of professionalism.

What Defines an IT-capable organisation?

While the creation of a mature, business-focussed IT profession is an essential element of the capability to exploit IT fully, it is not sufficient in itself. IT professionals can only be fully effective in organisations which have a wider professional culture and which are led by IT-competent business managers. Given this wider dependency it is important that the IT profession should take a proactive approach not just to improving its own professionalism but also to improving the business environment in which it operates. In the UK the BCS has done exactly that, working with other leading professionals, government, IT employers, institutions and trade associations to improve professionalism across a broad front.

In the area of business leadership, BCS has partnered with the Chartered Management Institute looking at the contribution of the Chief Executive in driving successful major change programmes. The report [9] from this project identified five key challenges facing senior executives in structuring, leading and implementing large and complex IT-driven business change.

- Creating transformational value rather than just implementing IT projects
- Building capability for ongoing change. Being able to predict future business needs and how IT can help shape new business models and deliver the desired benefits
- Creating a climate of open communication
- Managing confidence and risk - understanding the impact of external changes
- Building personal capability, learning and confidence.

The report concluded that CEOs need to have a growing understanding of the strategic use of IT to ensure that their organisations are ready to capitalise on the new opportunities it provides. Specifically, they need to have external environmental developments on their radar so that they can actively manage the implications for internal IT change programmes and in particular, active and visible leadership is required to avoid the twin traps of:

- extended implementation timeframes
- lack of full exploitation of business benefits.

A Professional Future

The work undertaken so far in the UK, has highlighted the enormous opportunity that now exists to create an IT profession driving a vastly improved

---

[9] Business Leadership of Technological Change : Five Key Challenges Facing CEOs © 2008 The British Computer Society

capability to exploit fully the potential of IT. The more recent work by the IFIP *International Professional Practice Programme Task Force* has demonstrated that this is a global opportunity – indeed the extent of globalization of the IT industry itself now makes it essential that we address this issue on an international basis.

The IT profession stands at a critical point in its development; responding to this opportunity will require a very different kind of IT profession and a body of IT professionals with a much wider range of knowledge and competence. Technical competence will remain important but there will be an increasing demand for IT practitioners with business, management and leadership skills.

This new IT profession must be focussed on business outcomes and play a full part at all stages of IT enabled business change programmes and projects. If the full potential of information and technology is to be realised, the IT function must move from being viewed as a support cost to being seen as an essential contributor to revenue generation, service improvement and business transformation.

Adapting to meet the challenge will not be easy for either the profession or the professionals. The changes for both are significant but so too are the potential benefits for all stakeholder communities. For the IT practitioner in particular the changes will mean higher rewards, improved career opportunities, increased recognition and the opportunity to play at a much more strategic level within organizations. And the IT profession which emerges from this process should be one which will stand alongside the accountancy profession in terms of influence and importance in the business world.

Turning this vision into reality will take both time and effort. As illustrated by the maturity model shown earlier in this article, we are still some way behind many of the older, more traditional areas of professional activity. But, unlike those other professions, we have the chance to put in place, almost from the outset, a coherent international professional structure to meet the needs of a global industry. That is a unique opportunity which we must now grasp and exploit.

European Universities and the ICT Industry

Vasile Baltac

Information Technology and Communications Association of Romania, Romania,
vasile.baltac@atic.org.ro

Abstract: Information and Communications Technologies (ICT) have a distinct and unique role to contribute to the overall advancement of Europe, in its efforts to ensure economic and social success. Europe needs continuous progress in information and communications technologies and its industry and universities contribute to this progress. The demand for professionals increases constantly and exceeds the offerings. Both in the industrial and university communities persists an opinion about a divorce between the formal existing educational institutions and the needs of ICT professionals by the industry. This divorce is considered by some to be at the origin of the scarcity of ICT professionals in many ICT specialties. While preparation of eSkills for basic ICT use is not the task of universities, but of high-schools, we may note also that there are still in several EU countries university graduates that do not have all the necessary basic skills to use ICT or E-business at work or at home. Policy makers, universities and industry have to increase investment in universities for preparing the right ICT skills. Europe has to bring its universities at the level of expectancy of the i2010 strategy.

Keywords: ICT industry, European universities, eSkills, certifications, CEPIS

1 Why a Paper on Universities and ICT Industry?

Information and Communications Technologies (ICT) have a distinct and unique role to contribute to the overall advancement of Europe, in its efforts to ensure economic and social success. This progress is based on the large deployment of technologies, a highly sophisticated workforce and the general training of users to fully exploit what the technologies offer. Entrepreneurship is fully embraced by enterprises in the ICT sector and the role of small and medium enterprises (SME) is remarkably important for the development of the sector, where challenge and competition are the main engines of growth.

Europe is under pressure from both the American and Asian continents. Higher salaries in Europe can be counterbalanced only by innovation and skills. The fresh

Please use the following format when citing this chapter:

Baltac, V., 2008, in IFIP International Federation for Information Processing, Volume 280; *E-Government; ICT Professionalism and Competences; Service Science*; Antonino Mazzeo, Roberto Bellini, Gianmario Motta; (Boston: Springer), pp. 81–94.

developments in Eastern Europe hardly compensate the impact of new sources of ICT manpower in Asia and South America. Europe needs continuous progress in information and communications technologies and its industry and universities contribute to this progress. Industry delivers the technologies and applications, but the core elements are the skills, and professionals having these skills. There is no other industry with such a high rate of evolution reflected in changes in the skills, and in the need for retraining, during the working life of a person.

It is the role of European higher education institutions, generally called universities, to produce the needed skills. Universities have the primary distinct role in producing the professionals needed by the ICT industry and they have to continue to strengthen their vital role in this respect. Despite a significant quantitative and qualitative offering by European universities, the demand for professionals increases constantly and exceeds the offerings. Estimating supply and demand levels in 2010 and 2015, CEPIS believes that Europe would face shortages of up to 70,000 ICT practitioners (CEPIS, 2007).

The cooperation of European universities with the ICT industry is very important and is of interest not only to the two actors, but public authorities should also be actively engaged. CEPIS notes that there persists both in the industrial and university communities an opinion about a divorce between the formal existing educational institutions and the needs of ICT professionals by the industry. This divorce is considered by some to be at the origin of the scarcity of ICT professionals in many ICT specialties. Other opinions take into account the fact that too few young people in developed countries want to study engineering subjects, to supply the needs of the industry. On the other hand, ICT professional educational background needs to be multidisciplinary to address student needs and highly specialised to address industry needs, a hard to reconcile dilemma.

While preparation of eSkills for basic ICT use is not the task of universities, but of high-schools, CEPIS notes also that there are still in several EU countries university graduates that do not have all the necessary basic skills to use ICT or E-business at work or at home.

Policy makers, universities and industry have to increase investment in universities for preparing the right ICT skills (Lamborghini, 2007). Most ICT graduates now come from Asia, a fact with deep impact on the future of the ICT industry.

Europe has to bring its universities at the level of expectancy of the i2010 strategy.

1.1 University – ICT Industry Partnership

The best way to interact between universities and the industry has been a much debated topic in Europe for decades. Universities enjoy, in general, a good relationship with the ICT industry. This is reflected in the high level of training of

ICT graduates and in the various forms of cooperation between university and industry.

There are still voices that affirm that universities and industry do not cooperate at a sufficient level. There are similar opinions in the USA, even if for European observers the US university-industry relations seem to be an ideal (Bavec, 2007). It is certain that universities and industry have different objectives and they might be naturally on different sides. But as industry is an important stakeholder of the university world it is worthwhile finding a compromise for the mutual benefit of all (Rovan, 2007).

European universities must be effective in their competition in information and communications technologies with the US and other world universities. This effectiveness can be achieved only through better cooperation with the ICT industry, in partnership with the relevant authorities.

1.2 Universities in a Changing World

Universities are moving in a changing world. Students are now less ready to accept what university delivers them if this does not fit with their set of values. There is a growing trend towards part-time studies. This is particularly true for computer related studies. The Digital Era started first in the universities bringing worldwide access to information and limiting the ex-cathedra approach to learning.

ICT is a vital element of the universities' infrastructure and courses tend to become world assets through Internet postings. In this way, and in many other ways, ICT has increased competition among universities. Europe should not be satisfied in this respect as US and Asian universities are making significant steps to update their courses and infrastructures.

Students have now unparalleled access to information and services and their expectancies are harder than ever to fulfil. The fast changes brought by on-line available teaching information changes the demographics of students. People may become students at any age and universities have to be prepared to offer them what they need.

Students are influenced in their demands by industry job offers. Skills need to be changed often, even in the same decade. ICT students graduating before 1995 were not exposed in university to some of today's concepts and technologies during their studies. Today, probably very few universities in the world still prepare skills in several old technologies, but the industry still needs them for legacy systems.

Universities are facing their most dramatic challenge yet, a highly connected, 24x7 digital worlds (Carrey, 2006). Industry creates competitors to universities, the so called 'infomediaries' (composite of information and intermediary) operating on-line 24/24 with very user-friendly portals, financially attractive for students needing more skills and less formal diplomas. Online course use is growing with a double digit figure.

Universities preparing ICT skills are confronted with even more increased reliance on technology. There is a discrepancy between universities that may afford the technological change needed without industry support and universities that need this support. One of the barriers to updating technological equipment in universities is the cost. Most European universities cannot afford to update their hardware, software and telecom infrastructure on an annual basis.

2 Universities and the ICT Industry

2.1 Universities and ICT High Innovation Rate

Universities keep up with the new technological wave and new applications. Any lack of adaptation creates or widens the gap between the level of skills industry expects from fresh graduates and the actual skills produced by universities. The ICT industry innovates fast and it is not quite clear to many to what extent the institutions of higher education should adapt to new trends and technologies. This does not imply that universities should follow every industry hype blindly; they have to be able to look "beyond the hype".

Many universities rely on research as a primary focus. From a simplified perspective universities would focus on science and reflective research, while leaving the ICT industry to handle the applicative angle. Nevertheless, one might question whether the professors and instructors should remain focused on fairly narrow PhD subjects for decades, while possibly excluding new market-relevant features from their research and their classroom lectures. This seems to be the present state of the differences between what European Universities offer and European ICT industry needs in the work force.

There is a natural trend for universities to favour basic research and leave applied research to industry. In some cases, European universities have researchers able to perform any kind of project and seek industry contracts as an additional source of funding.

This is why one solution might be for the universities to grant easier access to more practical expert personnel. This would require that universities set up expert panels to evaluate the way in which new technological waves could add to the knowledge of existing research fields or even constitute the basis for entirely new research grounds. These panels should be affiliated with ICT industry personnel who would support the integration of academic studies with practical up-to-date exercises. Similar models have been initiated, with quite some success, in the past. CEPIS is in the position to act as catalyst of such panels.

2.2 Universities and Entrepreneurship (SME)

ICT industry growth is fed by innovation carried out in small and medium enterprises. Most large ICT companies in the world, including Europe, started as SMEs. The SMEs act as innovation poles, they gather the skills and entrepreneurship attitudes that make ICT grow.

Universities are the main source of entrepreneurs. Most start their ventures, even before they graduate. European universities will better contribute to the increase of the SME sector in ICT, first by giving the students a solid scientific and technical background to allow them to innovate, and second by preparing them with the managerial skills needed in a small enterprise.

The universities are also the catalysts of entrepreneurship through technology parks established in the universities. This allows entrepreneurs to keep in contact with professors and benefit from their research output.

CEPIS believes that governments and the EU Commission should encourage, in any form, the development of such entrepreneurial centres around universities, nuclei of birth for many ICT companies in the industry.

2.3 Research in Universities

Universities are actively engaged in research. The research activity is the most important pillar sustaining teaching and bringing educators close to technology levels. The European R&D framework programmes have largely succeeded in bringing universities and industry together in funding research that is useful to both (Katsikas, 2007). Speeding up the application of the research characteristic to ICT is seemingly benefiting the industry and forcing the universities to industry-like time scenarios.

Universities accelerate innovation in learning and research as they understand the marketplace and develop new types of learning systems. This report is focused on the educational role of the universities and the research aspects will not be further developed.

2.4 Universities and ICT skills

Universities are the main supplier of ICT skills demanded in the marketplace. ICT skills are divided into 3 categories by the European Commission (EU, 2007):

• ICT practitioner skills: these are the capabilities required for researching, developing, designing, strategic planning, managing, producing, consulting, marketing, selling, integrating, installing, administering, maintaining, supporting and servicing ICT systems.

• ICT user skills: these are the capabilities required for the effective application of ICT systems and devices by the individual. ICT users apply systems as tools in support of their own work. User skills cover the use of common software tools and of specialised tools supporting business functions within industry. At the general level, they cover "digital literacy".

• E-business skills: these are the capabilities needed to exploit opportunities provided by ICT, notably the Internet; to ensure more efficient and effective performance of different types of organisations; to explore possibilities for new ways of conducting business/administrative and organisational processes; and/or establish new businesses.

The ICT industry counts on universities to produce professionals with ICT practitioner skills.

It is not the task of universities to prepare the people to use ICT applications, i.e. to have the user or E-business skills. However, Europe is not uniform as regards the level of digital literacy throughout the various countries and E-business development. There are significant differences in levels of digital literacy among the 27 EU countries and also compared with non-EU countries.

All universities, due to the high mobility of students, should ascertain the level of ICT skills that their junior freshmen students have on admission and bring all students to the necessary levels of basic user and eBusiness ICT skills. CEPIS considers ECDL to be an appropriate tool to asses this level.

This implication of universities in assessment or creation of basic skills is important as ICT is no longer a product or service for the elite, but as EU's eEurope states "Information Society is for all".

2.5 Universities and the increasing scarcity of ICT professionals

The strategic importance of the contemporary eSkills for Europe is widely recognized. Estimating supply and demand levels in 2010 and 2015 CEPIS believes that Europe would face shortages of up to 70,000 ICT practitioners, because of inadequate qualification and certification infrastructure (CEPIS 2007). Other reports confirm the gap in ICT skills preparation in Europe and underline that there is another gap in the so called e-business skills that mean effective competencies in using ICT and web technologies for business applications and for e-government applications.

Universities have the responsibility, not only for the qualitative aspects of ICT skills needed, but also to adapt and provide solutions for the increasing scarcity of ICT professionals within the market. The foreseeable lack of ICT skills in a few years shows that universities and policy makers are far from agreeing on what actions are urgent, both as diversification of ICT profiles and annual output. In some countries the supply/demand disequilibrium of ICT students is expected to deepen even more dramatically as the number of accepted ICT students continues to increase only marginally, or in some cases even drop. This contradicts the general trend for higher salaries and elite status of ICT graduates.

The different approaches of the universities and industry to the graduate skills required increases the gap between what universities offer and what the industry needs are. Industry has pragmatic goals and expectations. They look for young employees that are immediately employable and functional without much additional investments into their professional formation. So, they would like to influence curricula and make them more practical and relevant. Industry would like to identify the most promising students and potential employees in advance. An appropriate preliminary selection of graduates would significantly lower industry's risk in investments into new employees. In many companies this is the main objective in their relationship with the universities.

Within the university environment, especially in the new European Union states, there are still calls for a high level of student training for everybody. This is why some professors criticise the fact that very good students are hired by companies during their second or third grades, therefore neglecting theoretical education and moving away from a potential scientific career.

Conciliation among these divergent tendencies is vital for reducing the gap between the demand of industry and the offer of ICT graduates of the universities.

2.6 Profile of ICT graduates

The universities aim to produce well-qualified scientists and engineers with a strong scientific background in the basic sciences, thorough knowledge of current and emerging technology, coupled with communication skills, the ability to effectively interact and interoperate with scientists of other disciplines, and with management and leadership skills.

Normally this is what industry would need. This is not always the case and we see a gap between what ICT industry wants as a profile of graduates and what universities deliver. In fact, even industry has no homogenous requests. Large ICT companies ask for a solid scientific background as they have resources to further train their staff to undertake a broad range of tasks and projects. Smaller ICT companies prefer specialised ICT graduates ready-to-work providing return without further human resource training expenses. It is impossible to reconcile the two opposing requirements of the industry to have ICT graduates who are both flexible and immediately usable.

European universities train their ICT students in a variety of ways and a continuous process of interaction of universities with industry and society is of paramount importance. Every university has to decide what kind of professional they want to offer to the industry and adapt the curricula to best fit to that requirement within the type of profession chosen.

As regards non-ICT graduates, the industry (both large and small companies) demands graduates with basic ICT skills, e.g. having the ability to use ICT tools for simple tasks, and as an educational tool without further training. The same demand is presented by society at large, the administration, educational system, media, etc.

2.7 Graduate level vs. certifications

The industry needs highly skilled people ready to perform specific tasks and projects. A possible solution to this demand is the process of certifications. The ICT industry has developed a full series of vendor certifications asking people to pass examinations and tests. Most certifications are related to a particular company and product and are not suited for new graduates who will specialise later after some activity in the industry.

ICT graduates of European universities are characterised by a variety of specialisations and further certification is the only way of specialising them for specific tasks. It would be ideal if a graduate would have a certification, but this would mean a serious change of university role and duties towards students, making universities simply an industry service provider. This does not exclude a student to take a vendor certification while working in the industry or as an extra optional subject.

The main advantage of certifications can become their main drawback. From one side, a certification ensures that the defined competences are actually possessed by the certified (with a credibility given by the reliability of the certifying body). This increases the mobility of the certified, whose competences are easily recognised even abroad. From the other side, the certification hides any difference among certified people: it just tells the user that all certified people possess at least the competences defined by the syllabus, nothing about possible deeper levels of knowledge by one certified person with respect to another (Scarabotollo, 2007).

Universities have a natural tendency, for a variety of reasons, to keep away from vendor oriented industry certifications.

Industry vendor oriented certifications will continue when they relate to specific proprietary technologies in the ICT field, but those not related with proprietary technologies will end. Even in the USA it is viewed by many that industry certifications are useless from an employment point of view.

However, a more general certification based less on a specific company competence and more on general professional competence would possibly build a university-industry bridge.

Such a certification is proposed by CEPIS through EUCIP and in trying to bring closer graduate skills to EUCIP–like skills seems one obvious step to harmonise university-industry needs.

2.8 Curricula - is the Bologna process moving in the right direction?

Curricula are what differentiate universities and define the level of professionalism of the future graduate.

The rapid advance of information and communications technology and the specific high rate of innovation bring industry to ask universities, almost unanimously, to update frequently their ICT curricula. The present curricula are judged by many in industry as not being adaptive enough to the new trends in ICT industry.

A major consideration is that the university curricula give too much attention to the theoretical training and less to industry internships and thus tend to produce super-skilled graduates (Baltac, 2007). The industry needs such people, but in a small number, as those being too highly skilled become unsatisfied with routine work, predominant in many companies.

Universities should produce both practitioners and research oriented people. The practitioners' level would be set through graduate and post-graduate master programmes. The research oriented students will benefit from PhD programmes.

The Bologna process which has just started may solve this problem, but it is still on the table. The Bologna agreement is expected to be implemented all over the European Union by the year 2010 and hopes to eliminate obstacles to the free circulation of people and help them to find jobs consistent with their education, regardless of their original country.

In general, universities claim to have adapted their curricula to the requirements of the Bologna recommendations. While some of them consider revisions to be made at the end of cycles (3+2+3), others consider a curricula revision every year.

In some EU countries it is true that in ICT specialisations the new Bologna type scheme (3+2+3) does not yet produce the best results. The first 3 years are filled with many courses repeating high school topics and students are not given the specialisation skills required by the industry, with dissatisfaction on both sides.

There are many opinions that the European tendency to move toward three-year bachelor degree programmes, may be alright for the humanities, but is certainly not acceptable for those areas of study which cannot be imagined without serious internships (medicine and engineering, including computing). Several universities in various countries declared that for computer science or engineering they will continue with 4 or 5 year bachelor programmes.

The Bologna process has to be continued with curricula updated for ICT graduates in the best interests of European universities and industry. Curricula have to be revisited systematically for the best harmonisation of graduates with market demands in Europe. This is related to continuing education and mobility.

2.9 The role of continuing education and mobility

As an industry with short technological cycles, the ICT industry is particularly appropriate for lifelong learning. This is essential for e-skills competence-building and certification, as businesses face the need to respond to the shortening of the technology life-cycles in ICT and the accompanying obsolescence of related knowledge, skills and competences of their employees (Lueders, 2007). This opens new horizons to work based and non formal learning.

Updating professional training via a continuous educational process is not always undertaken by universities of most European countries, with some noted exceptions.

Master and doctoral studies are mostly aimed at students with high potential for research and rarely universities engage themselves in adult ICT education through university courses. One exception is represented by Executive MBA courses with ICT specialisations.

However, continuous education with short cycles is a necessity in ICT. On one hand, people who graduated 10-15 years ago received an education based on technologies that are now obsolete. Training in the new technologies, frequently requiring revising basic concepts, is left to industry training schools. Universities should be encouraged to offer master courses to students or graduates of other disciplines as a conversion course. Many of these could be offered through e-learning.

On the other hand, the lack of skills brings into the ICT field an important number of non-ICT university graduates, mostly in emerging countries. They enter the field mostly retrained through industry certifications lacking basic training in computing concepts.

Universities could play a major role in the ICT education of people who have already been working in the industry for years or are under professional re-conversion. They have to be opened to all groups needing ICT education.

New advances in e-learning technologies allow and favour distance learning, transforming the industry is a serious competitor of universities for adult and continuous education.

Proper financing can lead universities to offer high level free courses on new technologies, an approach reserved for the moment to several companies and professional associations. CEPIS believes that universities have to play a more important role in the post-graduate training of ICT professionals.

Mobility in the sense of movement of people between universities and industry is to be encouraged. Universities enjoy a large autonomy, but this should encourage people from industry to bring their fresh innovative ideas and experience to students and to people from universities to apply their ideas in industry.

This could change the opinion existing in many European universities, that the educators are civil servants with good and bad features, among which immovability, even when incompetent and lacking a business approach, and insisting on universities as essentially a scientific and research environment. This has a negative impact on updating with the needs of human resources by the ICT industry in particular, but one could say with the needs of industry and services in general.

CEPIS believes that mobility of people between universities and ICT industry is beneficial, will promote innovation, and has to be encouraged by a proper framework.

3 Universities and ICT basic skills

eEurope cannot be achieved without overall dissemination of basic ICT skills. Not only citizens are required to possess these skills, but the lack of these skills has profound economic impact especially for SMEs. Due to their limited resources, SMEs cannot invest in basic ICT education of their personnel and they have to be helped in this direction. e-Inclusion has different levels in the different countries of the European Union. There are still cases where not only secondary school graduates do not have these skills, but also some non-ICT university graduates do not have them (Baltac, 2008).

Training for basic skills for ICT and E-Business is not the task of universities, but belongs to secondary education. The largest part of the target group for spreading digital literacy is at an age where going back to secondary school is impossible. Universities cannot be asked to participate in the effort to disseminate basic ICT skills after student graduation, due to their highly qualified staff and their main research and education priorities.

Universities will bring a notable contribution to basic ICT skills dissemination, if all non-ICT graduates in Europe will have these basic skills. ICT and web technologies have to be considered as main enabling technologies for the preparation of all professions and in all industrial and social activities. Secondary and high schools should refocus their education programmes around these enabling technologies and redesign new partnerships with industry and public services for the dynamic preparation of the right skills in a permanently changing environment. Universities may help them with developing curricula and teaching materials.

The e-business skills are not also generally covered by universities; because they require a deep context knowledge originated by on the job experience and is frequently offered by some IT vendors as consultancy service. This is a category of professionals most appreciated by the market and it is also the most inclined to the certification approach.

CEPIS has developed a programme called European Computer Driving Licence - ECDL, now at Syllabus 5, based on the contribution of experts of national computer associations. We may strongly conclude that all European secondary school and university graduates have to be digitally literate, at least at the level of ECDL.

The role of universities in this area will end when all high school graduates will be at the required level of basic ICT skills.

4 Role of EU and Governments in university-industry relationship

Governments are the catalysts that can influence the 'universities/ICT industry' relationship. In Europe, a high number of universities are public universities, the role of the EU and Governments going far beyond being only catalysts of relations of the education system with industry. Particularly in the EU, where in addition to national governments the European Commission plays an important role with its financial incentives and different R&D and regional programmes. Their regulatory role has an important function to maintain and support an educational infrastructure that would provide a sufficient number of educated people for all social and economic needs.

Governments and the European Commission can dramatically change universities/industry relations with focused incentives, mainly derived from their funding schemes.

ICT skills now have a well defined impact on economy and society. The lack of e-business and ICT skills at country level could lead to a potential loss of at least 1% of the GDP (Lamborghini, 2007) and the delay of major national or European e-projects. A focus on ICT skills is therefore an action of paramount importance for national Governments and the European Commission.

5 CEPIS Call to action

CEPIS is the most representative non-governmental body of ICT professionals in Europe with 37 member association from 33 European countries representing more than 300,000 professionals.

CEPIS recognises the main role of the universities in ICT education. Universities and the ICT industry are partners and the success of this partnership is sought by all. CEPIS believes that some actions are bringing closer the universities and industry expectations.

• CEPIS offers its services with the participation of the European Commission in a multi-stakeholder partnership as a pan-European mediator between universities and industry to define requirements for ICT skills at graduate, post-graduate and distance learning levels. CEPIS is the right group to bring together academia and industry in order that the output from the educational institutions satisfies the needs of the industry.

- CEPIS offers its assistance in standardising and homogenising European mutual recognition of professionalism in the ICT sector.
- ICT curricula have to be adapted to reflect the actual needs of future graduates as industry employees. CEPIS offers its mediation through its EUCIP certification model that can be used as a tool for levelling up curricula of ICT studies in European universities.
- CEPIS believes that governments and the EU Commission should encourage, in any form, the development of entrepreneurial centres around universities nuclei of birth for many ICT companies in the industry.
- CEPIS supports the use of e-learning as a continuing professional development methodology.
- CEPIS considers that universities should be encouraged to offer master or other post-graduate conversion courses to non-ICT graduates.
- Universities have to check that their non-ICT students have the minimal ICT skills to act in the Information Society. CEPIS considers that its ECDL certification tool is very appropriate for checking the level attained by a non-ICT student.
- While recognising the positive role of the Bologna process, CEPIS asks for a review of the present content of curricula for ICT studies that could affect the future of the ICT industry by producing graduates without the proper theoretical background and practical training.
- CEPIS considers that the ICT vendor oriented professional certifications should be organised outside universities, offering graduates, after a certain experience gained in the field, a professional status. CEPIS offers its vendor neutral EUCIP certification programme enabling a unified assessment, across Europe, of professional level of ICT skills. Such vendor neutral certifications could be undertaken by universities at their evaluation.
- CEPIS believes that mobility of people between universities and the ICT industry is beneficial and it will promote innovation. This should be encouraged by a proper framework.
- CEPIS highly appreciates the e-Inclusion initiative of the European Commission. CEPIS thinks that all non-ICT students should be tested for their basic abilities to use ICT technologies at workplaces and at home. CEPIS considers its ECDL tool as an excellent solution for this assessment to be generalised in universities.
- CEPIS recognises the role of new countries that became EU members. They represent an important reservoir of ICT skills with proven competences and competitiveness. However, the e-Inclusion is not at the level of older members of the EU and ICT skills emigration affects these countries. CEPIS asks the European Commission to pay special attention to the ICT development needs of these countries, by implementing special programmes for ICT infrastructural development and ICT basic skills dissemination. CEPIS has member associations in all these countries and can define the actions and their implementation.

Acknowledgements

The above position paper was developed by the author during September 2007 – April 2008 as the chairman of a Task Force on Education set by the Council of the European Professional Societies CEPIS.

Contributions by comments and ideas by Fernando Piera – ATI Spain, Anders Linde - Dansk IT, Mary Sharp – ICS, Ernst Mayr – GI, Jos Baeten – NGI, Michael Schanz – VDE, Giulio Occhini – AICA and Andrew McGettrick - BCS are acknowledged. Special acknowledgment is to be done to members of CEPIS Execom, especially Geoff McMullen, Past President and Niko Schlamberger, President, who encouraged me and the work of the task force.

Debates at IT STAR 2nd IT STAR Workshop on Universities and ICT Industry UNICTRY 07, Genzano di Roma, 26 May 2007 and EU University Business Forum, Brussels, 28-29 February 2008 (European Commission 2008) had an important contribution to the clarification of the above ideas.

References

Baltac, Vasile, Universities and the Information Society, in L'Europe dans la Société de l'Information, Editions Larcier, Paris, 2008

Baltac, Vasile and Mihalca, Dan, On Romanian Experiences Related to Universities and ICT Industry, Proceedings of the 2nd IT STAR Workshop on Universities and ICT Industry UNICTRY 07, Genzano di Roma, 26 May 2007

Bavec, Cene, Universities and the ICT industry in search for innovativeness, Proceedings of the 2nd IT STAR Workshop on Universities and ICT Industry UNICTRY 07, Genzano di Roma, 26 May 2007

Carey, Patrick F., IBM's Higher Education Point of View – 2012, Executive White Paper Series, (2006), Available via IBM http://www-3.ibm.com/industries/education/doc/content/ /resource/thought/1737354110.html , Accessed 24 April 2008

CEPIS, Thinking ahead on e-skills for the ICT industry in Europe, eSkills Report, 2007 Available via CEPIS www.cepis.org/files/cepis/docs/20071217032722_Thinking%20Ahead%20on%20e-Skills%20in%20.doc Accessed 24 April 2008

European Commission, http://ec.europa.eu/education/policies/educ/business/index_en.html Accessed 1 May 2008

European Union, DG Enterprise and Industry, e-Skills FOR the 21st CENTURY: FOSTERING COMPETITIVENESS, GROWTH AND JOBS, Available via EU http://ec.europa.eu/enterprise/ict/policy/ict-skills.htm Accessed 24 April 2008

Katsikas, Sokratis K., Universities and the ICT Industry, Higher Education and the ICT Industry, IT STAR Newsletter May 2007 Available in printed form and via IT STAR www.itstar.eu

Lamborghini, Bruno, Keynote Speech, Proceedings of the 2nd IT STAR Workshop on Universities and ICT Industry UNICTRY 07, Genzano di Roma, 26 May 2007

Lueders, Hugo, e-Skills Competences, Proceedings of the 2nd IT STAR Workshop on Universities and ICT Industry UNICTRY 07, Genzano di Roma, 26 May 2007

Rovan, Branislav , Universities and Industry, Proceedings of the 2nd IT STAR Workshop on Universities and ICT Industry UNICTRY 07, Genzano di Roma, 26 May 2007

Scarabottolo, Nello, Certification of ICT skills: a bridge between Universities and Industries, 2nd IT STAR Workshop, Genzano di Roma, 26 May 2007

How to move forward and implement e-skills on a long term basis

E-skills are a strategic tool to develop innovation and meet challenges deriving from globalisation

Franco Patini

Confindustria, Confederation of Italian Industry

Nowadays, e-skills concern an ample group of interested parties, in fact, considering the "digital citizenship" we might conclude that we are all involved, from those who use basic levels of "digital access" to ICT specialists.

Many are therefore the stakeholders operating on issues related to e-skills development: schools, Universities, public administrations, enterprises, political makers, associations, local governors, just to mention some of them.

Amongst all initiatives that Italy is carrying out, we deem important to highlight some of them having a particular value: those carried out within "the system".

We believe essential, at a Country level, without willing to obstacle single initiatives, private or public, or which are the result of Public – Private Partnership, to disseminate a common and shared model to define, describe and evaluate e-skills, able to cover the whole scenario, from e-citizens to informatics experts.

In the light of the foregoing, we can confirm that our Country has made an accurate choice testified by various initiatives now ongoing, as hereinafter briefly pointed out:

- The Italian Ministry of Employment, in organizing the Labour Bourse as a meeting place to exchange professionals demand and offer, has adopted the EUCIP model as the framework according to which professional profiles are described
- the National Committee of Informatics in Public Administration (CNIPA) is about to publish a recommendation to be applied by Public administrations in order to adopt the EUCIP framework as reference scheme for the evaluation of professional skills to be used in ICT public tenders
- In the academic ambit, Universities of Information Science and Informatics Engineering are introducing the EUCIP model (and relevant recognizing mechanism of curricula credits) to try to align academic skills, typical of university courses, to main skills required by the market.

Please use the following format when citing this chapter:

Patini, F., 2008, in IFIP International Federation for Information Processing, Volume 280; *E-Government; ICT Professionalism and Competences; Service Science*; Antonino Mazzeo, Roberto Bellini, Gianmario Motta; (Boston: Springer), pp. 95–96.

Together with those « institutional initiatives » many best practices can be mentioned: certain public administration offices, particularly attentive, as well as enterprises and professional institutions (for example the Association and Register of Engineers) are developing strategies that not only tend to evaluate and develop ICT skills (i.e. e-skills) but are build recurring always more often to the shared model.

In conclusions is always more diffuse the assumption that – in order to create a favourable environment for e-skills development, on long term basis – is essential, at a national level, but this of course applies to other Countries at EU level, the existence of an "e-skills framework" that has to be:

- *shared*
- *not "owned"*
- *maintained and able to grow*
- *entrusted to an authoritative and not competitive entity*

all, hopefully on an European scale.

IT and Professionalism in Developing Countries

Focus on Africa

Moira de Roche

President: Computer Society South Africa, General Manager – Laragh Skills (Pty) Ltd, moirad@laragh.com

Abstract: Most of Africa is focused on alleviating poverty and starvation, so IT practice does not enjoy the prominence in Africa. However, developing the IT Industry, and ensuring that practitioners are professional, will provide an industry that can create wealth. After a brief discussion on what is meant by professionalism, this paper will explore the issues relating to IT in Africa, especially South Africa, and why Africa is the "forgotten continent" from a global IT perspective. It explores professionalism skills frameworks, and how proven skills levels can help change this perspective. Finally, it provides recommendations for a way forward.

Keywords: Information Technology, IT, Professionalism, Skills frameworks, Africa, standards

1. Introduction

In researching this paper, the author found very little research on IT in Africa, other than how it relates to the Digital Divide, or so called E-Development. According to the World Bank, E-development has two possible connotations - the development of the ICT related aspects of society (e.g. bundling egovernment, e-civil society, e-business and ICT infrastructure development) and using ICT as a tool within a holistic approach to social and economic development. The development of the IT Industry per se is largely ignored.

This is in stark contrast to other developing countries such as India and China. For this reason, much of its contents are anecdotal or the authors own opinions.

As the author lives in South Africa, is very involved with the Computer Society, and has been in the IT Training industry for many years, the paper will mostly relate to the situation in South Africa. It is also the most advanced nation in sub-Saharan Africa, with a flourishing IT Industry.

Please use the following format when citing this chapter:

de Roche, M., 2008, in IFIP International Federation for Information Processing, Volume 280; *E-Government; ICT Professionalism and Competences; Service Science*; Antonino Mazzeo, Roberto Bellini, Gianmario Motta; (Boston: Springer), pp. 97–108.

1.1 Africa in perspective

Let's look at some numbers.

Perhaps the most useful way of looking at Africa is to consider its population in contract to the rest of the world. Table 1 below shows the populations of the 5 most populous countries.

Table 1. Most populous countries (Source: Wikipedia)

Country	Population	Percentage of World Population
World	6,671,226,000	
China	1,323,436,000	19,84%
India	1,131,982,000	16,97%
USA	303,902,495	4,55%
Indonesia	231,627,000	3,47%
Brazil	186,576,380	2,80%

Table 2. Shows the total population of Africa.

Table 2 – Populations of Africa and some countries in Africa. (Source: Wikipedia)

Country	Total Population	Percentage of total	222 countries listed
Africa (53 countries)	922,000,000	13.82%	
South Africa	47,850,700	0.72 %	No 26 in world
Nigeria	148,093,000	2.22%	No 8 in world

South Africa has the highest GDP in Africa (see below) and Nigeria the largest population, which is why they have been listed in the above table.

And what about Gross Domestic Product?

Richest 10 African Countries 2006: GDP Per Country
1. South Africa $606.4 billion in international$ (up 8% from 2005)
2. Algeria $262.2 billion (up 8.5%)
3. Nigeria $181.8 billion (up 10.2%)
4. Morocco $150.8 billion (up 4.8%)
5. Sudan $98.8 billion (up 11.2%)
6. Tunisia $91.4 billion (up 7.4%)
7. Ethiopia $78.4 billion (up 12%)
8. Ghana $59.4 billion (up 9.1%)
9. Angola $53.9 billion (up 24.3%)
10. Democratic Rep. of Congo $50.4 billion (up 9.7%)

Out of 50 African nations, the top 10 countries above generated almost 40% of Africa's total GDP in 2006. Note that each experienced growth over the previous year.

1.2. ICT in Africa

According to the World Bank, Information and Communications Technologies (ICT) have now become an integral part and key enabler of today's development agenda. There is a growing and increasingly sophisticated demand for the Bank's support in this area. The Bank's capacity to respond to this demand is a "fundamental test of the World Bank's relevance in the years ahead" according to Jemal-ud-din Kassum, EAP Regional Vice President, at the recent e-government workshop (www.worldbank.org).

So it is clear that ICT is very relevant in Africa for two major reasons:
- As an enabler to development of communities and access to resources, such as e-government
- ICT skills become a marketable resource to increase the earning potential of a country, and move the economy from a largely agricultural economy to a knowledge economy.

1.2.1 SADC

Nowhere is this sentiment better illustrated than in the following Declaration on Information and Communications Technology (ICT) the level of commitment by the Southern Africa Development Community (SADC) countries.

PREAMBLE We, the Heads of State or Government of: The Republic of Angola; The Republic of Botswana; The Democratic Republic of Congo; The Kingdom of Lesotho; The Republic of Malawi; The Republic of Mauritius; The Republic of Mozambique; The Republic of Namibia; The Republic of Seychelles; The Republic of South Africa; The Kingdom of Swaziland; The United Republic of Tanzania; The Republic of Zambia; The Republic of Zimbabwe;

RECOGNISING that the Southern African Development Community needs a coherent regional policy and strategy on Information and Communications Technology (hereinafter referred to as "ICT") that promotes sustainable economic development, technology and bridges the digital divide within the Region and the rest of the world;

CONVINCED that a pervasive, reliable and affordable information and communications infrastructure is the foundation upon which the Southern African Renaissance can be built and sustained;

RECALLING the priority accorded to the challenge of bridging the digital divide in the Millennium Declaration adopted by the Millennium Assembly and statements made in the G8 Summit in Okinawa and the Southern African Economic Summit, 2001;

NOTING the capacity limitations in the Region, in particular shortage of skilled ICT personnel, high cost of development of ICT infrastructure, slow progress towards the deregulation of the telecommunications sectors leading to monopolies, unaffordability of universal access due to high tariffs and internet charges, lack of economic commerce readiness, reluctance of acceptance for ICT culture and innovations;

CONCERNED about the lack of regional policy and strategy on ICT and the digital divide between and within countries and the Region, which have the potential to widen the socio-economic disparity that exists;

FURTHER NOTING that international experience has shown that ICT, if harnessed, can contribute significantly to the economic development of countries and facilitate the provision of a better life for citizens;

AWARE that the digital divide does not only manifest itself economically or technologically but also culturally, creating a world that is increasingly less representative and reflective of the languages, cultures, ideas and diversity of the peoples of the world;

RECALLING Decision 52/2000 of the SATCC Committee of Ministers which urged Member States to give ICT priority for national and regional socio-economic development and accord such recognition in their national programmes in the effort of turning the Region into an information - based economy;

RECOGNISING that ICT is a fast, reliable, efficient and easy way of communication and information exchange;

ACKNOWLEDGING that effective information communication is best achieved under an environment characterised by:
- policy guidelines;
- legislation;
- well defined strategy;
- telecommunications deregulation;
- reliable, efficient and scalable network infrastructure;
- human resources development in the area of ICT;
- knowledge management;
- affordable access to information;
- natural way for collaboration and conversation;
- seamless integration;
- ubiquitous access; and
- security;

AWARE that the challenge for SADC is to ensure improved living standards for all its people, by harnessing the human, capital, technology and material resources at its disposal in the most productive and sustainable manner......, (Source www.sadc.int)

So at government level, there is awareness and some commitment to building IT capacity on the continent, and the benefits of doing so, especially the opportunity to grow the economies. It should be noted that this goes far beyond the necessity to lessen the Digital Divide. Unfortunately, and perhaps necessarily, aid to the continent remains focused on poverty and disease alleviation. Whilst this is understandable, it creates an additional "divide" – what Africa needs to save itself, versus the world simply providing food and medicines, and not looking at longer term issues.

2. IT Education and Skills in Africa

In their paper Description of Computer Science Higher Education in Sub-Saharan Africa: Initial Explorations, Marshini Chetty et al, state " Many countries in Sub-Saharan Africa (SSA) are in need of technology innovators who are equipped to leverage technologies in locally relevant domains such as health, government and education. To create skilled graduates who can build and shape locally relevant technologies, higher education institutes in Africa must have Computer Science (CS) education programs that meet local needs, for example, to satisfy the demand for entrepreneurs to build industry and strengthen an economy".

The Universities in South Africa produce, for the most part, skilled and knowledgeable computer science graduates. However, business and industry often level the accusation that these graduates are not "what is needed by business". This might or might not be true: what is very evident is that there are several graduates (and other apparently experienced individuals), who do not easily find suitable employment, whilst at the same time there is a widely reported "skills shortage".

There are other surprising examples of Centers of Excellence: The Computer and Information Technology Department, Makerere University, Kampala, Uganda is widely acknowledged as one of these.

In addition, each year, South Africa produces 1,400 engineers with B.Eng. and B.Sc. Eng. degrees. Only about half of these graduates go on to register with the Engineering Council of South Africa (ECSA) as practicing professionals (and very few join Computer Society South Africa). The Joint Initiative on Priority Skills Acquisition (JIPSA – a South African initiative to develop scarce and priority skills) has determined that to meet projected demand, the average annual output of engineers from the higher education sector needs to increase by 1,000 to a total of 2,400 a year. Measures need to be put in place to ensure that these graduates become registered professionals. (JIPSA report).

At the same time, enrolments into Computer Science and Bachelor of Commerce degrees with Information Systems as a major have been steadily declining. The author believes this can be attributed to the following:
• Poor quality of mathematics and science education at school level.
• Few school leavers with these subjects at an acceptable grade.

- No mechanisms for identifying talent in learners who don't have these subjects but still have an aptitude for Computer Science.
- Lack of understanding by learners (especially in poor communities) of what a career in IT involves.
- IT teachers are attracted to commerce, so there is a severe lack of Computer teachers at school level. The situation is worsening.

A Comptia report, developed by the Center for Strategy research, finds that:
- Companies in emerging markets report more skills gaps
- Emerging countries find all IT skills will increase in importance over the next five years and that their IT headcount will increase over this period.

This clearly illustrates that the emerging countries in Africa will need more and more IT practitioners, against a backdrop of reducing numbers of graduates.

In a report in ITWeb, a South African daily online publication, Harish Lala, country manager of ZenSar Technologies, says that while the local market is growing, SA stands on the back foot in the offshoring business. He says skills– more than other economic factors like the credit crunch and electricity crisis – is SA's biggest challenge. He goes on to say that SA is competing with markets in Eastern Europe, the Far East and South Asia to capture and retain business. "These countries are moving swiftly to develop skills, and Europe and the US are looking at the best options they can get. The reality is that skills (in SA) need to be developed at a faster rate than they are currently."

Jay Reddy, Managing Director at Dimension Data KZN, adds weight to the skills shortage argument, saying they have had to contract specialists from a sister company in India. Reddy said the increased demand for networking infrastructure skills across Africa has fuelled the demand for high calibre people. "From our perspective there are very few high end networking skills particularly around the Cisco networking technologies which require high end routing and advanced switching skills. The same goes for telephony and wireless skills in the massively growing IP sector." Reddy goes on to say that the gap is at least 60-70% or more. For every 10 vacancies only about 3 or 4 people would have the requisite skills. Mr Reddy points out that while SA does have learnership and graduate programmes to incorporate more skills, there is a big gap in output from tertiary institutions. "Tertiary institutions appear to focus their degree courses more on Business Analysis and programming techniques, with very little emphasis spent on networking and voice technologies within the IP space. Networking and voice, particularly in the IP space, is complex and requires sound theoretical knowledge of the IP Protocol to enable a candidate to grasp the concept and excel therein."[1]

Mr Reddy's comments put a different spin on the skills shortage issue, which is often thought to be only in the software development arena. Learnership

---

[1] Source: "Skills forum to focus on high end networking skills" www.smartxchange.co.za

programmes develop entry level skills, but the shortage lies in high-end skills in both software development and networking.

It should also be noted that there is an ongoing discussion on the difference between software development, and software engineering, with the majority of people using the terms interchangeably.

Furthermore, industry qualifications such as those offered by Cisco and Microsoft have enjoyed huge success in South Africa. It is possible that their popularity has been counterproductive in that several school leavers saw these certifications as an alternative to a degree or diploma, rather than as a means to enhance skills for those already in the workplace. At one stage (about six or seven years ago), South Africa had more Microsoft Certified Systems Engineers (MCSE's) than the United Kingdom!

3. ICT Hubs

Mauritius, an Indian Ocean Island off the East Coast of Africa, experienced a reduction of the GDP as a result of their two main crops, Cotton and Sugar, being produced more competitively elsewhere in the world. The government made a policy decision to develop towards becoming an ICT Hub. The government established the National Computer Board. In view of promoting Mauritius as a competitive location for ICT activities, marketing the Mauritian ICT industry abroad and assisting local operators with establishing contacts and partnerships with potential customers, joint venture partners and outsourcers, the NCB regularly participates in international events, such as the Salon Européen des Centres des Contacts et de la Relation Client (SECA) held in Paris each year, and proposes to participate in other fairs like the Birmingham Call Centre Expo in the UK , the Bangalore IT Fair, EBIT in Madagascar, Cyber in Reunion Island and COMDEX in South Africa. (source www.gov.mu). There are incentives for companies to provide training on ICT related subjects. And pay rates are fairly low when compared to developed countries (and even South Africa), so with continual marketing, and proof that their IT practitioners meet a minimum standard, combined with quality outputs, should provide the opportunity for Mauritius to compete globally.

South Africa has three organizations whose purpose is to create an ICT Hub in their respective regions: Innovation Hub in Gauteng Province; SmartXchange in Kwazulu-Natal (KZN); and Cape IT Initiative in Western Cape. Each one of these has a slightly different vision and goal:

Innovation Hub - A community of pioneers, inventors, entrepreneurs and free thinkers - challenged and inspired, breaking new ground, collaborating and inventing new technologies.

The **Cape IT Initiative (CITI)** is a networking and cluster development agency that brings together people, ideas and capital to grow the Western Cape, South

Africa's ICT sector. CITI's goal is to promote Cape Town as a global IT hub and gateway into Africa, thus facilitating the creation of jobs and prosperity through IT.

The Core Mandate for **SmartXchange** includes: Developing a quality ICT SMME base in KZN (Incubation and SMME support); Cluster Development and Promoting the region as an ICT hub of Africa; ICT Skills Development; and Supporting initiatives that work to bridge the digital divide

4. IT Professionalism in Africa – with emphasis on South Africa

We have the skills, but not in the numbers needed. Also, Africa has long been an exporter of raw materials, without beneficiation, and this culture persists in our thinking. Innovation is still a scarce commodity, although we have some amazing examples of world class technologies being developed, the most well-known of which is probably Mark Shuttleworth, who sold the digital encryption technology for millions of dollars.

According to the ICT Census commissioned by Cape IT Initiative in 2007, IT consultancy is the "product" most regularly exported, and the greatest percentage of IT exports are to elsewhere in Africa. This is encouraged, as Africa is an open market, less affected by the IT prominence of the Asian tigers than Europe or North America, but we need to become a global player.

So what can we do to improve our status as a center for excellence in IT? The author believes that finding a mechanism to confer an internationally recognized professional qualification on IT practitioners would be a firm step in the right direction.

There is often some confusion about what professional groups exist in IT. Peter J. Denning [2], writing for an ACM publication states that there are over 40 organized groups in computing and information technology. IT-specific disciplines are the core technologies of computer science and engineering, and include; Computer Science, Software Engineering, Operating Systems, to name only a few. ITIntensive disciplines are the other branches of science, engineering and commerce that innovate in IT as part of their work. Examples include: Aerospace engineering; Banking and financial services; and Telecommunications. The third group - IT-supportive occupations - are relatively new professional specialties that support and maintain IT Infrastructure. They include Help Desk technicians, Web Masters, IT trainers.

What do we mean by Professionalism in IT? Charles Hughes, past President of British Computer Society, and Chairman of the IP3 Task Force, in his paper "Characteristics of a the profession and IT Professionals" states that "A profession is a vocation or pursuit, especially one which involves some branch of advanced learning, and the body of people engaged in it.

---

[2] "When IT Becomes a Profession" Peter J Denning , 2001

(Furthermore), a profession must:
- be a community controlled by regulation or by a governing body/bodies (most usually
- professional institutions or associations) which directs the behaviour of members of the
- community in professional matters
- determine the knowledge, skills, attributes and experience required by professionals
- give leadership and deliver on its promise to the public it serves in its specific field of activity
- adhere to the general standards of professional communities and define those attributes and
- characteristics that distinguish a specific profession from others
- be valued for its contribution to society

The definition of a professional adopted by the British Computer Society Professionalism in IT programme is:

A fully established IT professional is a practitioner who has specific skills rooted in a broad base and appropriate qualifications, belongs to a regulated body, undergoes continuous development, operates to a code of conduct and recognises personal accountability.

Although Computer Society South Africa (CSSA) has had a Professional grade of membership for some years, they have only recently implemented a professional qualification. The Computer Professional Education qualification was developed in Australia by the Australian Computer Society ACS. The learning materials are provided online, so they can be accessed from anywhere. The qualification is aimed at practitioners with a bachelor level degree, and at least 18 months' working experience. Recognition of prior learning procedures are in place for those who have experience or other studies that are deemed equivalent to a B degree.

The IP3 Task Force, set up by IFIP, started its work in January 2007. The Task Force is working towards creating an International Professional Practice Programme. This is global programme led by IFIP (The International Federation for Information Processing) to promote professionalism in IT, define international standards and create a global infrastructure that will encourage and support the development of both practitioners and employer organizations and give recognition to those who meet and maintain the required standards for knowledge, experience, competence and integrity.

IP3 certification schemes, of which the first will be the 'gold standard' *International IT Professional (IITP)* certification will be:
- Vendor independent
- Operated by accredited IFIP member bodies
- Available worldwide

- Based on consistent global standards for professionals in all areas of IT activity
- Built around a requirement for complete professional formation – including relevant knowledge, experience, competence and commitment to a code of professional ethics
- Dependent on the maintenance of competence through a programme of continuing professional education and development
- Supported by a disciplinary code with a process for public complaint and sanctions where appropriate.

Within this overall independent framework IP3 certification schemes will recognize and give credit to other certification schemes, including vendor certification, wherever these provide appropriate and valuable assurance for part of the overall professional formation.[3]

For developing countries in Africa, such a programme will have significant benefits; the most important of all is "guaranteeing" the standard of IT professionals who have received the qualification. So "where you come from" will be less important than the professional qualification you hold.

Other benefits include:
For the Practitioner
- increased recognition and reward – IT staff at all levels often feel they are undervalued
- greater mobility – people should be able to work where they want to, and not be disadvantaged because of where they come from
- career path - professional practitioners will increase their opportunity to reach c-level positions in their organizations
- professional accountability – as with other professions, IT practitioners should have a sense of accountability for the success and quality of the work they are engaged in
- Be part of a global community of professional practitioners

For Employers
- improved risk management and corporate governance
- more successful IT enabled business change
- enhanced recruitment and talent management
- global companies can be assured that all internationally qualified staff meet a minimum professional standard, thus enabling a mobile and agile workforce.

It is hoped that South Africa will lead the way in providing a qualification that will be accredited by the international body. The model we are using – using the ACS qualification, is easily replicable and transportable. We can modify the learning materials at a later stage if deemed necessary: however, we find that the

---

[3] IP3 – Building an International Professional Practice Programme, Colin Thompson, IP3 Task Force

materials are not country specific as they have been designed for a global audience.

IP3 has a long term goal to, with assistance and guidance from IFIP, SADC and the African Union, and mentoring from Computer Society South Africa, Australian and other member Societies, to roll-out a qualification which meets the standards to other countries in Africa.

The Skills Framework for the Information Age (SFIA) is the high level UK Government backed competency framework describing the roles within IT and the skills needed to fulfil themSFIA is the widely used two-dimensional IT skills framework, which is made available at no cost to the end user (www.sfia.org).

It is envisaged that a recognized professional in IT will:

- belong to a recognized, regulated professional community for information and communications technology workers
- share with other professionals the understanding of a core body of knowledge (CBOK)
- have knowledge of one or more specialist area
- demonstrate the capability to operate at the equivalent of SFIA Level 5 or above

5. Recommendations

IT has much to offer Africa, in terms of economic development. We have to ensure that we are not left behind, or perceived as lacking in the requisite IT skills.

It is therefore essential that African Computer Societies, and relevant government departments throughout the region work towards setting up skills frameworks, based on SFIA (adapted rather than reinvented). We must also implement a professional standard and qualification that is mandated or chartered by the government.

IP3, together with IFIP, and Societies that already have a professional qualification, should engage with African Societies - where they exist - and government departments to share best practice, and actively assist them with becoming professional bodies with a relevant qualification. IFIP and IP3 must:

- Use forums and conferences such as WITFOR to get the message out to emerging African countries.
- IFIP, in partnership with CSSA, should continue in its quest to set up an African consortium. This has been in the plans for some years now, but funding is essential to its ongoing success.
- Find early adopters for the IP3 programme in Africa. Computer Society South Africa is already on its way, and Botswana and Ethiopia have expressed interest.
- • IFIP must assist African Societies in ensuring the elements of professional practice are embedded in their constitutions: an enforced code of conduct, ethics, responsibility; suitably stringent entry requirements for professional membership,
- Africa must use and adapt existing frameworks, and resist the urge to create their own.

- Using an online offering, such as that offered by the ACS CPE, is highly recommended for the following reasons:
  1. It can be adopted in a short space of time
  2. There is no need to recreate infrastructure
  3. The standards of delivery are consistent
  4. Candidates can interact with practitioners around the world, sharing best practice, and thus are not constrained by the boundaries of their own country.
  5. Regional societies can provide mentoring – with the possibility of creating a revenue stream.
- Encourage aid monies and skills toward this end.

From an IT perspective, Africa does not have to stand in anyone's shadow. We are capable of playing on the world stage, and must to do because IT can be true creator of wealth.

A Model for Rating and Certifying Competences in the EUCIP Framework

Andrea Violetti [1]**, Susanna Daddi** [2]**, Stefano Hajek** [3]

[1] AIP-ITCS
[2] Jobnet SpA
[3] Perugia University, Insubria University

Introduction

Italian Computer Society - acronym AIP-ITCS - is a trade association which allows its members, through a "network of social relationships", to communicate with and between different environments with the purpose of increasing the intellectual capital of computer professionals and the social capital of the association.

While waiting for better policies for innovation and ICT to be identified, we are aware that an "objective" and "merit based" management of knowledge, although difficult to achieve, should constantly be pursued, in opposition to the natural tendency of man to develop a "subjective" and "patron-and client" management of knowledge. We consider a merit based system the ideal system; in practice this means a constant tendency towards a merit based management.

The guideline for policies of social and economic development will therefore be a merit based and corporative rewarding welfare applicable to the "market of knowledge." This is how the model for measuring and certifying competences originates. The aim is to achieve, in an objective and merit-based manner, a system for the assessment of competences, in this case those concerning the ICT sector, without leaving out, next to distinctive competences, relational and communicative skills.

The purpose of this model is to elaborate a standard method for the issuing of competence certificates in accordance with the EU directive 92/51 of 18 June 1992 and subsequent modifications and with the national regulations of reference, in order to show the market that a certain professional is competent in a specific or general profession and that that competence can be used all over the EU.

This model was first conceived in July 2005 with the purpose of finding a strategic and merit-based solution that fulfils the need for certification of competences in all intellectual jobs.

It has been necessary to reduce the complexity of the issue through the implementation of a model easily understandable and usable by the work, training, service, industry, trade and consumer markets and in all cases by any interested organization.

Please use the following format when citing this chapter:

Violetti, A., Daddi, S. and Hajek, S., 2008, in IFIP International Federation for Information Processing, Volume 280; *E-Government; ICT Professionalism and Competences; Service Science*; Antonino Mazzeo, Roberto Bellini, Gianmario Motta; (Boston: Springer), pp. 109–122.

Basically, the idea is to calculate the average quality index of a professional organization and the position of the professional above or below this average, obliging those who wish to receive a competence certificate as general computer professional, to keep their index above the average through life-long training. Next to this we can identify specific profiles for which it is possible to obtain a further specialist competence certificate by verifying, through matching, the competence achieved in a specific sector.

1. Model for measuring and certifying competences

The model is a simplified and stylized representation of the reality which is being analysed, i.e. the measurement and certification of ICT competences; all elements considered irrelevant have been eliminated in order to focus on the essential through verbal, graphic and mathematical descriptions.

The model should be read in two ways:

as a description of what happens given the real values of the "exogenous elements" the results obtained for the "endogenous elements"	(measurement and certification of competence) (titles, experience) (which certification)
as an instrument for deciding what is to be done given the desired values of the "endogenous elements" values that the "exogenous elements" gain	(life-long training and self assessment) (in what I would like to evaluate myself/certify) (what I should study)

Meets
- The requests, standards and guidelines of the CEPIS
- Is compatible with the Eucip frameworks
- The law requirements and best practices of the sector
- The expectations of professionals, clients and enterprises
- Market expectations in terms of professional ethics and deontology
- Requests of both private and public training structures
- Practicality and functionality criteria
- Other professional associations

Supplies
- General criteria for the development of a data base of training paths in order to manage the relative credits
- General criteria for the development of a data base of professional competences in order to manage the relative credits

- Objective basis for issuing the competence certification in accordance with the EC directive 92/51
- A simple and objective classification of the competences of members
- Registration of the life-long training activities of the single members

The model results from the considerations of thousands of members during the last 15 years and does not expect to be conclusive or exhaustive but wants to make up for a serious deficiency in the ICT sector, i.e. the one of competence evaluation. Every association must be able to plan an independent and efficient implementation of the model in order to manage, measure and certify the competences of its members in the interest of professionals and of the market. Every training and professional activity must be adequately supported by computer instruments updated on –demand on training needs in order to overcome the complexity and heterogeneity that the society of knowledge interprets, and professionals must guarantee a minimum standard both with regards to knowledge (training) and to competence (experience), considering the paradigm: knowledge + experience = competence.

Considering that, as by article 8A of the EU treaty, the internal market means an area without internal barriers and that, pursuant to article 3, letter c) of the treaty, the elimination of barriers between member States for the free circulation of people and services is one of the objectives of the Community; that for the citizens of the member States this elimination implies the possibility of carrying out a profession, independently or dependently, in a member State different from the one in which they acquired their professional qualifications; considering moreover that according to the definitions specified in letter c) article 1, Title 1 of the EU directive 92/51, "competence certificate" means any title:

- ratifying a training path not part of a system constituting a diploma according to the EEC directive 89/48 or a diploma or certificate according to the present directive, or
- issued after an evaluation of the qualifications, aptitudes or knowledge of the requesting party considered essential for carrying out a profession from an authority appointed in accordance with the legislative or administrative regulations of a member State, without the request of the demonstration of a preliminary training;

The competence certificate issued with the aid of the above model has become fundamental to operate on the markets.

1.1 Certification of competences

The model for Measuring and Certifying Competences is preparatory to the issuing of the competence certificate in accordance with the EC provision 92/51 and subsequent modifications. The certificate is issued if the applying candidate's final evaluation is above the average (considering a margin of tolerance for acceptation) of all the final evaluations of the members of a professional association; this certification is general and certifies the professional ability of the candidate in the field of computers. After the issuing of the general certificate the professional can apply for a supplementary specialist certificate. The dynamism both of the data base of the candidates (on which the model is based), profiles, titles and certificates supplies a valid support both for the planning of life-long training and for the constant assessment of the "validity" of the granted certificate.

Compelling the candidate to remain always within the range complying with the minimum quality index automatically calculated.

As the evaluation is acceptable only if the average exceeds the minimum accepted level, the second candidate will necessarily have to be superior to the previous. This creates a mechanism of self-control on the skill status and professional capacities of the candidate and subsequent candidates. For this reason the model does not pay too much attention to the obligatory or obvious education that a professional ought to have, but focuses on the ability of the professional to keep himself updated and remain in the average of this organization which, in its turn, is forced to declare to the market its objectives in terms of average quality index of its members by publishing these indexes on an official web site. Depending on the organization's and professionals' requirements, the publication of the evaluation results for the certification of the candidate can be public, private or partially public; nevertheless they will be indicated on the competence certificate which can expire or be suspended if the candidate's indexes of quality should go below the levels of non-acceptability indicated by the organization. This dynamic system forces the professional to follow constant training and to record his training; only through supplementary training hours and further titles or certificates can the depreciation of knowledge be compensated and constant improvement be generated with the introduction of new professionals with further qualifications and skills. All this applies to the minimum and general training of the professional; regarding specialist training, starting from 100 for the highest qualification in a specific field, the professional can be certified with 100 or below 100. The representation of the general profile is a dot situated on a Cartesian axis where the ordinates represent the RPC and the abscissas time (the age of the professional), while the graphic representation of the specialist profile is represented by a circle whose centre is situated where the general profile is located and the diameter representing the total coverage of the profile declared with a self-certification of skills.

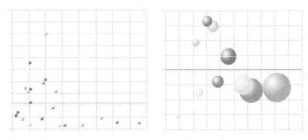

1.2. Distinctive elements and definitions

Competence certificate (ACK)	Issued by the association The competence certificate is a certificate issued after an evaluation of the personal qualifications, aptitudes or knowledge of the applicant considered fundamental for carrying out a profession by an authority appointed in accordance with the legislative and administrative regulations of a state. It rests upon the solid basis of life-long training, professional experience and deontology, providing an overall evaluation of the professional. The professional's competences will therefore be enhanced and evaluated differently. The market will finally be able to assess the true value of the professional to whom it has turned.
Relative Professional Credits (RPC)	Assigned to each item of the scientific committee in relation to computer sciences.
Relative Training Credits (RTC)	Number of hours of constant and compulsory training necessary each year to overcome deficiency of competences and relative professional credits (RPC)
Relative Deontological Debt (RDD)	Assigned by the industrial tribunal in relation to computer sciences (it must tend to 0)
Overall evaluation of the member (OEM)	Evaluation of the member from the scientific committee by means of an interview to assess, among other things, relational and behavioural skills.
Coefficient of devaluation or re-evaluation of the competence (CDR)	It is an indicator of devaluation or re-evaluation, therefore negative or positive, which assesses how much the value of the RPC/RTC given to a certain item decreases or increases in the course of the year.
Bonus malus index (BMI)	Positive and negative corrective index of the RPC/RTC at the disposal of the overall evaluation group of the member
Average quality index (AQI)	Average of all the overall evaluations of the professional (OEM), index above which the professional is associable and below which further training or certifications are required for the preservation or renovation of the certification
Percentage departure quality(PDQ)	Indicates how many percentage points of departure from AQI are accepted
Index Professional Quality (IPQ)	Index resulting from the application of the model; it represents the index of quality achieved by the professional

1.3. Level of competences

The levels set by the model are two:

General Computer Professional
All professionals with an average RPC above the average index of the organization (AQI), represented on the graphic by dots.

Specialised Computer Professionals
All professionals with RPC>AQI and 100% matching with one of the assessed profiles
(Example: Eucip Elective profiles – Business Analyst), represented on the graphic by circles.

Thanks to the very nature of the model, based on a data base and with a numeric measuring system of competences in a specific profession, if the simplification should prove to be insufficient, it is possible to elaborate further levels of competences and further competence certifications.

1.4. Data base

	% Incident of Section	Coefficient of deva-luation or re-evalua-tion of the com-petence (CDR	Relative Professional Credits (RPC)	Bonus Malus Index (BMI)	Relative Professional Credits (RPC) Calculate
Training Section					
Certification Section					
Skills section					
Pubblication Section					
Association Section					

Index Professional Quality (IPQ)

The model includes the management of Curriculum Vitae through the acquisition of information divided in sections, with a unit of measurement, weight, devaluation or re-evaluation coefficient for a positive or negative correction and a criteria for the assignment of RPC for each section.

1.5. Implementation level

The model has already been implemented in our association, has already lived its first cycle and has passed the four processes of innovation showing low levels of difficulty in the first phase, medium in the second and high in the tow final phases; now it is important to identify accelerators for all processes and to improve what has been achieved up to date.

2. Bayesian neural networks in human resources pattern recognition

Analysis of correspondences between job requirements and personal skills plays a central role in Human Resources Management; lacking skills can be filled by addressing training programs to people "potentially" interested in.

A way to discover professional potentiality is to explore skills patterns, making inference about the relevance of each skill "given" other skills.

Neural Networks are pattern recognition tools we used to investigate skills' reciprocal support; instead of traditional maximum likelihood based learning we adopted Bayesian learning to avoid overfitting shortcoming: forecasting is integrated all over weight posterior distribution.

Being involved integration, analytically unfeasible, Hybrid Metropolis Algorithm was adopted; it numerically treats complex integrals making use of net gradient information to speed Metropolis random walk runs.

Real case simulations are commented with focus on approach's robustness.

2.1 Job profiling

The case study we're treating refers to iJobnet, a framework for human resource management that classifies professional skills, collects skills into a database and measures the fit of each skills aggregate (cv items) to ideal "job descriptions"; fit degree is a measure of distance between singular cv's items and items in job descriptions.

iJobnet's taxonomy for IT professionals follows EUCIP international standard; it is based on expert rules periodically updated by a scientific committee.

A fundamental iJobnet's mission is to reduce skill supply - demand mismatching through development of targeted training programs to IT professionals; so iJobnet explores learning needs in that professional community to improve profiles'adequacy . This is accomplished by discovering recurrent skills patterns in the community and "completing" patterns in individuals: basic idea is to "fill in" lacking skills in profiles belonging to common knowledge areas (patterns), addressing training sessions to people "potentially" interested in.

Aim of this work is to design a pattern recognition tool that makes inference about the support of groups of skills to a singular skill so to evaluate the relevance of a skill given other skills.

2.2 Neural Networks and pattern recognition

2.2.1 Neural Network paradigm

Well established tools for pattern recognition are neural networks.

Neural networks are non-linear regression models inspired by natural metaphor of brain structure in which information is represented and stored through activation maps in a set of connected nodes.

Formally, define the node

$$y\left(\bar{x}_{l-1}, \bar{w}_{i,l-1}\right) = x_{i,l} = \left(1 + e^{-\sum_{j=0}^{m} w_{i,j,l-1} x_{j,l-1}}\right)^{-1}$$

Where $x_{i,l}$ is the ith node at layer l, $\bar{x}_{l-1}$ is the vector of nodes $x_{j,l-1}$ at layer l-1, $\bar{w}_{i,l-1}$ is the vector of weights $w_{i,j,l-1}$ at layer l-1 "linking" $x_{i,l}$ with $x_{j,l-1}$ [1]

Being the node x defined recursively, the weighted sum of nodes along consecutive layers gives the overall network value for a set of inputs $\bar{x}_0$.

Network's learning is a "reinforcement" process that updates connection weights according to the minimum distance between observed examples and model's representations.

Let Err be the net training error over a set of observation patterns: learning consists of training error reduction:

$$Err = \sum_{n=0}^{N}\left[\sum_{i=0}^{\omega} x_{i,l} - t_{i,n}\right]^2 = \sum_{n=0}^{N}\left[\sum_{i=0}^{\omega} y(x_{n,l-1}, w_{i,l-1}) - t_{i,n}\right]^2$$

being n $(0 \leq n \leq N)$ the number of observations patterns and i $(0 \leq i \leq \omega)$ the number of net output.

Traditionally training error reduction is obtained via least squares, hence reaching the maximum likelihood of observed data given parameters. [D.E. Rumelhart et Al - 1986].

This approach to inference is well known to be affected by overfitting: the training sample could be not representative of the full population's behavior and too detailed models have the shortcoming to tradeoff a low in-sample approximation error with high variance – i.e. not acceptable out-of-sample (prediction) error.

2.2.2 Bayesian Neural Networks
Maximum likelihood criterion is reliable only when observed samples are the most likely; it is the most probable circumstance, but it is not certain. Conversely, a way to take into account parameters' uncertainty is to consider the maximum

---

[1] The choice of sigmoidal function as "activation function" ensures neural network's "universal approximation" property as stated in [K.Hornik et Al. 1989].

probability of parameters given data, parameters themselves following a distribution law.

Bayesian learning is based on this idea deriving posterior parameters distribution from the Bayes rule:

$$P(w|x, y) = \frac{P(x, y|w)P(w)}{\int P(x, y|w)P(w)}$$

In neural networks frame bayesian approach integrates predictions from all possible weights vectors over the posterior weight distribution rather than use a single "optimal" set of network weights.

With integration a weight vector that fits the data only slightly better than others will contribute only slightly more to prediction without exclusion of alternative models [R.M. Neal - 1992]:

$$\hat{y}_{n+1} = \int y(x_{n+1}, w)P(w|(x_1, y_1), ..., (x_n, y_n))dw$$

Posterior distribution evaluation requires expressions for prior distribution and for likelihood function. Assume for the prior a zero-mean Gaussian function for the weights of the form:

$$p(w) = \frac{1}{Z_w(\alpha)} exp\left(-\alpha \frac{1}{2}\|w\|^2\right)$$

In which the normalization factor $Z_w(\alpha)$ is given by:

$$Z_w(\alpha) = \frac{\left(\frac{2\pi}{\alpha}\right)W}{2}$$

Where W represents the total u of weight parameters. [C.M. Bishop - 1995].

Likelihood function represents here the distribution of target values for a given input vector; again we consider a Gaussian with mean given by the output $y(x,w)$ of the network and variance governed by a parameter β^{-1} so that:

$$p(t|x, w) = \left(\frac{\beta}{2\pi}\right)^{1/2} exp\left(-\frac{\beta}{2}[y(x, w) - t]^2\right)$$

Looking at the entire dataset D we assume that the patterns are drawn independently from this distribution, and hence that joint probability is multiplicative:

$$p(D|w) = \prod_{n=1}^{N} p(t_n|x_n, w)$$

$$p(t|x, w) = \frac{1}{Z_D(\beta)} exp\left(-\frac{\beta}{2}\sum_{n=1}^{N}[y(x_n, w) - t_n]^2\right)$$

Where the normalization factor $Z_D(\beta)$ is given by:

$$Z_D(\beta) = \left(\frac{2\pi}{\beta}\right)^{N/2}$$

2.3 Montecarlo numerical integration

Integral involved in Bayesian prediction is generally hard – if not impossible - to evaluate analytically; numerical methods, namely Montecarlo methods, are available for this purpose.

The fundamental idea is to approximate $\int y(x, w)p(w|x, y)$ with the

$$I = E[y(x, w)] \approx \frac{1}{N}\sum_{i=1}^{N} y(x, w_i)$$

corresponding expected value

where $\{w_i\}$ represents a sample of weight vectors generated from the distribution $p(w \mid x, y)$.

2.3.1 Metropolis Algorithm
This basic computation is for Bayesian neural networks infeasible due to the multi – dimensionality and multi – modality in the posterior probability density for w; Metropolis algorithm is an effective way to arrange for the distribution of weight vectors to correspond to $p(w \mid D)$.

Metropolis Algorithm generates candidate steps from Markov chains:

$$w_{new} = w_{old} + \varepsilon$$

but reject a proportion of the steps which lead to a reduction in the value of $p(w \mid D)$.

This must be done with great care, however, in order to ensure that resulting sample of weight vectors represents the required distribution. In the Metropolis algorithm this is achieved by using the following criterion:

If $p(w_{new}|y, x) > p(w_{old}|y, x)$

Then accept

Else   accept   with   probability

$$\frac{p(w_{new}|y, x)}{p(w_{old}|y, x)}$$ 2

2.3.2 Hybrid Montecarlo algorithm

A critical point in Metropolis Algorithm and in any other MCMC samplers is the number of initial steps until the chain approaches stationarity; being that number related to the distance of starting value from the distribution's mode, the length of so named "burn-in period" can be reduced using back-propagation (gradient descent) to find starting values.

Hybrid Montecarlo method improves efficiency in Metropolis algorithm taking account of information concerning the gradient of $p(w \mid D)$ and using this to choose search directions which favour regions of high posterior probability. [D. MacKay - 1999]

It is inspired by energy evolution dynamics in physical systems as described by Hamiltonian equations.

Set $U(x) = -P(w|x, y)$; willing to draw Montecarlo Samples from $\pi(x) \propto e^{-U(x)}$ introduce a fictious "momentum vector" p with corresponding

$$K(p) = \sum_{i=0}^{d} p_i^2 / m_i$$

"kinetic energy"   where mi represents the "mass" of components i.

System's total energy is: $H(x, p) = U(x) + K(p)$; sampling (x,p) from $\pi(x, p) \propto e^{P(w|x, y)} = e^{-H(x, p)}$ target distribution $\pi(x, p)$ is obtained from marginal distribution $\int \pi(x, p)$.

---

[2] Convergence proof for Metropolis algorithm shows that sample generation process attains stationariety at reached distribution; see: [N.Metropolis et Al - 1956]

Omitting theoretical motivations – far beyond the scope of present work - Hybrid
Metropolis algorithm proceeds schematically as follows:

- Generate a momentum vector p' from the Gaussian distribution $\pi(p) \propto e^{-K(p)}$
- Reach a new configuration in phase space (x', p') running the following
  leapfrog algorithm:

$$p' = p' - \frac{1}{2}\delta\frac{\partial U}{\partial x}$$
$$x' = x' + \delta p'$$

For m = 1 to l -1

$$p' - p' - \delta\frac{\partial U}{\partial x}$$
$$x' = x' + \delta p'$$

End For

$$p' = p' - \frac{1}{2}\delta\frac{\partial U}{\partial x}$$

$$K(p) = \sum_{i=0}^{d} p_i^2$$

$$H(x,p) = U(x) + K(p)$$

- Let $(x_{n+1}, p_{n+1}) = (x', p')$ with probability:
  $$P = min[1, exp\{-H(x', -p') + H(x_n, p_n)\}]$$
  and let $(x_{n+1}, p_{n+1}) = (x_n, p_n)$ with probability 1-P

3. Application to skills pattern recognition

3.1 Network setup

We tested Bayesian neural network model accuracy on a sample of 200 curricula
splitting the sample in two: a learning sample consisting of 150 curricula used to
update the weights, and remaining 50 curricula used as validation set to evaluate
model's generalization error.

A curriculum is, for our purposes, a collection of professional skills related to a
specific technical area; in this experiment we cover IT development area feeding
the network with 14 skills in input – each assuming value 1 in presence of the
respective skill, 0 elsewhere - and one skill as target.

The network is structured – after trying alternative configurations searching for
better bias / variance tradeoff - with a single hidden layer of 28 nodes; Hybrid
Metropolis runned along 50.000 iterations reaching a stationary distribution.

3.2 Results and conclusion

Figure 1 depicts the in-sample error distribution originated by all models (weights vectors) applied to skill absence/presence forecasting.

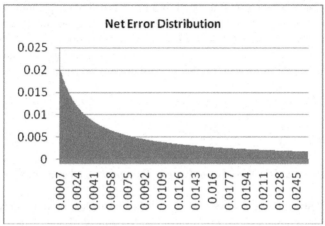

Fig. 1 – BNN error distribution

The network correctly predicts "in sample" the presence of a skill in the % of cases of effective presence and the absence in the % of cases of effective absence. Cross validation test (out of sample error) report a % right "presence" forecasting and a % right "absence" forecasting; this result confirms the good generalization property of Bayesian neural network especially when compared with results obtained with traditional approach (back propagation learning): as expected, while the in-sample error is lower in back propagation than in HMC, it becomes appreciably larger in back propagation than in HMC when measured out of sample (see table).

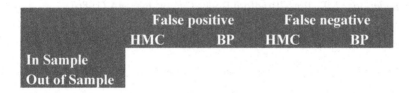

	False positive		False negative	
	HMC	BP	HMC	BP
In Sample				
Out of Sample				

Bayesian learning reduce out of sample error taking into account the uncertainty of the model, hence integrating prediction with respect the posterior weights distribution.

This learning strategy is particularly interesting in situations – like this – where the learning sample is necessary limited in size and not fully representative of the whole domain characteristics.

A further added value – only mentioned here - in Bayesian learning paradigm is the opportunity to incorporate in the model prior information from expert knowledge; opinions can be translated into prior distribution parameters value or directly or "forcing" the network to learn opinions: so obtained posterior distributions can be assumed as new priors in a new network.

Considered the central role of expert advisors in human resource analysis and selection this research direction will be seriously examined in the proceedings of our enquiry.

References

Bishop C.M.: *Neural Networks for Pattern Recognition*, Clarendon Press, Oxford, (1995).

Hornik K., Stinchombe M., White W.: "Multilayer feedforward networks are universal approximators", *Neural Networks* Volume 2, Issue 5, p. 359 – 366 (1989)

Metropolis N., Rosenbluth A.W., Rosenbluth M.N., Teller A.H., Teller E.: "Equations of State Calculations by Fast Computing Machines". *Journal of Chemical Physics*, 21(6):1087-1092, (1953)

MacKay D.: "Introduction to Monte Carlo methods." *M. Jordan, editor, Learning in Graphical Models*, pages 175-204. The MIT Press, Cambridge, MA, USA, (1999).

Neal R.M.: "Bayesian training of backpropagation networks by the hybrid Monte Carlo method'", Technical Report CRG-TR-92-1, Dept. of Computer Science, University of Toronto (1992)

Rumelhart D.E., McClelland J.L., & the PDP Research Group: *Parallel Distributed Processing: Explorations in the Microstructure of Cognition. Vol. 1:Foundations*,: MIT Press/Bradford Books Cambridge, MA (1986).

The need for a standard qualification of ICT professional competences

The reasons that urged CEPIS to create the EUCIP model are even more pressing today than they were in 2000

Paolo Schgör

Certifications manager at AICA, Italy, p.schgor@aicanet.it

Abstract: Standards are, generally speaking, a sensible way of simplifying a number of issues; this is also true for ICT professional competences, the standardization of which could bring huge benefits to all stakeholders, including education & training providers, employers, candidates and agencies for employment, freelance professionals, ICT associations, governmental and statistical institutions, and - finally - the ICT industry at large. The EUCIP model is certainly one of the most interesting proposals for a possible multi-stakeholder solution to this incredibly complex issue.

Keywords: Europe, ICT certifications, ICT competences, professionalism, professional societies, standardization

1. The Need for Standards in ICT

1.1 Standards in a Layman's View

I'm not sure whether a specific professionalism regarding the definition of standards has ever been defined (or even can be); anyway, I do not consider myself a professional "standardizer", and the following introductory statements are offered as a layman's view.

On the other hand, I have been progressively involved in international teams and task forces having an implicit – or sometimes explicit – focus on the definition of standards around ICT competences; thus, the main part of this script is dedicated to the description of the current proposals devised by CEPIS on this subject.

Please use the following format when citing this chapter:

Schgör, P., 2008, in IFIP International Federation for Information Processing, Volume 280; *E-Government; ICT Professionalism and Competences; Service Science*; Antonino Mazzeo, Roberto Bellini, Gianmario Motta; (Boston: Springer), pp. 123–132.

My thesis is that **having one recognized standard may not be a vital issue, but it is much better than having several**.

I don't even want to take into account the total absence of standards, simply because this means somehow that anyone decides one's own (possibly a different one every time): all these cases can be seen as degenerate forms of "several" standards.

Just a couple of trivial examples taken from personal "ICT user" experience: a negative instance and a positive one.

- Negative: every traveller knows the frustration related to the absence of one global standard for electric power plugs; if you carry a laptop computer or any other mobile device, it is usually much easier to get connected to the Internet (by wired or wireless access protocols) than getting your device's battery recharged!

  The only currently available solution is to use specific adapters (see picture) that reflect the need for a "translation" between conflicting local standards about the physical shape of sockets and plugs.

- Positive: the recent victory of the Blu-ray Disc standard over the HD DVD standard is generally seen as a quite beneficial outcome of the Sony-versus-Toshiba conflict on formats for High Definition movies in the "Home Theater" consumer market.

  Regardless of who wins and who looses, and leaving asides disputes on which format was better (in terms of technical features, quality, prices, flexibility, de facto market position, etc.), most analysts agree on the positive effects of Toshiba's unexpected surrender, that crowns Blu-ray as the industry standard; all players – including Toshiba, Nec and the other partners in the loosing front – are now expected to benefit, more or less, sooner or later, from a faster-growing market.

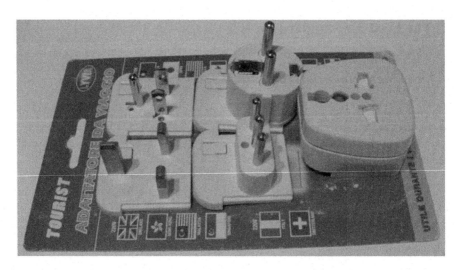

From a user's perspective, in the short term it might be really annoying to be forced to change a previously adopted standard, if the match winner is not "yours"; but in the medium and long term, the benefits of cross-border, cross-producer, cross-anything compatibility exceed by far the nuisance caused by a possible transition.

1.2 The Idea of a Standard Structure for the ICT Profession

The idea of establishing a European common ground for the definition of ICT professionalism and for the classification of related professional skills is now 20 years old: as a matter of fact, some records [1] of such discussions between Computer Societies date back to 1988. In that year, during an IFIP Congress in Rio de Janeiro, the delegates from 8 European countries started thinking of a possible cooperation, having in mind the increasing role of the future European Union in national policies. Still in 1988, a 'historical' meeting in London set the basis both for the foundation of CEPIS (whose Articles of Association were signed in 1991) and for the development of a **European Informatics Skills Structure**, EISS, then published in May 1992 [2] with the following subtitle: "A Set of Performance Standards Covering all Functional Areas of Work Carried out by Professionals in Informatics".

In other words, the idea of a standard framework for the ICT profession was born in the very same moment as CEPIS, and by the same parents, so that they can be thought of as twins: and there's no surprise in considering that the need for an international standard rose in a climate that was strongly conditioned by expectations on the announced progressive convergence of 12 independent states into a new European Union (officially signed-off with this name at Maastricht, on 7 February 1992). With some simplification, we might say that such cross-border standardization attempts are a consequence of a perceived enlarged market space for ICT professionals.

If this was true in 1988, it is even more pressing today, 20 years later, when a progressive globalization seems to be inevitable, whatever you may think of it.

1.3 Further European Endeavours

In more recent times, starting with the new millennium, several different initiatives addressed the issue of a unified approach to ICT professional skills.
I'll mention here only the four most significant attempts that had (or still do have) an explicit ambition to formulate super-national proposals at a European level.

Career Space: this initiative rose during the hype of the so-called new economy, when ICT companies had very serious problems in finding new graduates to hire; half a dozen of the major multinationals created the Career Space consortium and specified 18 Generic Skills Profiles; their goals were both to describe the characteristics of some typical ICT jobs in an interesting way (so as to attract young people), and to drive the attention of universities to the most critical subjects that the ICT employers could hardly find in a graduate's preparation. A very practical approach led to a set of deliverables which are interesting in terms of ICT skills requirements (directly described from the demand side of the job market), yet poor in terms of scientific rigour; however, the results produced by this consortium were adopted by CEN (see below) and incorporated in CWA 14925 and CWA 15005.

e-Skills Forum: in parallel with the rise of the Career Space initiative, the European Commission launched the e-Skills Forum, and asked the Governments of EU member states to appoint an official national delegate for discussions in the area of ICT skills and their improvement through e-learning. The main merit of this very interesting initiative is to facilitate the dialogue between stakeholders.

e-SCC / ILB: following the launch of the e-Skills Forum, the main international operators offering ICT certification formed a consortium called e-Skills Certification Consortium (e-SCC), which was recently replaced by the Industry Leadership Board (ILB); its the main goal is to support the concept of "Multi-Stakeholder Partnership" initiatives, involving public and private entities in joint projects bringing tangible results in the diffusion of key ICT competences.

CEN/ISSS: CEN is the European Centre for Standardization, and the specific ISSS line of business focuses on an Information Society Standardization Structure. CEN members are the national standards bodies of Austria, Belgium, Cyprus, Czech Republic, Denmark, Estonia, Finland, France, Germany, Greece, Hungary, Iceland, Ireland, Italy, Latvia, Lithuania, Luxembourg, Malta, Netherlands, Norway, Poland, Portugal, Romania, Slovakia, Slovenia, Spain, Sweden, Switzerland and United Kingdom.

Within CEN/ISSS a stable "workshop" is dedicated to ICT skills, and it is managed with the support of the European Commission (DG Enterprise), Cedefop (the Centre for the Development of Vocational Training, a EU agency) and CEPIS.

Since 2004, the CEN/ISSS Workshop involved several stakeholders, and reached consensus about some intermediate results: the afore mentioned recognition of Career Space results, plus a document on an "ICT Skills Meta-Framework" (CWA 15505) recognizing the relevance of various national frameworks, namely SFIA in the UK, AITTS in Germany, and CIGREF Nomenclature in France.

Although this is currently the most serious endeavour to define a European standard, unfortunately the Workshop does not seem to be in a position to achieve results that can really be used to address the practical issues of ICT skills management. This is, of course, a personal opinion, but it could be supported by two arguments: firstly, the discussion is more and more abstract and far from the ICT domain (the main focus seems to be on terminology and methodological issues); secondly, there is an insufficient commitment of some of the main stakeholders, i.e. the various authorities working on national/local qualification standards and the international operators offering ICT certification.

In any case, the problem is really complex, also due to the reasons presented in the next section.

1.4 Factors Affecting the Complexity of Resolution

The definition of a standard system for the qualification of ICT professional competences is not a trivial subject: it requires a large team of experts who can guarantee a reasonable coverage of all technical aspects of the ICT domain, plus a few experts in the definition of a coherent and balanced framework. Yet, the most arduous factors of complexity in having a standard accepted seem to be the political aspects: a list of such factors is presented here.

Multiple purposes: as pointed out by Matthew Dixon [3], classification of professional profiles and competences are relevant for a number of different applications, and e-competence frameworks typically reflect a specific purpose for which they were designed.

Ministerial jurisdiction: for the same reason mentioned just above, different governmental departments (Education, Industry, Trade and Competition, Labour, Justice...) are involved in the definition of competence standards.

Territorial jurisdiction: several levels of local autonomy exist, and there's no common consent on whose guidelines are binding. In the worst cases, we could think of 5 or 6 levels of local authorities defining norms:

- global (ISO norms, UNO resolutions...),
- "continental union" level (by EU, NAFTA...),
- national (in France, Germany, Italy, UK...),
- "regional" (in Bavaria, Lombardy, Scotland...),
- "sub-regional" (French departments, Italian provinces, UK counties),
- township...

In the recent past, the hierarchy was certainly led by the national governance, with possible recommendations from international bodies and some tolerance for minor local adjustments. Nowadays, in Europe, two diverging trends seem to be shifting more authority both to super-national entities (the EU) and to regional governments.

Sectoral and corporate-level jurisdiction: many standards – including the above mentioned Blu-ray Disc format – come from industry associations or even from single companies; eventually, if they find a clear way ahead, they are officially recognized as official norms and sometimes referenced by specific laws.

Notwithstanding all of the above complexity factors, a solution could (and should) be found. It is a fact that a number of large companies and Public Administration entities are working separately on these issues, and it would be nonsense not to join forces and continue to restart every time from scratch. Unfortunately, this is still the current practice.

2. The EUCIP Model

2.1 Origins and Parallel Developments

The EUCIP model, briefly presented here, can be seen as the result of two decades of work done by CEPIS, the Council of European Professional Informatics Societies, through task forces involving several Member Societies from various countries.

In such a considerable time period (compared to the very recent history of ICT) some words have changed, so that what was once referred to as "skills structure" would now be called "competence framework", but the concept is basically still the same: to provide a comprehensive reference for classifying and qualifying the various elements of knowledge, ability and demonstrated professional performance characterizing an ICT professional.

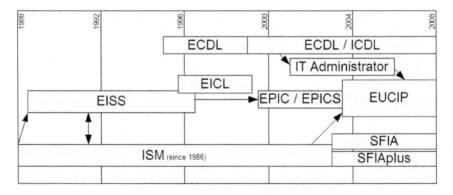

The figure shows how CEPIS's efforts are inspired and supported by parallel activities promoted by the British Computer Society (BCS), whose leading position within CEPIS was always recognized. Nevertheless, a distinction between

UK-centric and Europe-wide proposals and applications was constantly kept, also taking into account the different institutional stakeholders (i.e. the Crown in UK, the European Commission in the EU, etc.).

Although each project would deserve a dedicated explanation, we will just take a single instance that gives an idea of the interlacement between different initiatives, which is much more complex than the figure can render.

The IT Administrator certification programme was first conceived as a unification of two separate ideas: based on several inputs from the market, the ECDL Foundation had involved experts from Greece, Ireland and the UK in the initial definition of an "ECDL Advanced Specialised" programme (something in the middle between ICT user skills and professional skills certification); in the meanwhile, the Italian government had asked AICA to develop the guidelines of a LAN administrator profile for decentralized branches of Public Administration entities. The task forces merged, and a single product – with 5 certification modules – was developed. A few years later, the experts working at the definition of the European Certification of Informatics Professionals (EUCIP) approved the merger of the IT Administrator programme into the EUCIP programme itself.

The whole new model was built with direct inputs from all of the above shown CEPIS-internal efforts and the experts involve were fully aware of the various endeavours listed under the subtitle 2.3: **EUCIP can therefore be considered as an original synthesis of a number of different researches and initiatives**.

2.2 Specific Features of the EUCIP Model

The EUCIP model synthesizes many previous and parallel works. The originality of such a synthesis is primarily related to the specific viewpoint of the expert groups that defined it: they were formed by ICT professionals, university professors and managers of international certification programmes, who had in mind both the theory of informatics and the business view of ICT; the main focus was on certification (drawing from the ECDL/ICDL experience and from constant research on the ICT certification market).

As a consequence, EUCIP is extremely **ICT specific** (hardly portable to different industries), **vendor independent**, but it acknowledges a high role to technology providers, **business oriented**, having a focus on applied technology for business effective information systems, and **practical-minded**, because all professional skills requirements were specified with a concern on possible examination forms.

From an academic point of view, the EUCIP model might be deemed weak in terms of "purity" in definitions, lacking in cross-sectoral generality, and scarce in the description of attitudes, behavioural skills and levels of responsibility: in my view, these are not really disadvantages, but characteristics associated with a model focusing on ICT skills.

EUCIP defines a **Core Level** (the inner circle in the figure below); this might be intended as the common body of knowledge that any ICT professional should be familiar with. The competence requirements specified in the Core Level syllabus are grouped into 3 knowledge areas, which correspond to the main phases in an Information System's life cycle: plan, build, and operate.

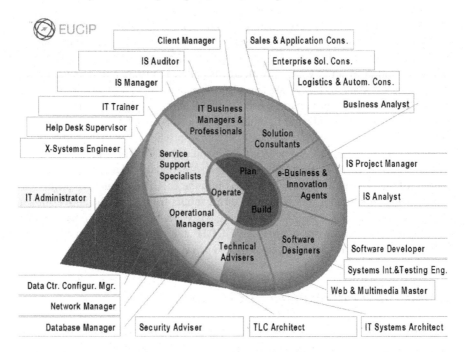

The total number of competence items specified for the core level is around 500, grouped into ca. 100 topics, further grouped into 18 categories, each of which belongs to one of the 3 main knowledge areas.

In addition to the Core Level, an ICT professional should be characterized by a specialisation, i.e. by deeper competence in some selected areas and categories (using the EUCIP terms). The EUCIP **Professional Level** certification can only be achieved by candidates who demonstrate additional competences earned through a mix of formal studies, "elective" certification modules (i.e. certificates issued by non-EUCIP organizations like Cisco, Microsoft etc.), plus some practical work experience. The EUCIP Professional Level defines 7 branches of professionalism and a total of 21 profiles; each of them is specified through a 20-page document, describing the typical tasks, the competence requirements and the cross reference to the classification systems used in the 4 main European countries.

The total number of competence items specified at the elective level is approximately 2500, grouped in over 150 categories, each of which refers to one of the 18 core categories.

The **IT Administrator** programme includes 5 certification modules, that can either be seen as a stand-alone series or taken as elective modules in a candidate's progression towards one of the 21 elective profiles.

Most of the official documents specifying the EUCIP standard are publicly available without restrictions through CEPIS and ECDL Foundation's websites.

2.3 Sample Applications and Benefits

In this section, a few EUCIP application examples are listed; each of them could be described in a dedicated article, but our objective here is only to catch the variety of possible (and real!) uses of a standard model for ICT competences, on the supply side of ICT education and training, as well as on the demand side, i.e. for governmental organizations and private companies aiming at a more effective management of their human capital.

Cisco / EUCIP cooperation: in 2005 Cisco was looking for a third-party certification to be offered to the European students attending IT Essentials courses at a Cisco Networking Academy; after some talks with the ECDL Foundation, some further studies and pilot projects, three EUCIP IT Administrator modules were chosen as the best solution. As a consequence, the most recent version of Cisco's IT Essentials curriculum – produced in the USA – was enriched taking EUCIP syllabi as one of the main sources of input.

IT vocational training in Estonia: vocational high schools in Estonia (one of the most advanced EU states in e-Government innovation) have adopted the EUCIP Core syllabus as the main reference for ICT students.

EUCIP at the University: several universities (remarkably in Italy and Ireland) have compared the contents of their courses for ICT students with EUCIP syllabi; the typical outcome is that some more attention should be paid to the subjects grouped in the "Plan" area of EUCIP, i.e. to the value of IT from a business perspective. As a consequence, students are invited to complement their studies with some dedicated training, and to prove their competence by getting EUCIP certified.

Professional development in Norwegian companies: unlike all other countries, in Norway EUCIP has always been proposed firstly to non-ICT companies as a way to improve the professional value of their ICT staff. This means, in practice, that every EUCIP project was planned in co-operation with one or more companies, i.e. working on the demand side of ICT employment.

EUCIP for ICT Governance in Italy: various Public Administration (PA) entities and governmental agencies in Italy have adopted EUCIP as the reference framework for ICT professional competences. Pilot projects have involved ICT employees of the Ministries of Finance, Defense, Justice, Education.

Italia Lavoro, the agency in charge of regulating the national employment market, has designed the national ICT professional profiles based on EUCIP profiles.

CNIPA, the governmental agency for ICT in PA, is about to release a complete set of guidelines for the procurement of ICT services, where professional profiles reflect EUCIP standards. It is likely that most invitations to tender from PA entities will recommend tenderers to refer to EUCIP profiles. By the way, some private organization like Generali, one of the largest Italian insurance groups, are working exactly in the same direction, recommending all internal ICT project managers and buyers to use EUCIP profiles as a benchmark when evaluating professional services proposals from their suppliers.

3. Conclusion

The EUCIP model offers a comprehensive set of concepts (including a body of knowledge for the whole scenario of ICT professions) and tools for an effective management of the human capital.

It can either be seen as a traditional certification offering (competing in a narrow market, where customers are disorientated by an excess of proposals) or as a **shared model around which a number of stakeholders are finding solutions** to the complex issues of professionalism and effective management of ICT competences and profiles.

The second option has an evident higher value, but the extent of its success depends only partly on CEPIS's ability to present the EUCIP "product": in fact, it mainly depends on an open attitude from other stakeholders, who can either exploit the value of this thorough model, or continue to conceive new projects from scratch, and cope with the arduous task of defining and measuring ICT professional competences.

References

1. Hamburg, Inge, 10 Years, CEPIS internal booklet, London, UK (1998).
2. CEPIS Task Force on Professional Qualifications and Development (led by the British Computer Society, 12 EU countries represented), European Informatics Skills Structure, CEPIS, Amsterdam, The Netherlands (1992).
3. Dixon, Matthew, "The potential Uses, Benefits and Costs of a European ICT Skills Meta-Framework", Annex A to the CWA 15515: "European ICT Skills Meta-Framework - State-of-the-Art review, clarification of the realities, and recommendations for next steps", CEN, Brussels, Belgium (2006).

EUCIP Driving the IT-Professional Competence in Norway

Renny Bakke Amundsen, CEO of EUCIP Norway

Norwegian Computer Society, Oslo, Norway

Abstract: EUCIP[1], the European Certification of Informatics Professionals, is a professional certification and competence development scheme aimed at IT practitioners and undergraduates. Like ECDL[2], EUCIP was developed by CEPIS[3], the Council of European Professional Informatics Societies. This article gives an overview of the experiences of the EUCIP Operator in Norway, EUCIP Norge[4], in targeting the corporate market through the use of collaborative partners.

Keywords: EUCIP, CEPIS, Certification, ICT Skill, ICT-Competence

1. Introduction

With a population of nearly 5 million in Norway, an estimated 100,000 people are IT-professionals and approximately 3,000 IT students. EUCIP Norge started with the corporate market as EUCIP would appeal to those who either lacked or had an out of date formal certification of IT-professional skills. The syllabus definition in colleges and universities is mainly driven by government which takes time to change. As a result, there has been good interest in EUCIP in the private sector, which should increase following the release of the full range of EUCIP Professional Profiles in late 2007.

2. Launching the EUCIP scheme in Norway:

As an early adopter of EUCIP, the initial work involved promoting the certification concept. Based on DND's (The Norwegian Computer Society[5])

---

[1] www.eucip.com

[2] www.ecdl.com

[3] www.cepis.org

[4] www.eucip.no

[5] http://dataforeningen.no/FgdLS4k.ips

Please use the following format when citing this chapter:

Amundsen, R.B., 2008, in IFIP International Federation for Information Processing, Volume 280; *E-Government; ICT Professionalism and Competences; Service Science*; Antonino Mazzeo, Roberto Bellini, Gianmario Motta; (Boston: Springer), pp. 133–138.

credibility as a vendor neutral IT-professional organisation, the society's network was used to promote the concept. This was achieved through:

- Meetings with CIOs or HR managers in companies within the computer industry as well as the user industry (where the highest amount of IT-professionals are working) and also in public service.
- Establishing a separate website http://www.eucip.no, to promote and explain the concept. As one of the most important marketing channels for DND is through mails and newsletters, it was important to have websites to refer to, instead of using extensive mails with attachments. In addition, EUCIP was also well presented on DND's own website[6].
- EUCIP was promoted at DND conferences and seminars and was introduced to some relevant work- or task- groups.
- DND formed a 100% owned Ltd. Company "EUCIP Norge" and its CEO presented EUCIP at relevant conferences hosted by DND or others.

With a geographically spread population, it was essential to authorise Test Centres in the major cities. EUCIP Norge went to the biggest ECDL Test Centres and was able to have 20 operating during the first year spread throughout the country.

3. Courseware to fill the competence gap:

Soon the demand for courseware appeared and EUCIP Norge found a courseware partner, **TISIP**[7]; a foundation cooperating with the Faculty of Information Technology and E-Learning at **Sør-Trøndelag University College**. They wrote text books (in Norwegian!) and E-learning programs for each module of the EUCIP Core syllabus.

There are also ongoing discussions with universities and college universities about incorporating some of the 21 Professional vocational profiles in their bachelor and master programs. They will probably first be available for the corporate market.

4. Significant Norwegian IT-Organisations as Partners

The EUCIP concept is now fairly well known among IT professionals in Norway. However, EUCIP Norge hasn't yet reached critical mass. EUCIP Norge is currently in a process of inviting the largest employers of IT-professionals to a partnership programme. To date three Norwegian IT organizations, **DND**

---

[6] http://dataforeningen.no/?module=Articles;action=ArticleFolder.publicOpenFolder;ID=748
[7] http://www.tisip.no/public/EUCIP/indexEUCIP.jsp

(Norwegian Computer Society), **IKT-Norge**[8] and **Abelia**[9], have agreed to support EUCIP as a general industry standard for professional skills.

In a press release in September 2007 they said: *"The majority of professions set standards which, when met, provide an indication of the skills and level of competence a worker possesses. You would probably be reluctant to let a person without a builder's certificate be the building contractor for your house. Even so, Norwegian businesses purchase IT services worth billions of kroner without requiring formal documentation of the competencies of the persons hired in to do the work. The industry clearly wishes to address this problem"*.

"This is a big step forward, for both the industry and the industry's customers" says IKT-Norge's Secretary General, Per-Morten Hoff. *"Certainly there are a number of certification programs which document competence within specific products, but a general competency standard has been sorely missed."*

Paul Chaffey, Managing Director of Abelia, also welcomes the adoption of the EUCIP standard in Norway. *"EUCIP is a common language for describing skills. We strongly recommend that our members start speaking this language"*.

Geir Horn, former President of the Norwegian Computer Society, is pleased for the support from the other organizations. *"The Norwegian Computer Society aims to be the leading certification body for IT professionals in Norway, and this co-operation is a breakthrough in achieving this heady goal"*.

Adoption of EUCIP implies significant cost reductions for the IT industry. Many companies have found it necessary to develop their own internal standards, and have found that they are of little value outside their own four walls.

"In Software Innovation we used millions of kroner on internal systems for describing the competence of each of our co-workers, without this being worth anything to the co-worker on the day he or she left the company" says Per Kveim, former chief executive of Software Innovation[10] and now Chairman of EUCIP Norge AS.

For those that employ IT workers or purchase IT services, EUCIP provides a more general view of competence than today's confusion of certifications for skills within specific products. A certification from EUCIP says much about a candidate's abilities, providing they fall in under one of the 21 job descriptions where EUCIP defines formal and practical competency requirements.

The Norwegian Computer Society has an exclusive license agreement for the programme in Norway and has established EUCIP Norge AS to administer the standard. IKT-Norge and Abelia acknowledge EUCIP as an industry standard and, through co-operation with the Norwegian Computer Society, are aiming to achieve the following goals:

- Recognize, document and protect industry standards for IT professionals

---

[8] http://www.ikt-norge.no/Engslish-infopage/

[9] http://abelia.no/english/

[10] http://www.software-innovation.com/en/pages/default.aspx

- Further develop a process for mapping and measurement of IT professionals' competencies
- Develop goal-oriented training plans and stimulate professional development
- Promote knowledge of the EUCIP standard within the media and public authorities
- Create enthusiasm for EUCIP as a general competency standard within the membership of the co-operating organizations
- Assist recognized educational institutions in developing EUCIP training programmes by identifying the industry's needs for skills development

EUCIP Norge is optimistic about the EUCIP initiative following the positive responses received from those visited so far. Essential to this success is the fact that the full range of EUCIP Professional Profiles is now available. This will open further opportunities as these organisations will have an industry standard to use for competence mapping, measuring and development for their IT-professionals.

5. Establishing EUCIP Examination boards in Norway

Essential for providing EUCIP Professional certification is to establish Examination Boards for each of the 21 profiles. Assistant Professor, Ragnvald Sannes[11] at BI[12] Norwegian School of Management, and a member of the EUCIP Board of Directors, has taken a leading role in this.

Each of the Examination Boards has minimum three members: one from the academia, one in Norway with credibility for his or her skills relevant for the EUCIP Professional Profile - preferably one from The Norwegian Computer Society - and one with the same credibility from the user industry. So far, there has been no problem filling these positions as it is seen as an asset to be titled: *A Member of EUCIP Examination Board.*

EUCIP recognise formal education as well as working experience relevant for the applied profile and both behavioural and competence skills are measured. In this, candidates are also given credit for holding other (including vendors) certificates if they prove relevant competence. E.g. a candidate gets credit for a Cisco certificate if applying for EUCIP Network Administrator. Due to this, we have started mapping all other certificates for exact EUCIP points for each of the 21 profiles. Vendors now start to show interest in this and are of course eager to assure their certificates are properly mapped.

---

[11] http://www.bi.no/Content/AcademicProfile____63388.aspx?ansattid=/fgl88001
[12] http://www.bi.no/Content/StartPageEnglish____56401.aspx

6. Early adopters for the EUCIP scheme in Norway

The first EUCIP Professional Certified as Business Analyst in Norway was Senior Consultant **David Thomstad** in **Ciber**[13] **Norway**. His substantial experience within ICT is highly recognised and he has a lot of other vendor- and vendor neutral certificates. He also has significant education, however from earlier time so he wanted an updated proof of his ICT professional skills. He says the rest of the Ciber's consultant staff with follow during the next years to give the company a head start in offering consultancies with highly recognised advisers in the Norwegian market.

Next out is **Devoteam daVinci**[14], starting with four experienced consultants who will complete the EUCIP Certification programme in June. Two of which are applying for EUCIP Business Analyst, one for Security Adviser and one for Project Manager. daVinci wants a head start in the Norwegian market as well, but also like to see their colleges in the rest of Scandinavia as well as Europe on board.

Another interesting case is **Microsoft Norway**[15] as their Chief Security Advisor **Ole Tom Seierstad**[16] wants to focus on security in Norway in 2008. As a part of his campaign, he is sponsoring four highly skilled consultants from some of Microsoft Norway's partners for EUCIP Security Adviser certification. He would like to make them leading figures within security and says the best way to prove their skills is for them to obtain a neutral accreditation, in addition to their Microsoft certificates.

Next in line is Aker Kværner[17], a leading global provider of services related to design, construction, maintenance, modification, and operation of both large and small industrial facilities. **Stein Schjerve**, Manager - Application Management, in Aker Kværner Business Partner wants to try the scheme with a handful in their staff on different EUCIP profiles during 2008. What drew Schjerve's attention to EUCIP was the standard for categorizing ICT skills useful to define, measure and develop their staff worldwide. Aker Kværner is extremely project oriented and needs an efficient way to put together sufficient project teams with participants from their 35 branch offices all over the world.

These are examples of how candidates as well as their companies make use of EUCIP's ability to a neutral way of documenting IT-Professional skills. It's useful for candidates for proving and for their companies to have the staff categorised as a base for developing individual competence according to the markets need as well as being able to describe their competence when offering their services.

---

[13] http://www.ciber-europe.com/

[14] http://www.davinci.no/index.php?lang=2

[15] http://www.microsoft.com/nb/no/default.aspx

[16] http://www.microsoft.com/norge/about/pr/portfolio.aspx?folder=/portfolio/Kontaktpersoner%20i%20Microsoft/Seierstad,%20Ole%20Tom

[17] http://www.akersolutions.com/internet/default.htm

7. Prelaunch of EUCIP IT-Administrator scheme in Norway

IT Administrator is a standalone certification programme that measures practical and theoretical knowledge of computer technicians. The programme is aimed at small to medium-sized companies, including educational institutes, which require in-house expertise in IT as well as individuals who wish to broaden their IT knowledge and be able to administer networks. This matches the company structure in a small country like Norway which means that it's perfect both for the industry and for public sector.

As a pilot, TISIP (se paragraph 3), will start a class for computer technicians and undergraduates in September this year enrolling about 50 students. The duration of the course will be one year and will cover all five modules from *PC Hardware* and *Operating Systems*, to *LAN and Network Services*, *Expert Network Use* as well as *IT Security*. Temporary employment services have shown great interest in this and The Norwegian Labour and Welfare Administration will be invited to enrol candidates as well.

8. Conclusions

This describes in short how The Norwegian Computer Society has decided to approach the Norwegian market. The most important was to achieve acceptance for EUCIP's way of categorising IT-Professional skills as well as the substantial way of measuring competence. In discussions with a lot of companies, even the biggest, it shows that they need and want a regime like this. They all admit it's important as a base to develop IT-Professional competence for an innovating market approach. They all have tried on individual basis to develop such a regime, and are interested in adopting this European standard as it is open and free with no risk to implement. The biggest and of course the multinational companies benefit the most as they work on a global market and need to describe, measure and develop their IT-skills on a worldwide basis.

By establishing EUCIP as a standard, we believe there will be a pull instead of a push for certifying candidates according to the vocational structure.

The EUCIP Scheme in the Italian University System

Marco Ferretti

C.I.N.I., Consorzio Interuniversitario Nazionale per l'Informatica, and University of Pavia, Italy, marco.ferretti@unipv.it

Abstract: This paper reports on the approach of Italian universities to the Eucip ICT certification. The Italian academia has taken a proactive mode: it has decided to work with AICA to support the scheme in all its levels, and to contribute to the quality of the certification with some specific projects, among which the development of e-learning material for the Core level. The cooperation has lasted for four years now, and will continue. It is unique within the European scenario, and it can offer at least a worked-out example of the relationship between a professional ICT certification and the university world.

Keywords: Certification, curricula, degree, university credit, e-learning.

1. Introduction

This contribution describes the approach of the Italian university system to the Eucip certification scheme. The paper discusses the issue of certification vs university degree, the approach to the Eucip scheme in the Italian academia, the projects that have been carried out, the role of e-learning in supporting the certification, and possible future developments. The Eucip scheme will not be described here: the reader is assumed to know the Eucip framework, useful references are the Eucip web site [1] and a summary description [2] available on AICA website.

As will be described later, a few institutions played a major role: AICA, the Italian society affiliated to CEPIS, that holds the right to distribute and to promote the Eucip concept in Italy; CINI, the consortium of Italian universities active in ICT [3], that operates the Eucip programme within universities [4]; Fondazione CRUI, the operative branch of the Conference of Italian Rectors, that worked with AICA and CINI in the Eucip4U project (2005-2007) [5]. AICA, CINI and Fondazione CRUI also run an "Observatory on ICT certification" (2000-2008) [6], that includes Eucip in its reports.

Please use the following format when citing this chapter:

Ferretti, M., 2008, in IFIP International Federation for Information Processing, Volume 280; *E-Government; ICT Professionalism and Competences; Service Science*; Antonino Mazzeo, Roberto Bellini, Gianmario Motta; (Boston: Springer), pp. 139–148.

2. Certifications vs University degrees

In this section, we discuss the relationship between professional certifications and university degrees, and we report on the Italian approach.

2.1 Why certifications in Universities?

At the very beginning, a few questions stand out that must be given proper answer. Why should universities take care of, or even participate, in certification schemes? Is certification of ICT skills an alternative to the assessment of ICT knowledge that comes along with university degrees in informatics?

Certifications are important within the ICT community. The first certification schemes were devised by *vendors* to enhance the perceived quality of their products. Both hardware and software were covered. A large market developed during the 90's: vendors, companies offering ad-hoc training, publishers, all contributed to creating a very strong business. An insightful analysis of the history of certification [7] shows the shift from "product" certifications, to "competence" certifications. Currently, many efforts are being put into the attempt to create a shared scheme to classify competences in a broad sense. The E-skills Forum [8] is one such, long-standing effort promoted by the EU. If we agree that "the true value of a certification is its ability to verify that a person possesses skills that are important to an employer" [7], we must show that indeed a certification and a university degree differ with respect to this.

Broadly speaking, university degrees in ICT have a two-fold task: i) creating a deep ground knowledge that allows a student to enter the profession with skills for being creative and effective in the use of technologies; ii) preparing the individual to handle changes and shifts of paradigms, that are a distinctive feature of ICT. None of these is the purpose of a certification. Yet, the university must signal students the relevance of certification: after getting their degree, students enter a profession and often the employer or the market demand that the professionist's competences be verified against a *syllabus* that details specific skills.

2.2 The approach in Italy

In the Italian university system, an ICT curriculum must allocate some effort to preparing students to enter the profession. This is usually obtained by setting up stages with companies, by offering short courses on the ethics of the profession, and by other similar offers. This is where certification can be effectively located within ICT curricula. It serves many purposes: it helps students perceive the role of the certification in the profession, it offers advantages when they apply for a job, it exposes them to an independent, non-academic way of assessing competences.

Eucip was considered particularly attractive because it is a flexible scheme, with a vendor-independent approach. It combines a unified ground knowledge level (the Core) with a multi-face vocational scheme (the profiles of the Elective level). Even vendor specific certifications can be a embedded in the Elective level scheme, thus opening up the way to striking a correct balance between long term skills and practical capabilities on specific software suites or hardware products.

For these reasons, a number of universities belonging to CINI, joined AICA in 2003 in the task of assessing if and how the Eucip scheme could be offered within the university system. After a preliminary assessment carried out within 5 universities, CINI and AICA agreed to launch a three-year project with a number of goals: i) to set up a network of university certification centres for the Eucip Core; ii) to produce a set of e-learning courses to support candidates to the Core certifications, both within universities and in the general market; iii) to examine the whole certification scheme (including the Elective level) and its relationship with ICT curricula. From 2005 to 2007, Fondazione CRUI, the operative branch of the Conference of the Rectors of Italian University joined with AICA and CINI in the Eucip4U project, with the specific goals to map the coverage of Eucip Core syllabus in a significant number of the degrees of informatics in engineering and in computer science, and to favour the granting of university credits to students that got the Core level certification. Recently, AICA and CINI signed a new two-year agreement to continue the cooperation; while the first project was focused on the Core level, the new one will address mainly the Elective.

3. Implementing the Core Level within ICT curricula

According the initial agreement, AICA granted CINI the exclusive right to operate the Eucip certification scheme within universities. The certification scheme was supported by CINI by setting up a network of University Competence Centres. In a university CINI establishes a single centre, though many test sites can be active, even in different locations within the same university. This structure is directed locally by a professor in informatics. A central coordinating structure manages all the project, and maintains a web site. Students sign-up to the certification programme at a special reduced fare, and have two years to complete the set of three exams that lead to the Core level certificate.

The Eucip Core level certification addresses knowledge areas, such as the BUILD and the OPERATE, that are at the "core" of any degree in informatics. The PLAN area, instead, is largely ignored by curricula, both in engineering and in computer science. So, at the outset, the project was targeted to students enrolled in the ICT curricula, on the assumption that at the end of the three-year curriculum, just before getting their degree, or possibly one year later, at the beginning of the subsequent two-year curriculum, they could successfully pass at least two of the Core level exams without any specific Eucip training. The university courses should have prepared them well beyond the level of the Core certification, as far as ICT is concerned. Instead, the PLAN area was expected to be mastered only to a very small degree.

These assumptions have been checked in the years 2004-2007 through the synergic actions of CINI centres of competence examination structure and the Eucip4U work on mapping actual coverage of syllabus in the curricula. The network of examination centres rapidly grew from the 9 universities already active at the end of 2004, to the 26 of late 2007, with altogether more than 40 sites delivering the tests. The universities that joined in the Eucip4U project were 30, with 66 tracks (39 from engineering, 23 from computer science and even 3 from economy, plus a master).

The detailed analysis of the coverage of the Eucip Core syllabus confirmed the initial assumption. The PLAN area was found totally or partially disregarded in all its modules by a minimum of 36 tracks (in the A1 module on "Organizations and their use of ICT") and by a maximum of 47 (in the A7 module on "Legal and ethical issues"). Furthermore, the OPERATE C7 module on "Service Delivery and Support" was found uncovered in 42 tracks; this was also expected. The true surprise comes from the unexpected low coverage declared by some 30 tracks in the BUILD B4 module on "User Interface and Web Design" and in the OPERATE C5 and C6 modules on "Wireless and Mobile Computing" and "Network management".

On another side, the groups of university professors active in informatics in engineering and computer science (GII and GRIN) recommended that the Core level certification be assigned university credits within ICT curricula. 41 of the tracks in the Eucip4U project complied, and granted an average of 5 credits (a three-year degree accounts for 180 credits).

Students started to enrol in the certification programme in autumn 2004, with a special fare that packaged the skills card and three exams. Table 1 shows the progress in time of enrolment, actual certifications issued, success percentages in the three knowledge areas.

Table 1. The diffusion of Eucip Core certification.

	Students		Exams			
Year	enrolled	certified	success	PLAN	BUILD	OPERATE
2004	226	71	62,0	52,4	70,7	65,4
2005	657	33	60,1	57,8	63,3	61,2
2006	444	52	62,5	56,4	66,8	64,9
2007	161	76	60,2	57,6	63,6	62,4

The numbers show a few interesting facts. If one considers success rates, the Eucip examinations proved to be more difficult than expected in the BUILD and

OPERATE areas. This effect was larger than what one could speculate on the basis of the coverage analysis carried out within the curricula. No surprise comes from the PLAN area. Among the reasons for this poor performance one must take into proper consideration the language issue: the exams were (and still are) delivered in English. The certification programme has attracted a good number of students up to 2006; in 2007 enrolment has declined strongly. Examination activity continues, since the programme allows for two years to complete the three tests, so a certain number of students are in process of completing the sequence. During 2006 CINI offered its e-learning courses for free to students (more on this sub-project in the following section); from 2007 the courses must be paid for, though at a price considerably lower than what the average Italian student spends for cell phones and the like!

Feedback was collected within the CINI network of university competence centres to assess the situation at the end of 2007. The decline in enrolment is most probably due to some concurrent facts: i) students perceive the Eucip scheme as a whole as something potentially important to their future profession, but they have been offered so far only the least "professional" part of it, namely the Core; ii) the Elective level certification has been completely specified in its 21 profiles in mid 2007, and has not been deployed consistently neither in the universities, nor in the market; iii) only in 2008 the Eucip scheme has been recognized in a few Italian institutions either in the private area or in the public one. It is likely that the trend will return to positive slopes when the diffusion of the Elective level outside the universities will be effectively perceived. A possible contribution form the university system to the Elective level is described in a subsequent section.

4. The CINI e-learning courseware for EUCIP Core

As anticipated, one of the tasks CINI planned to support the Core level of the EUCIP certification scheme was the design, production and operation of set of e-learning courses. CINI held this part of the mutual cooperation with AICA so important and relevant for the world of the academia involved with informatics that it decided to share with AICA on equal basis the costs (known !) and benefits (speculative !). Among the motivations that lead CINI to this position were: i) the desire to support a certification that, at the Core level, is by nature "vendor independent" and that shares so much with all degrees of informatics in Italian university curricula; ii) the hope to contribute to set at a high level the perceived quality of the EUCIP scheme as a whole, mainly outside the university world; iii) the hope to offer the ICT community in its broad sense a set of high quality courses on introduction to informatics, that could *also* serve as a tool for preparing candidates to the certification;   iv) the desire to experiment the e-learning techniques already used within some of the universities in a *nation-wide* framework, by running national virtual classrooms.

4.1 Design principles

Many Italian universities have produced e-learning material for official courses in various tracks, and there are a few degrees, especially in the ICT area, that offer on-line classes only. So there is widespread knowledge on setting up e-learning "university course".

Designing of Eucip Core is another matter. For one thing, the estimated effort for the various "modules" of the three knowledge areas is usually much smaller than the comparable effort for a university course. Furthermore, the target audience can be quite different: in a university environment, the profile of students of ICT degrees is known, while the prospect usage of Eucip courseware can call for attendees with good ICT practice, but no or little formal training, or for people in public administration that are involved with ICT processes but have no training in informatics at all, or even for students in business schools that want to complement their economics degree with training in informatics. Finally, one can conceive the material using the syllabus as a guideline, or one can adopt a more wide approach designing the courses without strictly adhering to the breakdown of the subjects suggested by the syllabus, meanwhile guaranteeing that all topics in the syllabus are indeed covered by the courses.

Since the profile of the would-be user of the courseware was so various, CINI decided to design the material with a "quality first" criterion and with the ultimate purpose to create a repository of elementary *learning objects* that could be re-used in more environments.

4.2 Courses structure and development

At the coarse level, the e-learning material developed is currently organized into 18 courses, each associated to one of the EUCIP "modules". Within a course, the material is broken down into *learning objects*, that is self-contained units that can possibly be assembled to set up different learning paths. Each learning object contains many items: *units of content* (text with graphics and figures, each some $600 \div 800$ characters), *self test questions* structured according to Eucip guidelines for examinations questions (multiple choice questions, with feedback for each choice); off-line *exercises* (short problems with an annotated solution), along with intended *learning outcomes*. The set of learning objects are accompanied by the *conceptual map*, a precedence graph that show the precedence among the concepts used within the learning objects themselves. The user of a module has a clear description of the sequence of learning paths that are available within each course. Coverage of the syllabus is guaranteed by proper references to the "topics" from within the learning objects.

The material has been produced in a year by a team of university professors and some professionals (the latter mainly for the PLAN Area). Authors were provided with proper guidelines and detailed instructions. A thorough reviewing process was set-up, with reviewers chosen among PhD students in ICT, technicians with operative skills and even staff with little or no formal education in ICT. An editorial board collected the review forms filled each by each of the reviewers on each learning object and routed feedback to the authors when necessary. The process was indeed a fairly huge one, as well as the output.

The learning material produced consists of 193 learning objects, containing a total of 2000 units of content with 725 drawings and pictures, 2000 self-test questions and 400 exercises.

4.3 The technologies

The whole e-learning project was conceived to be an all in-house one, that is CINI wanted to leverage the capabilities and skills available within its member universities. So, an open software approach was followed consistently. The delivery platform was chosen among the open software based ones, and Dokeos turned out to be the most apt to the goals of the project. Among the key features, it supported fairly well SCORM 1.2 and allows for a fairly flexible setup of the virtual classes and for the tracing of the learning progress of the users.

The learning objects have been produced through software chain that has targeted re-use: the intermediate result of the developing project is a repository of XML documents embedding the various types of learning material. The final HTML pages (with proper javascript code for managing, among other things, self-test questions) also comply with accessibility requirements.

4.4 The e-learning model

One of the most important choices for this sub-project was the design of the e-learning model. The first use of the courses was within university students enrolled in computer engineering and computer science tracks. This audience was scattered throughout many universities and there was no practical possibility to create local classrooms obeying the blended mode e-learning paradigm. So the model adopted was based on virtual classrooms, assisted by a *tutor*, with the support of a domain *expert* and the overall assistance of a *controller*. Both the tutor and the student enrolled in the classroom were bound by an *agreement*. The tutor had to guarantee proper assistance to the classroom by regularly logging onto the platform, by answering questions with one of the asynchronous communications tools available (forums, FAQ, messages) or by forwarding them to the expert, by checking on the progress of each individual and by reporting on a weekly basis to the controller. The student accepted that he could access the courses for their whole duration provided that he actively participated in the experiment: he had to log on the platform within two weeks from the start, meanwhile reading a number of units of contents from at least one learning object, and he should complete three of the seven courses within the first two months.

The classroom was scheduled to last for three months: the tutor was active for the first two months, and the student could continue on his own for one more month. At the end of the period, the student was asked to fill in an assessment form.

The *expert* was the author of the module. His services were considered necessary only occasionally, should a tutor be unable to answer directly the questions raised by course attendees. The subjects covered by the courses are indeed very wide; while the BUILD and OPERATE area are somehow homogeneous and insist strictly on ICT, the PLAN area requires a different expertise. So, in a virtual classroom that is associated to all the Eucip Core courses, the tutor is unlikely to be in command of all subject matters.

The *controller* was given the task to control the work of the tutors. This function has proven very important for the experimentation phase, and can be used profitably when an e-learning process involves many virtual classrooms that are active at the same time. Basically, the controller checks that the tutor complies with the duties of his agreement.

Of course, the actual work of tutors and of the controller and the quality of the service offered to the student depends on the features of the delivery platform. This is were the combination of technologies (standard SCORM 1.2) and open software played its role at the most: the type of data collected by the platform and the modes of analyzing these data were not suited to the intended scopes but have been properly tailored and extended.

4.5 The experimentation

The first use of the e-learning course was within universities. We chose to offer students of informatics degrees learning material for the PLAN area of the syllabus (and of module C7 on Service Delivery and Support) because these knowledge areas are not covered or treated only shortly in the official course of their curricula. Also, the BUILD and OPERATE course were offered to students in electronics and telecommunications: their curriculum indeed covers only introductory informatics.

From November 2005 to June 2006 CINI ran 9 nation-wide virtual classrooms. Some 800 students were involved in the experiment. They were offered free access to the classrooms, provided that they had enrolled in the Eucip certification scheme, and that they belonged to one of the tracks that supported the Eucip4U project. The experiment worked fairly well; the management of the process was smooth, some initial technical deficiencies in the platform were identified and corrected (slowness due to improper DBMS usage by Dokeos, unreliable collection of tracing data).

The student perspective has been analyzed on the basis of the questionnaires filled in and with the help of the tutors. It turned out that the courses have been perceived useful and suited to the certification. The one thing that disappointed most students is the use of the Italian language: since the certification exams are delivered in English, the user of the courses receives proper cultural assistance, but experiences true difficulties with the sometimes puzzling terminology of the English questions issued during the exams, mostly in the PLAN area.

A small experimentation was also carried out in a classroom of ICT professionals, mostly engineers or public servants in ICT agencies. Their feedback was altogether different: they considered the material very useful to rehearse and update "ground knowledge" in ICT; yet, the shear volume of the 2000 web pages (for the whole Core) was perceived as a major hurdle. Actually, a proper profiling of the candidate can help extract from the large repository of learning objects those really necessary to an individual learning path. Work is in progress!

5. Perspectives on the future

The cooperation between AICA and CINI continues and a new agreement for the year 2008-2009 has been signed. On his side, AICA is setting up a set of services for companies and the general market based on the 21 profiles of the Elective level with the "Cantiere dei Mestieri" [9]. Accordingly, the approach to Eucip within universities will be more focused on the Elective level, in many directions.

The Elective level is the real professional part of the certification. Its 21 profiles detail competences that typically can be attained only after proper work in the field. The candidate to the certification must produce a "portfolio" that lists competences along three dimensions: formal training/education, work experience, accredited specific Eucip modules (beyond the Core, that is mandatory). If this "portfolio" is rich enough (there exist a very precise sets of rules to assess in objective way the dimensions), the candidate is admitted to a final examination.

The university system can help in many ways, within this scenario. Clearly, students at the end of their degree are well below the competence level of a professionist, in any profile. Yet, if they have got their degree by preparing their final dissertation as a result of a stage within a company on subjects strongly related to a profile, they could be interested in being awarded an "assistant" certificate, should their "portfolio" have the required characteristics.

The dimension on accredited Eucip module is currently the most weak one in Italy. The university system can help in three ways: i) by setting up master degrees that are closely shaped after one of the profiles; ii) by analyzing current university courses in the two-year Laurea Magistrale curricula for coverage of profile sub-areas; iii) by designing new courses well matched to the profiles that are most appealing in the ICT market. Two are the criteria: on one side, students enrolled in a university degree get not only university credits, but also Eucip "points" to be later spent for the certification; on another one, specific new didactic proposals can be modelled after the requirements of the ICT market, clearly specified by a set of professional profiles widely accepted and recognized.

6. Acknowledgements

Many are the persons that contributed to the Eucip effort within the Italian university system. The first workgroup established by CINI in 2003 was composed P. Ciancarini, P. Della Vigna, B. Fadini[†], M. Ferretti, A. Martelli, D. Nardi, P. Prinetto, F. Turini and G. Ventre. The 2004-2007 project was directed by a committee with M. Ferretti (project leader), P. Ciancarini, B. Fadini, P. Prinetto and S. Russo. The same group with the further contribution by A. Chianese led the e-learning subproject, with a specific role played by Chianese, Ciancarini and Ferretti in the editorial board. The central operative structure was run by P. Ferrari, and G. Meregaglia constantly took care of the financial management. The joint AICA-CINI-Fondazione CRUI Eucip4U project was steered by a committee with C. Alfonsi, M. Calzarossa, P. Ciancarini, N. Cimitile (group leader), M. Ferretti, F. Patini, D. Pedreschi, N. Scarabottolo, with the constant support by M. Leo. These projects would not be possible without the voluntary effort of the university professors and personnel that actually run the network of CINI centres and that acted as reference persons during the Eucip4U sub-project. Not to mention the over 40 people that authored the modules of the CINI e-learning courses ! A final special acknowledgement is due to the late B. Fadini, Director of CINI up to mid 2007, who strongly supported the Eucip scheme and the collaboration of the university with AICA.

References

1. Eucip website, www.eucip.com
2. The EUCIP Model, A standard approach to the definition and measurement of ICT Competences, AICA report, March 2007, available at: http://www.eucip.it. (as of May 2008)
3. CINI website: www.consorzio-cini.it
4. CINI Eucip website: eucip.consorzio-cinit.it, in Italian.
5. Eucip4U website: www.fondazionecrui.it/eucip4U, in Italian.
6. AICA-CINI-Fondazione CRUI "Observatory on ICT Certifications Universities" website: http://osservatorio.consorzio-cini.it, in Italian.
7. Shore J., Why Certification? The Applicability of IT Certification to College and University Curricula. Available at www.developer.ibm.com/university /scholars/**certification**/ebusiness/pdfs/why-**certification**.pdf , (as of May 2008).
8. E-Skills website, http://ec.europa.eu/enterprise/ict/policy/ict-skills.htm
9. "Cantiere dei Mestieri", available at http://aicanet.net/soci/il-cantiere-dei-mestieri-ict (as of May 2008)

IT skill requirements in Public Administration

A model of IS Function for Public Administrations in order to identify professional requirements and training needs. The experience of the Department for National General Accounting of the Italian Ministry of Economy and Finance.

Pietro Paolo Trimarchi

Ministry of Economy and Finance – Department for National General Accounting (RGS), Italy, pietropaolo.trimarchi@tesoro.it

Abstract: In the last twenty years, the role and the organization of IS function has been undergoing profound changes. Both firms and Public Administrations have not always been able to adapt successfully to new realities. In particular, IS staff often do not have appropriate skills, on the one hand, to translate business needs in IT solutions and, on the other hand, to deal competently with suppliers. The Department for National General Accounting of the Italian Ministry of Economy and Finance is trying to fill these competence gaps through a re-training program for its IS human resources. For this purpose a model of IS function was built. It is the starting point and the goal of the project.

Keywords: IS function, public administration, EUCIP

1. The IS function in today's organizations

Realizing what the role and the structure of IS function is within modern organizations is the first step to identify IT skill requirements. In fact, not only technical competences, but also business needs have been changing rapidly.

The weight of IT within organizations has been growing. However, the actual change is not the scope of its presence but what it is used for.

Today, automating operational activities represents normality; whereas the new goal of information systems is to support decisions in order to enhance their quality. Therefore, the current purpose of IT is no longer and not only to increase

Please use the following format when citing this chapter:

Trimarchi, P.P., 2008, in IFIP International Federation for Information Processing, Volume 280; *E-Government; ICT Professionalism and Competences; Service Science*; Antonino Mazzeo, Roberto Bellini, Gianmario Motta; (Boston: Springer), pp. 149–157.

processes efficiency but also more and more to improve management effectiveness.

This is true for firms as well as for public administrations. In fact - although they have different aims (firms are subjected to market competition while public administrations are submitted to the consent of the people) – they both need meaningful and well-timed information to achieve, given the resources available, the best results. Therefore, IT requirements of an organization often depend more on its size than on its private or public nature. And, in principle, dealing with the information system (or the IS function) within a public administration or within a firm is substantially the same.

This does not mean there are no differences. Nevertheless, if the level of analysis remains general these differences are not significant. For example, it is known that IT strategy should not only be aligned to business strategy but also should be an active part of it. This concept is valid for firms as well as for public administrations. Of course, suggestions coming from IT will be different in the two different cases, but shouldn't it be the same scenario when speaking about two firms, one having its business in a competitive and the other that has its business in an oligopolistic or a monopolistic market?

The reason is that IT is an instrument as well as IS function is a support function. So their link with the core business of the organization is slack and guidelines about their role and organizational structure can be adapted to different real applications.

As explained, the role of IT within organizations has been changing over time. This is evident when looking at the evolution of enterprise information systems: from transaction processing systems (TPS) to management information systems (MIS), to decision support systems (DSS), to executive support systems (ESS), to supply chain management systems (SCM), to customer relationship management systems (CRM), to knowledge management systems (KMS), etc.

It also follows that the role of IS function has changed, so new skills are required of the people who work in the function. Particularly, there is demand for professionals who are able to translate business needs in IT solutions and to suggest IT opportunities to improve business.

But another important change has occurred in IS function: it is IT outsourcing.
In fact, complexity of new technologies, on the one hand, and necessity to concentrate on core business and to reduce expenses, on the other hand, have pushed many organizations to entrust specialized firms with most of information systems management.

In this case there are not significant differences between public and private organizations (except for the rules of outsourcers selection) too.

Even though it is not the aim of these pages to examine pros and cons of outsourcing, many authors have underlined that it can bring about losing control over IT strategy. Moreover, the consequent reduction of internal competences can cause IT suppliers to take advantage of clients.

Finally, there are three items useful in identifying IT skill requirements for modern organizations: state of technology, role of IT and form of sourcing. Furthermore, experience of firms is also applicable to public administrations.

2. Organizing the IS function

The state of technology and the role of IS function within the organization determine IT skill requirements, and the form of sourcing determines which skills internal staff must possess and which skills IT suppliers must possess.

Moreover, the form of sourcing should be chosen according to the role of IS function within the organization and the state of technology. For this reason, an appropriate structure of the function can be determined only by reconciling these three items.

2.1 Tasks and processes of the IS function

Various models of IS function management can be found in specialized literature. Usually, they effectively describe processes that must take place in order to assure correct functioning of information systems and suitable support to business. These processes sometimes are placed in a life cycle based framework, other times are classified according to the value chain method.

On the contrary, contributions about tasks assigned to the different units of the IS function are more generic.

Of course, that is for internal structure of the function depends from peculiar needs of each organization; furthermore IT processes pass through the whole IS function, so it is very difficult to synthesize such a complexity in a sort of organization chart. Nevertheless, determining *who does what* within the IS function could help to give some guidelines for organizing it and, afterwards, for identifying skill requirements.

To these aims it could be useful to build a model of IS function based on a functional point of view, composed by sets of homogeneous activities, that - according to the characteristics of each organization - can represent organizational units, persons or, more simply, critical tasks ensuring success of IT processes.

Generically, each of those sets could be viewed as the owner of distinct processes described in other models based on processes.

2.2 A model of IS function[1]

The model proposed in these pages has been built beginning from well-known models based on processes (like COBIT, ITIL and others), by disassembling these processes in activities and by assembling these activities in homogeneous areas.

As well as every model, this is a simplification of realty, in fact - depending on the effective needs of each organization - every set of activities can be further split or, alternatively, can be joint with other sets. However, being based on appreciated models based on processes, this model probably maps all the activities that are performed in the IS function. Moreover, its structure points out functional connections among the distinct units without referring to hierarchic relations, so that it is abstract enough to be adaptable to different actual cases.

2.2.1 The general model

The general model, that includes all activities without considering the event of outsourcing, is represented in *Figure 1*.

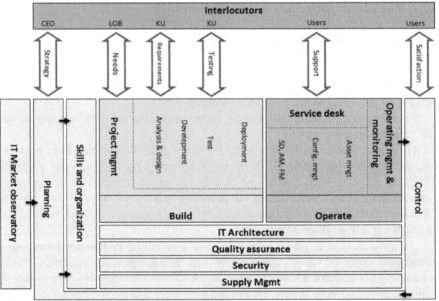

Figure 1 A model of the IS function.

---

[1] A detailed description of the model is not the aim of this document, so it will be only outlined. It is the result of a work performed by the IS staff of the Italian Ministry of Economy and Finance (MEF) - Department for National General Accounting (RGS) as a contribution to a project for IT professionals reviewing, still in progress, run by the IT National Centre for PA (CNIPA).

In a few words, each module of the model – that represents an homogeneous activities area - could be viewed like an IS sub-function that is the process owner of one or more processes. For example, the IT annual planning is a process shared by many units within IS function, but it is coordinated by the sub-function "Planning and control", that is its process owner.

Within the model it is possible to distinguish three macro-areas: *Build* and *Operate* , respectively, include systems development and service delivery and support; the third, that could be called *Governance*, includes activities assuring the consistency of the whole information system.

2.2.2 The model with outsourcing

As said, owing to complexity of new technologies and exigency to cut costs, most of the organizations outsource information systems management.

Even though typology and intensity of IT outsourcing are very different, in principle, it is wise at least to keep inside a skilled staff able to decide and govern the IT strategy. But the strength of this advice, after all, depends on how much strategic IT is considered by each organization.

With regard to outsourcing, one property of the model under discussion is that, being modular, it is adaptable to every concrete situation.

In *Figure 2* is represented a typical case of IT outsourcing, where technical activities are delegate to outsourcers while strategy, leadership and service level management are due of the "internal" IS function.

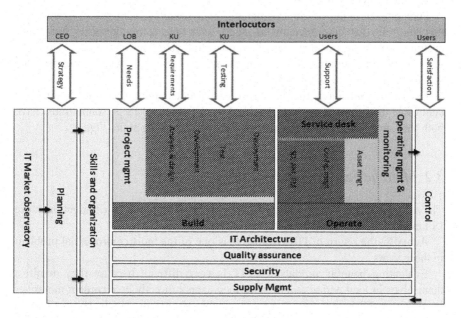

Figure 2 The model with a typical case of IT outsourcing.

3. IS function personnel's skills and training needs

Another property of the model under discussion is that it is composed by sets of homogeneous activities, so each of them requires homogeneous skills too. That is why such a model, besides representing a framework for organizing the IS function, is also useful to build a map of skill requirements.

Even though going into each area of the model thoroughly is beyond the aim of these pages, it is important to underline that IS personnel should have competences both in technical and managerial/financial subjects.

3.1 Technical skills

Technical skills are not only referred to IT but also to the business that IT supports. In fact, the IS function (more than others) regard the rest of the organization as an external customer, so it is not sufficient that IS personnel know how to implement solutions, they must also be able to analyze problems, that means to understand customers business requirements.

Sometimes these competences are not to be possessed together (for instance this is true for software developers); other times, for finding the best solutions that fulfill the requirements of the organization it is essential to know jointly both the IT and the subject of the business.

Personnel working in the area called *Project management* are an example of this: they are just like account managers who receive requirements from their customers (or better: who suggest them new strategic opportunities that IT offers), who find the suitable IT solution and, afterwards, who supervise the implementation of the whole project.

Even in organizations that have recourse of outsourcing (but want to keep the control of the information system and of the IT strategy) IS personnel must have both the kinds of skill. This is particularly evident looking at the *Figure 2*.

3.2 Managerial and financial skills

The more organizations are large and IT spending weigh upon the budget the more IS function needs managerial and financial skills.

Actually, the return of IT investments is one of the most controversial problem in these years.

Evaluating benefits produced by IT is very difficult because they manifest themselves in long period and because they cannot directly be recorded; moreover investing in IT is sometimes an unavoidable choice to remain competitive in comparison with rivals. So, when results of IT spending do not come up to expectations, it is not so clear if it happened for wrong evaluations in choosing investments or, rather, for disproportionate expectations.

In any case, this problem implies that IS function needs personnel able to run economic and financial aspects of IT management, at least with regard to activities of programming and management control, cost-benefit analysis within feasibility studies and supply management.

In fact, if these activities were done out of IS function, the consistency between the choices taken for technical reasons and the choices taken for financial reasons could not be assured. For example, in the event of reduction in expendable founds, it would be hoped that cuts in IT spending were decided within IS function.

With particular regard to public administrations, the problem in discussion is even greater. First of all, because the return of investments in literal sense does not exist for public administrations; so benefits deriving from IT are necessarily intangible. Secondly, because supply management is usually subjected to precise rules and regulations, especially concerning suppliers selection; so, in addition to drawing up and managing contracts, it is necessary to draw up calls for bids really assuring the best trade-off between quality and price.

Finally, on the subject of managerial skills, it is enough to say that today IS personnel must knows topics like project management, team working, communication, etc.

4. The experience of MEF-RGS

In 2006, a re-training program for IS personnel of the Department for National General Accounting (RGS) of the Italian Ministry of Economy and Finance (MEF) started.

The aim of this program, that is still in progress, is not to improve the activities that IS personnel are already doing, but to develop skills really required to make effective the IS function work. For this why, it cannot be only based on the current IS function organization; on the contrary, the very organization need to be revised. So a model like the one represented in *Figure 2* has been used as a reference.

Actually, when the training program started a revising of the IS function was already being carried out, so some skill gaps came out. Nevertheless, by building an abstract model like the one described above, a systematic vision of the matter has been enabled.

Synthetically, the aims of the training program in discussion is making IS personnel able:

– to analyze customers' problems and to understand which IT solutions can be suitable[2];

---

[2] Customers of RGS IS function are mainly internal customers.

- to identify which among new technologies can be useful to improve customers' activities and, in that event, suggest them to customers;
- to deal competently with IT suppliers;
- to oversee all the different stages of IT projects (IT development is outsourced);
- to carry out a full control over the IS operational management (that is outsourced).

After fixing targets, a market research was carried out to select an appropriate system of training.

Finally, the system called European Certification of Informatics Professionals (EUCIP) was chosen, an independent framework of certifications consisting of two degrees: the Core level, that makes a survey of IT and enterprise information systems, and the Elective level, structured in different specialized profiles[3].

Such a system of certifications has seemed to be suitable to the aim for mainly three reasons:

- being independent of specific IT producers;
- because the syllabus of the Core level gives a synthetic but complete survey of information systems, so that people attending the training program can formalize their knowledge and fill up their gaps; moreover, this help to have a basic IT culture common to all IS personnel;
- because the different professional profiles of the Elective level cover a large part of the competence objective of the training program.

At this point, the training program has started.

In the first stage, concluded in 2007, a group of personnel has obtained the Core level certification, some of them with marks good enough to be qualified for teaching.

In following stages - just starting - some of those personnel will attend different courses to obtain the Elective level certifications (prevalently, as business analyst and IS project manager). At the same time, other personnel will attend new courses for the Core level certification, where the first personnel, that obtained the qualification, will be the teachers.

5. Conclusions

EUCIP Core level Syllabus is made up of three modules: Plan, Build and Operate, so each candidate must pass three exams to obtain the certification.

In the experience of RGS-MEF the results of these exams have shown that most of competence gaps regarded the Plan module. This comes up to expectations and confirms that subjects like IT alignment to business strategy,

---

[3] More information are available on http://www.eucip.com.

specific instruments for enterprise information systems, IT spending, project management, etc. are not well known by personnel of IS function.

Of course, this is a serious problem for people that every day, on the one hand, deal with suppliers who sell new technologies like enterprise resource planning, data warehouse, business intelligence systems, etc., and, on the other hand, have to fulfill more and more exigent customer's requirements. So that such a training program, including basic knowledge, is proving to be really useful.

Furthermore, an organization based on a model like the one discussed in these pages seems to be suitable to make the IS function really effective and aligned to the business.

References

Agarwal R., Sambamurthy V.: Principles and models for organizing the IT function. In MIS Quarterly Executive Vol. 1 No. 1 /March 2002.

Camussone, P.F.: Il sistema informativo aziendale, ETASLIBRI, 1998.

Camussone, P.F.: Informatica organizzazione e strategie, McGraw-Hill, 2000.

Hoffer, J.A., Prescott, M.b., McFadden, F.R. and Morabito, V.: Management delle informazioni aziendali, Pearson Education, 2005.

IT Governance Institute: COBIT Mapping: Overview of International IT Guidance, 2nd Edition. Available on http://www.itgi.org.

McFarlan, F.W.: Information technology changes the way you compete, Harward Business Review, May-June 1984.

Mintzberg, H.: Structure in five. Design effective organization, Prentice Hall, 1983.

Porter, M.E., and Millar,P.E.: How information gives you competitive advantage, Harvard Business Review, July 1985.

Rudd, C. and Hodgkiss, G.: An introductory overview of ITIL, Alison Cartlidge Xansa, 2004

Sciarelli, S.: Fondamenti di economia e gestione delle imprese, CEDAM, 2004.

Tagliavini, M., Ravarini, A. and Sciuto, D.: Sistemi per la gestione dell'informazione, Apogeo, 2003.

International Professional Practice Partnership (IP3) - Overview

Charles Hughes

Chairman, IFIP, International Professional Practice Partnership (IP3) Task Force
President BCS, 2005-2006
Charles.Hughes@emanagement.ltd.uk

Abstract: The IFIP International Professional Practice Partnership is embarked on the ambitious task of creating an international profession to provide the key leadership in all parts of the global IT industry – both supplier and user sides. Globally, society is utterly dependent on the IT industry for maintaining and enhancing the quality of life in the developed world and the developing world is looking to leverage IT to move rapidly forward. IT is a quintessentially global industry. For example, no e-business user can have any knowledge of where their transactions are processed or their data stored. Only the creation of a strong global profession of qualified and experienced practitioners gives confidence to all users of IT systems that they can trust the systems on which their whole lifestyle depends.

Keywords: International Professional Practice Partnership (IP3), IT professionalism, International Federation for Information Processing (IFIP),

1. Introduction

The International Federation for Information Processing (IFIP) is a global federation of over 55 member societies and, through its regional affiliates, linking almost 100 national IT bodies with an aggregate membership of almost 1 million individuals. It has as one of its strategic objectives the promotion of a professional approach to IT practice.

This paper sets out the background to the current major initiative and summarises its objectives and achievements to date.

2. IFIP and Professionalism

For more than 10 years IFIP has taken a series of actions to promote this objective. The first stage was the creation in the mid 1990s of a Task Force to look at issues

---

Please use the following format when citing this chapter:

Hughes, C., 2008, in IFIP International Federation for Information Processing, Volume 280; *E-Government; ICT Professionalism and Competences; Service Science*; Antonino Mazzeo, Roberto Bellini, Gianmario Motta; (Boston: Springer), pp. 159–163.

of Professional Harmonisation. The purpose was to establish a shared understanding of professional practice globally and then to seek to specify a minimum standard. The long term objective being to achieve sufficient formalization to be able to use General Agreement on Trade in Services (GATS) procedures to facilitate mobility of suitably qualified and experienced IT practitioners.

Arising from this work, in 2002, IFIP co-sponsored, with the World IT Services Association (WITSA) and the Organisation for Economic Cooperation and Development (OECD), an international workshop on Global IT Skills Needs. This brought together 35 experts from 14 countries. This conference, entitled "Meeting Global IT Skills Needs – the Role of Professionalism", looked IT skills needs from three angles – demand, supply and constraints. The summary proceedings are available on the internet, [1].

The next step was a meeting hosted by IEEE-Computer Society in Vancouver in late July 2006 to which they invited a number of the world's leading computer societies to meet together with representatives of IFIP to discuss a range of topics of common interest. One strong theme to emerge was the shared interest of the Australian Computer Society (ACS), British Computer Society (BCS) and Canadian Information Processing Society (CIPS) in sharing their mutual experience and practice in promoting and recognizing professional standards among individual IT practitioners. This was followed by a plenary presentation by the then President of the BCS, Charles Hughes, at the World Computer Congress, August 2006 in Santiago, Chile

It was subsequently agreed at the invitation of the IFIP Executive that the three societies would meet again at an early date. The next meeting took place in Cape Town in January 2007 attended by representatives of IFIP, ACS, BCS and CIPS together with the local Computer Society of South Africa (CSSA). At this meeting each society outlined its current progress in promoting professionalism and in recognising suitably qualified and experienced IT practitioners. The societies also agreed to propose to IFIP that it should formally establish a Task Force on IT professionalism. Further, the societies agreed to work together to devise an approach to provide a global minimum standard of individual IT professional practice. This has been designated as International IT Professional (IITP).

The Task Force has since met in London in May 2007, Montreal in September 2007 and Dublin in April 2008.

At its Cape Town meeting the Task Force adopted the name of the International Professional Practice Programme (I3P). However, trademark investigations and other considerations led to the adoption in Dublin in April 2008 of the name International Professional Practice Partnership (IP3).

The remainder of this paper summarises the Task Force's objectives and progress to date.

3. IP3 Project

IFIP's International Professional Practice Partnership (IP3) is working to create an international IT profession, equivalent in prestige to established professions such as law, accountancy and architecture, that will:
- enable organizations to exploit fully the potential of IT;
- be respected by its stakeholders, including employees, employers, customers, academia, governments and key international bodies; and
- be a source of real pride and aspiration for IT practitioners.

IP3 promotes the accomplishments of IT professionals around the world. It is seeking to raise public awareness of the vital role of IT in our modern world and the work of IT professionals in delivering the IT services on which our modern world depends.

4. What is a Professional?

One critical step in this process is to provide a well defined and understood method to recognise individual members of this profession. IP3 is therefore preparing a scheme under which any IFIP Full Member or Professional Affiliate body may seek accreditation to recognise their own individual members who have appropriate qualifications and experience as an "International IT Professional" (IITP). Each IITP designated practitioner will be understood to be a **trustworthy advisor** within the discipline of IT.

The IITP standard will:
- be based on a **clear set of criteria** establishing a **global standard** which incorporates the credentials established by accredited national associations;
- be **universally recognized**, helping enable **worldwide mobility** for the IT workforce; and
- establish **credibility and stature** for those who have met its requirements.

However, it will do more. IITP will help ensure that employers have **a standardized set of prerequisites** for specific IT roles within their respective organizations. This will help professionals and their organizations achieve a **higher project success rate,** thereby reducing cost overruns and project failure for organizations. They will help to ensure **corporate governance** in IT, and to help business, government and society gain maximum benefit from IT.

Finally, these credentials will establish **professional accountability,** governed by a code of ethics and a code of conduct that all those who are accredited must follow.

Those who hold these credentials demonstrate their commitment, expertise, and a desire continually to expand their knowledge. Most important, they demonstrate the substantial contribution IT Professionals can bring to organizations worldwide—because leadership in IT knows no borders.

5. Accreditation Procedure

Any IFIP Full Member or Professional Affiliate member can apply to IP3 for accreditation. The member body will be visited by a small party of trained IP3 assessors who will ensure that it has appropriate procedures for assessing applications from individual members for recognition as IITPs.

A fuller discussion of the IP3 Accreditation process will be given later in this session.

IP3 recognises the wide variety of patterns of professional development and regulation around the world. Consequently, IP3 specifies what standards have to be met but leaves to individual bodies the task of demonstrating that those they wish to designate do meet the IP3 criteria. Thus IP3 respects the different practices and traditions that operate in different jurisdictions.

6. Benefits of an International Standard

IT is beyond doubt the most international of technologies and industries. While other professions need global standards, no other combines the global reach of IT. IT supply and usage is global, furthermore, the location is unknown to the user. Any e-business user cannot help but be aware that they can have no knowledge of where their details are being transferred to or from where IT services are being provided.

The value of addressing the international challenge through an international organisation such as IFIP is discussed further in Roger Johnson's paper later in this session, [2].

7. IP3 Membership and Industrial Support

IP3 is seeking the support of leading IT suppliers and users by giving support, both in cash and kind. The reaction of industry to the IP3 programme has been almost universally supportive.

The Task Force is especially grateful to Microsoft for the considerable support and encouragement they continue to give to the programme. Graham Watson explains the value of IP3 to Microsoft later in this session.

8. Conclusions

Society's utter dependence on IT services in support of almost every aspect of our lives means that we are all dependent on countless IT practitioners and IT systems spread right around the globe. Never has there been a greater imperative to start putting in place standards for all practitioners on whom our society depends wherever in the world they work.

The International Professional Practice Partnership aims to ensure that worldwide suitably experienced and qualified IT professionals can be recognized so that humanity can have confidence that those, individually and collectively, responsible for the IT services can be trusted to deliver the highest quality of service and be held accountable to their peers when they fall seriously short. Only in that way can society be confident of the IT systems on which it is utterly dependent.

References

1. Meeting Global IT Skills Needs – the Role of Professionalism. Woking, UK, October 2002. Sponsored by IFIP, OECD and WITSA. IFIP, 2002. www.globalitskills.org
2. Johnson, R.G IP3: Member Societies' Role and Engagement. Proceeding of the WCC 2008 Professionalism Conference.

IP3 - National Societies' Roles and Responsibilities

Roger G. Johnson

Birkbeck College, London University, UK, r.johnson@bcs.org.uk

Abstract: This paper discusses the nature of the global IT industry and explores the issues of attempting to impose minimum standards of competence, knowledge and conduct on such a disparate workforce. The paper proceeds to explain the rationale for the approach taken by the International Federation for Information Processing's (IFIP) International Professional Practice Partnership (IP3) and how it is being implemented. It is compared with the International Professional Engineer (IntPE) scheme of the International Engineering Alliance. Finally, the paper explains how IP3 understands that IITP will bring additional member benefits for IFIP member societies and also additional candidates coming forward to sit for suitable examinations offered by a arrange of third parties.

Keywords: International Professional Practice Partnership (IP3), International IT Practitioner (IITP), International Federation for Information Processing (IFIP), professional designation.

1. Introduction

This paper sets out the way in which the International Federation for Information Processing's (IFIP) International Professional Practice Partnership (IP3) operates its International IT Professional (IITP) programme. It explains why an international designation for IT professionals is needed. It will describe the operation of IITP and why IFIP and its member societies are uniquely placed to implement such a scheme. The paper explains the ambitions of the scheme and the need to build on what already exists. The paper concludes by outlining some of the prospective benefits from a successful implementation of such a scheme worldwide.

The International Federation for Information Processing (IFIP) is a global federation of over 55 member societies and, through its regional affiliates, linking almost 100 national IT bodies with an aggregate membership of almost 1 million individuals.

Please use the following format when citing this chapter:

Johnson, R.G., 2008, in IFIP International Federation for Information Processing, Volume 280; *E-Government; ICT Professionalism and Competences; Service Science*; Antonino Mazzeo, Roberto Bellini, Gianmario Motta; (Boston: Springer), pp. 165–171.

2. IT – the ultimate International Industry

Modern advanced societies are entirely dependent for their quality of life on the IT industry – both supply and user sides. Developing nations are rightly keen to harness IT in support of achieving their development goals. The very large attendances at IFIP's two-yearly World IT Forum (WITFOR) conferences focussing specifically on how IT can be leveraged for development bear testimony to the universality of the ambition for IT-led solutions, [1].

No invention has transformed our world so comprehensively as the computer. It is only 60 years since the successful running of the world's first stored-program computer at Manchester University. From that pioneering work have flowed computer applications that touch all our lives every minute of every day.

The scale of the achievement comes from the ability to integrate computer technology with communications technology which together can deliver information almost instantaneously around the globe.

No other technology has advanced so fast. Every year new advances make possible information systems that were previously impractical. Building the vast systems that run on today's computers is an engineering activity that stands comparison with the greatest achievements of the nineteenth-century engineers who transformed that society. Modern information systems are now the most complex artefacts yet made by human beings.

2.1 Ubiquitous IT

Nothing illustrates the power of IT as well as the airline industry which so many of us have come to take for granted. Long gone are visits to travel agents to make bookings with many airlines now having over 80% of ticket sales online and many charging extra for telephone bookings.

E-tickets have replaced check-in desks apart from luggage drops. While we are going through security, the aircrew are agreeing their flight plans with Air Traffic Control, the aircraft is refuelled and the provisions for the flight are loaded, with details of the passengers' seats for special meals, all managed by a series of information systems.

When we board the aircraft we enter another world, where information systems rule. Increasingly for much of the flight the pilots do not fly the aircraft but monitor its behaviour against their preset flight plan.

Yet in the past few years airlines have been able to make further major advances. Minor faults detected by onboard systems on the previous flight and notified automatically to the destination can be quickly fixed so that aircraft can depart on schedule for their next flight. The latest aircraft have replaced many of the mechanical control systems with digital systems.

One of the most remarkable aspects of this whole revolution is that the computer systems, apart from at the check in, are largely invisible to the passengers and yet without them mass commercial air transport would be impossible. Everywhere around us, at home with the telephone, car and domestic appliances, travelling to work by train and traffic control, and at work with all kinds of applications our lives are affected by information systems. In every case we barely notice their presence. Consequently IT practitioners have often been referred in articles to information systems engineers as 'invisible engineers'.

2.2 Public Information Utility

Starting from nowhere in the early 1990s, the Internet revolutionised the availability of information of all sorts. Companies rapidly advanced from just giving information to offering extensive e-business opportunities.

The Internet has become a public information utility. However, this introduces a crucial issue about designing and maintaining public information systems. The professionals who build and maintain such systems have a special responsibility of care in their construction. Like many other engineers, information systems engineers derive satisfaction from seeing others using the artefacts they have built. However, without understating the complexity of building a bridge, an information system is a much more complex artefact. In particular, the interaction between it and its user is far more complex.

Early computerised information systems often had several groups of employees between the computer and the customer. The modern system, such as one on the Internet, however, has no such intermediaries to check its output. Erroneous data supplied to Internet users may cause serious inconvenience.

2.3 Professionalism

Information systems professionals carry major responsibilities on their shoulders. This is why a career in information systems can be rewarding. But it is not to be undertaken lightly.

IT professionals have overcome a number of challenges in the past ten years, notably mostly avoiding problems from the "millennium bug" and the introduction of the euro throughout much of Europe. These two challenges provided serious challenges to information systems professionals. They also demonstrated another key attribute of information systems: information systems evolve. There are always changes to be made and facilities upgraded.

Information systems are at the heart of every developed society. They are essential to the standard of living we have all come to expect. Only properly trained professionals can ensure that the world has the information systems it needs to ensure the well-being of every citizen.

3. Regulating an International Profession

To understand what it means to create a regulated profession we need first to understand the nature of the professional. The British Computer Society defines professionalism as:

> *A fully established IT professional is a practitioner who has specific skills rooted in a broad base and appropriate qualifications, belongs to a regulated body, undergoes continuous development, operates to a code of conduct and recognises personal accountability.*

Thus to regulate IT professionals and thus to create a *regulated profession* it is essential to deal with each of the points in this definition. This means that there must be a means to:

- *ensure that members of the community obtain and maintain an acceptable standard of professional competence*
- *define the profession's core body of knowledge and competences*
- *set appropriate minimum codes of conduct and professional standards set and enforce rules and standards which recognise and protect the public interest*
- *take disciplinary action should the rules and standards not be observed or should a member be guilty of unprofessional work*
- *support members in their commitment to adhere to the rules and professional standards*
- *provide sufficient capacity to implement and manage the above conditions*

The historic professions have addressed these for many years. In the UK, the BCS has been accepted as a full member of the engineering community and BCS Professional Members can seek registration as a Chartered Engineer which is in turn fully recognized internationally. However, the UK is the only jurisdiction in which this has been achieved.

Implementations of professionalism vary from country to country and discipline to discipline. In some there are autonomous professional institutions while in others there are combinations of nationally approved qualifications and statutory regulation. IP3 does not advance any particular model but is concerned only that, whatever the mode in a given jurisdiction, the professional community can fulfill the minimum standards identified above.

For individual practitioners, who seek registration as a professional, this means that they must:
- *conform to a published code of conduct*
- *know, and work within, the limits of their capabilities*
- *be accountable for and submit to peer review of their actions*
- *undertake continuous professional development*

- *have their competence to practice re-assessed on a regular basis*
- *explain the implications of their work to stakeholders*
- *recognise obligations to the profession as well as to their employer*
- *have regard to the public good*
- *contribute to the development of the profession*
- *support other professionals in maintaining professional standards and developing professional competence*

These requirements mean that any attempt to establish a global minimum standard for IT professionals must identify criteria to assess whether a member society operates appropriate procedures. These must cover, amongst other issues, individual knowledge compared to core body of knowledge, compliance with a Code of Conduct including an appropriate disciplinary procedure, together with availability and uptake of continuous professional development. Individuals also need to demonstrate their commitment to developing their profession and mutual support to fellow practitioners.

4. How IITP will operate?

The IP3 partners at their first meeting in Cape Town, ([2] includes a short background to the IP3 project to date), examined the challenge of creating a scheme for a global IT professional designation for individuals and recognised that it could only be done by a process of accrediting member societies to designate suitably qualified and experienced individual members.

Thus the Task Force recognised that it needed to establish accreditation criteria in each of the areas listed above as requirements of a regulated profession. The Task Force has recently produced an accreditation procedure which is the subject of another paper in this session.

IP3 will maintain a central register of all members of member societies who are eligible to use the designation International IT Practitioner (IITP).

The IP3 accreditation procedure applies to the procedures of the member body applying for accreditation and not to an individual. Typically member societies will seek accreditation for an existing grade of membership. Initially, this is expected to be Computer Professional (CP) by the Australian Computer Society (ACS), Chartered IT Practitioner (CITP) by the BCS and Information Systems Practitioner (ISP) by the Canadian Information Processing Society (CIPS).

If all are successful, it is expected that by autumn 2008 around 25,000 individuals will hold a member society designation which meets the IP3 criteria and hence be eligible to describe themselves as IITP.

The costs of operating IP3 will be met largely by an annual fee levied on the accredited organisations and which will reflect the number of individuals eligible to use the IITP designation.

5. Comparison with IntPE

The IP3 international accreditation procedure is ambitious for a profession which has historically lacked even national standards. However, it has much in common with the procedures operated by the International Engineering Alliance (IEA), [3]. This body is responsible for the operation of the Washington Accord which, since 2001, "recognises substantial equivalence in the accreditation of qualifications in engineering technology" at tertiary level. They also operate a scheme for designating individuals as International Professional Engineers (IntPE) by a scheme which appears very similar to the proposed IP3 procedures for IITP.

At present IP3 does not have the equivalent of the Washington Accord but its standards for the tertiary level qualification are informed by BCS practice in this area which are compliant with the accord by reason of the BCS' membership of the UK Engineering Council which is a Washington Accord signatory.

Furthermore, IP3 is actively supporting the activities initiated in late 2007 to establish a "Seoul Declaration" which it is expected will achieve for computing courses what the Washington Accord has done for engineering courses.

Finally, the IEA shows that it is possible for a variety of different implementations of professionalism to cooperate successfully in promoting professional standards across the world in a robust manner.

6. What IITP is not

It is important to state several things which IP3 is not intending to do with IITP.

Firstly, it is not creating a new body to which individuals can belong. Individuals seeking the right to be designated an IITP must go to an IFIP member society and join at an appropriate grade. Thus IITP is an additional member benefit which should, if successful, lead to increased membership and higher levels of member retention.

Secondly, IP3 is not seeking to "re-invent wheels". Wherever possible, IP3 will seek to adopt existing material giving suitable acknowledgments to the original authors for granting the right to its use. For example, the Skills Framework for the Information Age (SFIA) has been adopted as the skills framework, [4].

Thirdly, IP3 is not an examining body. IP3 will set standards for member societies to apply to their members in terms of demonstrating competence with the Core Body of Knowledge and also with Continuing Professional Development (CPD). However, the way in which accredited bodies determine the competence of individuals they wish to designate is a matter for them. This could include traditional tertiary qualifications, which may in due course be covered by the "Seoul Declaration" or a combination of other qualifications, national or regional such as European Certification of Information Professionals, (EUCIP) [5]. What IITP accreditors will wish to ascertain is that alone or in combination they achieve the minimum standard set down. Again, IP3 believes that IITP can increase interest in professional and vocational qualifications to the benefit of a range of existing examining bodies.

Finally, IP3 is not yet another new body but a partnership amongst member societies in IFIP. All bodies seeking accreditation must be either Full Members or Professional Affiliates of IFIP.

7. Conclusion

IT is totally ubiquitous in our lives and increasingly worldwide, not just in developed countries. Consequently we are seeing the emergence of a uniquely global profession.

The mission of IP3 in promoting IITP is to offer the first global standard which IP3 member societies can use to designate suitably qualified and experienced individual practitioners as having achieved the right to describe themselves as an International IT Professional.

References

1. World IT Forum (WITFOR 2007), Addis Ababa, August 2007, www.witfor207.org
2. Hughes, C. International Professional Practice Partnership (IP3) – Overview. Proceeding of the WCC 2008 Professionalism Conference.
3. International Engineering Alliance, 2008 see www.washingtonaccord.org/
4. Skills Framework for the Information Age (SFIA), 2008 www.sfia.org.uk
5. European Certification of Information Professionals, (EUCIP), www.eucip.org

The Emerging ISO International Standard for Certification of Software Engineering Professionals

Juan Garbajosa

Universidad Politécnica de Madrid - Technical University of Madrid (UPM).
E.U. Informática. Cra. Valencia Km. 7 E-28031 Madrid. Spain.
E-mail: juan.garbajosa --at-- upm.es

Abstract: The emerging standard ISO/IEC 24773, Software Engineering – Certification of Software Engineering Professionals – Comparison Framework, is at its final stage of development. The coming International Standard will establish a framework for comparison of schemes for certifying software engineering professionals. It is expected that ISO/IEC 24773 will facilitate the portability of software engineering professional certifications between different countries or organizations. At present, different countries and organizations have adopted different approaches that are implemented by means of regulations and bylaws. The intention of this International Standard is to be open to these individual approaches by providing a framework for expressing them in a common scheme that can lead to understanding.

Keywords: certification scheme, qualification scheme, body of knowledge, competences, skills, code of ethics, software engineers

1. Introduction

Software intensive systems are becoming, more and more, critical components of most aspects of our life. This phenomenon started a few decades ago but it is unmistakably clear at present.   Cell phones, automotive industry or medical systems are everyday examples of the ever increasing role of software. At the same time, these systems have become increasingly complex. Similarly to other engineering disciplines, and partly as a reaction of the relevance of software in everyday life, the recognition and codification of effective practices software development processes and products started a few years ago in the field of software engineering. This effort has led to the development of systems and software engineering standards by ISO and IEC [1], by professional societies [2],

Please use the following format when citing this chapter:

Garbajosa, J., 2008, in IFIP International Federation for Information Processing, Volume 280; *E-Government; ICT Professionalism and Competences; Service Science*; Antonino Mazzeo, Roberto Bellini, Gianmario Motta; (Boston: Springer), pp. 173–178.

and by national standards bodies. It has also led to the definition of an internationally recognized body of knowledge for software engineering [3].

A concern that has been coming up for years is related to the identification of the required competences and qualifications of the professionals who develop software intensive systems. This has included the establishment of software engineering degrees at Universities, extension of professional engineering qualifications, e.g. licensed or chartered status, to software engineers and the creation of qualification and certification schemes for software engineering professionals. Certifications schemes have different mechanisms to assess candidates' competences. Most usually it is either by examination, or review of a candidate's competences, including education, experience, and mastery of specific skills.

The increasing globalization of the software industry implies that a software engineering professional is likely to work in different countries over the course of a career. It is therefore important to develop ways to increase the portability of professional certifications in this domain.

ISO/IEC JTC1 SC7 subcommittee agreed to establish a Study Group to consider the subject of standards and/or technical reports for certifications of software engineers. As a result of the study group job, a report was produced [4].

This report analyzed the fundamental principles of certification, described in ISO/IEC 17024 [5], went into studying, available at the time, approaches to certification of software engineers. One of the conclusions was that an international standard for the professional software engineering certification process would make mutual recognition of professional credentials much easier, enabling professionals to move easily within an increasingly global software industry. At the time the report was produced recognition could only be achieved by bilateral negotiations. Despite some regional successes, such as in the case of Japan, bilateral approaches would not be able to scale to the entire world. It was also concluded that it would be the easiest to begin by developing a standard that would provide a reference model for the technical bases. That is the standard would not describe an exam or the technical issues themselves but would provide a framework for mutual comparison of schemes. SC7 submitted a new work item project for ballot. The project started by the end of 2005. It received project number 24773. At the time of producing this paper the project is under Final Draft International Standard Ballot (FDIS ballot).

The rest of the paper presents the structure of the future standard, and the design guidelines. At the end of the paper a number of conclusions are included and some ideas for future work are provided.

2. Overview of *Software Engineering* — *Certification of Software Engineering Professionals* — *Comparison Framework*

ISO/IEC FDIS 24773:2007 (in short FDIS 24773) refines and supplements the processes for certification of individuals included in ISO/IEC 17024 [5], *Conformity Assessment – General requirements for bodies operating certification of persons*. The management and implementation of the Scheme developed under this International Standard can also take into account the processes and definitions of ISO/IEC 17024.

In some countries, governments and other bodies assess the qualifications of software engineering professionals by evaluating candidates' knowledge, skills and job experience and issuing certificates of qualification to those demonstrating competence as defined by an assessing organization. Such an organization is defined as qualification body in FDIS 24773. A qualification body will be able to use appropriate components of the future standard document for comparison with other such schemes or as a delegated qualification body. Educational organisations will be also able to use a Scheme developed under FDIS 24773 for comparison purposes.

The Guide to the body of knowledge ISO/IEC TR 19759:2005, Software Engineering – Guide to the Software Engineering Body of Knowledge [3] is utilized in FDIS 24773 for comparison of software engineering bodies of knowledge. Education bodies, qualification or examination bodies and certification bodies are not required to use, or comply with, SWEBOK, but are required to map a software engineering body of knowledge to SWEBOK.

FDIS 24773 This International Standard is not intended to discourage or diminish the role of universities in developing and offering diverse and innovative software engineering programs. Rather, it encourages universities to participate in the initial and continuing development of software engineering professionals. At the same time, certification bodies are encouraged to consult with and work with universities in establishing schemes under this standard.

FDIS 24773 contents basically include, as well as introductory stuff, the following sections:
a.   Requirements for a Certification Scheme
b.   Knowledge and skills
c.   Evaluation of competence
d.   Codes of ethics and professional practice
e.   Maintenance of certification

2.1 Requirements for a Certification Scheme

The certification body shall produce a certification scheme that contains a description of the software engineering professionals to be certified. The Scheme shall include a title, a list of the tasks that the software engineering professional described in the title would be expected to undertake; a description of characteristics of the work associated with the title, a description of the competences, and how these competences will be evaluated.

An important issue is that any minimum educational qualification or experience should be also explicitly stated. That is, a university degree could be either required or not. Additionally, details of any delegations to a qualification body, codes of ethics and professional practices required, and how the certification is maintained should be described.

2.2 Knowledge and skills

The evaluation component of the scheme shall be based on a body of knowledge. At this stage FDIS 24773 does not enforce or preclude the use of any specific body of knowledge. ISO/IEC TR 19759 [3] is only used as a reference. That is, the only condition requested is that the body of knowledge used is to be mapped onto [3]. The use of [3] is included only to provide a common reference point for comparison.

For each component of this body of knowledge, the scheme shall state the cognitive level expected of a successful candidate for certification. This is an important issue. The objective is that the required knowledge is associated to a cognitive level, e.g. description or evaluation. Actually the expected professional performance will be determined by this cognitive level. Additionally, other technical knowledge requirements, e.g. information systems, could be considered. Knowledge of appropriate standards should be included. Finally it is possible to include knowledge on a specific domain.

Concerning skills both software engineering and generic skills, such as the ability to apply knowledge or the ability to communicate should be included.

2.3 Evaluation of competence

The certification body shall consolidate the information described in section 2.2 into a set of competences. It is required to explain how each competence can be attained or mastered, i.e. training, education and/or experience. It is also necessary to describe how competences will be evaluated.

2.4 Code of Ethics

Code of ethics is always potentially subject to dispute, and varies between cultures. FDIS 24773 provides a specific set of matters that should be included in any code of ethics for software engineering professionals. These include descriptions of the minimum standards of conduct and occupational ideals that guide the actions of software engineering professionals, the goals of the software engineering profession, and the rights and duties of software engineering professionals with respect to the public, employers, peers, and clients. However, no specific item is specifically enforced.

2.3 Maintenance of certification

Requirements for maintaining and renewing certification should be considered. This includes clauses for renewal of certification, and continuing professional development.

3. Conclusions

This paper has highlighted the main guidelines for FDIS 24773; hopefully the current draft will become International Standard ISO/IEC 24773 in a short future. FDIS 24773 has been depicted to respond to the needs of national and multi-national organizations or suppliers for developing software in an ever growing global market.

The coming International Standard 24773 will facilitate the portability of software engineering professional certifications between different countries. At present, different countries have adopted different approaches on the topic that are implemented by means of regulations and bylaws. The intention of the future International Standard 24773 is to be open to these national approaches by providing a framework for expressing them in a common scheme that can lead to understanding between different countries.

Important to underscore, the editorial team has always intended to reach the highest level of consensus. This has always been considered essential for the success of the coming standard.

It is expected that, as soon as the development of the standard is finalised, its deployment will start. As most of the standards, the International Standard 24773 will not contain details on usage or application. However, a document intended as a guide for usage, containing examples, will be started, hopefully very soon.

References

1. ISO/IEC JTC 1/SC 7 - Software and systems engineering catalogue.
        http://www.iso.org/iso/iso_catalogue/catalogue_tc/catalogue_tc_browse.htm
        ?commid=45086&published=on. Read April 30th, 2008
2. IEEE Standards Association. Software Engineering – Descriptions
        http://standards.ieee.org/reading/ieee/std_public/description/se/
3. ISO/IEC TR 19759:2005. Software Engineering -- Guide to the Software Engineering Body
    of Knowledge (SWEBOK)
4. ISO/IEC JTC1/SC7 /N3190. International Certification of Software Engineers Study Group
    Final Report. Available at http://www.jtc1-sc7.org. 2005-03-28
5. ISO/IEC 17024:2003. Conformity assessment -- General requirements for bodies operating
    certification of persons.

Acknowledgements

The author of this paper is indebted to all the members of ISO/IEC JTC1 SC7 WG20 who have contributed with their effort to produce the current draft of the 24773 project document; hopefully in a short future, it will become an International Standard. Special appreciation has to be paid to the editorial team formed by three co-editors: Stephen Seidman, Robert Hart and Hiroshi Mukaiyama. The author is also grateful to all countries that submitted or will be submitting comments since this was, and will be, a helpful source for improving the document.

European Standardisation Process

Outline of presentation concerning the CEN/ISSS workshop on e-skills

Noel Geoffrey McMullen[1], John O'Sullivan[2]

[1] CEPIS Past President, Chairman CEN/ISSS ICT Skills Workshop
[2] Consultant for CEN/ISSS ICT Skills Workshop

The CEN/ISSS workshop on e-skills was established in 2003 and exists to deliver CEN Workshop Agreements (CWAs) in its area of interest. The workshop has moved from general reviews of the field to the development of specific frameworks. It is now likely that the workshop will have a long life delivering CWAs embodying consensual expert opinions as precursors to full standards in this growing field.

Geoff will review the history of the workshop, its deliverables to date and the current projects, as well as work planned for 2009/10. He will cover the range of participants and the historical knowledge they bring to the workshop deliberations. He will also describe briefly the network of other active participants in this field in Europe.

He will then hand over to John O'Sullivan who will speak about the CEN/ISSS Workshop Agreement on ICT Certification.

John will start by reviewing previous work in this field, in particular the recent CEPIS project HARMONISE which reported at the end of last year. He will present updated data on that project's four main themes:
- Labour market for professional e-skills
- e-Skills certification processes
- Market for e-skills certification
- Quality standards

HARMONISE concluded that the present situation of many overlapping qualifications was a "certification jungle", with poor information, lack of

Please use the following format when citing this chapter:

McMullen, N.G. and O'Sullivan, J., 2008, in IFIP International Federation for Information Processing, Volume 280; *E-Government; ICT Professionalism and Competences; Service Science;* Antonino Mazzeo, Roberto Bellini, Gianmario Motta; (Boston: Springer), pp. 179–180.

clarity, confusing to prospective candidates and employers, to the detriment of the labour market.

He will go on to present a current follow-on project under the CEN/ISSS Workshop Agreement (CWA). This project aims to:
- Provide updated metrics on the current state of play of the main certifications in the major markets in Europe, with a methodology for annual updates
- A methodology for mapping e-certifications onto the emerging e-Competence Framework and European Qualifications Framework, with one or two worked examples
- A proposed European standard or reference model for e-certifications

By working with the main stakeholders in the field, it is hoped that industry, users and academia will welcome the new standard, and that current vendor and independent certification schemes will converge towards it.

SERVICE SCIENCE

Compliance Requirements for Business-process driven SOAs

Michael P. Papazoglou

INFOLAB, Dept. of Information Systems and Mgt., Tilburg University, The Netherlands, e-mail: mikep@uvt.nl

Abstract: Business processes form the foundation for all organizations, and as such, are impacted by industry regulations. Without explicit business process definitions, flexible rules frameworks, and audit trails that provide for non-repudiation, organizations face litigation risks. This requires organizations to review their business processes and ensure that they meet the compliance standards set forth in legislation. In this paper we discuss compliance-aware implications for Service Oriented Architectures and present open research problems.

1. Introduction

TCompliance regulations, such as HIPAA, Basel II, Sarbanes-Oxley (SOX) and others require all organizations to review their business processes and ensure that they meet the compliance standards set forth in the legislation. This includes, but is not limited to, data acquisition and archival, document management, data security, financial accounting practices, shareholder reporting functions and to know when unusual activities occur. In a broader perspective compliance can pertain to any explicitly stated rule or regulation that prescribes any aspect of an internal or crossorganizational business process; including for example public policies, customer preferences, partner agreements and jurisdictional provisions.

Currently compliance to such rules and regulations is typically achieved on a percase basis. Often compliance solutions are hand crafted for particular compliance problems. Although such ad-hoc solutions achieve their objective, from a management perspective they have several undesirable characteristics. They are:

- hard to maintain as they do not follow a well established architectural pattern;
- hard to evolve as the solutions usually involve hard coding requirements across multiple systems with ill defined dependencies among components;
- hard to reuse as they are custom made to target specific compliance problems;
- hard to understand because a compliance solution often addresses several compliance requirements in a tangled manner;
- hard to formally verify that they guarantee overall compliance.

Please use the following format when citing this chapter:

Papazoglou, M.P., 2008, in IFIP International Federation for Information Processing, Volume 280; *E-Government; ICT Professionalism and Competences; Service Science*; Antonino Mazzeo, Roberto Bellini, Gianmario Motta; (Boston: Springer), pp. 183–194.

Business processes form the foundation for all organizations, and as such, are impacted by industry regulations. Without explicit business process definitions, flexible rule frameworks, and audit trails that provide for non-repudiation, organizations face litigation risks and even criminal penalties. Where business processes stretch across many cooperating and coordinated systems, possibly crossing organizational boundaries, technologies like XML and Web services are making system-to-system interactions commonplace and Service Oriented Architectures (SOAs) serve as a logical integration framework for connecting loosely coupled software modules into on-demand business processes.

2. Business-process driven SOAs

Service orientation utilizes services as constructs to support the rapid, low-cost and easy composition of distributed applications. Key to this concept is the Service-Oriented Architecture (SOA), which is a logical way of designing a software system to provide services to either end-user applications or to other services distributed over a network, via published and discoverable interfaces. Business processes form the foundation for SOAs and require that multiple steps occur between physically independent yet logically dependent software services. Underlying the need for flexibility in SOA is the ability to dynamically grow application portfolios quickly by rapidly assembling new services to address business needs.

To effectively align technical initiatives with the strategic goals at the business level, SOA is combined with Business Process Management technologies [1]. BPM is a natural complement to SOA, and a mechanism through which an organization can apply SOA to high-value business challenges. Layering BPM on top of a solid SOA allows actions within business processes to be exposed via automated services. With BPM orchestration, the exposure of key business events, processes and information to users at the appropriate times and in the appropriate contexts adds tremendous business value that might not otherwise be achieved with a conventional SOA.

When combining SOA with BPM technologies, service composition is typically provided by a process engine (or workflow engine), which invokes the SOA services to realize individual activities in the process. The main goal of such business process-driven SOAs is to increase the productivity, efficiency, and flexibility of an organization via (business) process management. Business process-driven SOAs help deliver control over business processes, fostering standardization across a company or an end-to-end process chain and compliance with regulations, policies, and best practices.

3. Compliance and Business-process driven SOAs

An important characteristic of SOAs is that they are impacted heavily by industry and sectorial regulations. Without explicit business process definitions, flexible rules frameworks, and audit trails that provide for non-repudiation, organizations face litigation risks.

Compliance regulations, such as HIPAA, Basel II, Sarbanes-Oxley (SOX) and others require all organizations to review their business processes and ensure that they meet the compliance standards set forth in the legislation. This can include, but is not limited to, data acquisition and archival, document management, data security, financial accounting practices, shareholder reporting functions. It also requires to know when unusual activities occur. In all cases, such new control and disclosure requirements create auditing demands for SOAs.

SOAs should play a crucial role in corporate governance, allowing management to ascertain that internal control measures that govern their key business processes can be checked, tested, and potentially certified with their underlying Web services.

Internal control constitutes a fundamental cornerstone in auditing, which is used to assure business process compliance, delivering objective and independent guarantees regarding virtually all accounting aspects of service-enabled business processes, including risk management, financial checks and governance processes [2].

A typical financial reporting control might mitigate the risk of misstating revenue due to inadequate physical or electronic security over sales documents and electronic files. This helps implement a compliance regulation act, such SOX section 404, which mandates that well-defined and documented processes and controls be in place for all aspects of company operations that affect financial information and reports. To achieve this functionality requires: (i) controlling and auditing who accesses financial information, (ii) controlling and auditing what financial information is accessed, and (iii) ensuring financial information is not compromised during transmission. Due to the inherent complexity present in compliance regulations, such as SOX, most companies cannot address these requirements without a strategy for automating the integration of the diverse business processes and their accompanying internal control systems throughout the enterprise.

4. Research Directions for Business-process driven SOAs

Novel service technologies should play a crucial role in allowing various types of users (including management) to ascertain that internal control measures that govern their key business processes can be checked, tested, and potentially certified with their underlying business processes. All of this requires continuously adjusting and aligning services within end-to-end business processes that span organizations to cater for regulatory needs. Such changes should not be disruptive by requiring radical modifications in the very fabric of services or the way that business in conducted. This poses enormous methodological and technological challenges as the complexity and scale of service-based applications will expand by orders of magnitude due to the increasing need for flexibility and dynamicity posed by distributed service policies and regulatory compliance.

The challenges of compliant business processes constitute a vibrant area of service research, which has so far received only limited attention and has never been addressed to its entirety. For a holistic approach to compliant business process management (one that covers the entire compliance life-cycle from design time checking to run-time monitoring and adaptation of services) we have identified the following pressing research challenges (themes) which require real innovation:

1. Advanced mechanisms for auditing SOAs.
2. A sound methodology and an associated technology support framework to manage compliance-centric business processes.
3. A more "human-centric" approach to compliance-driven software development that allows stakeholders to express their requirements in terms of typical compliance concerns.
4. A framework that supports the execution of high-level requests that are associated with compliance expressions and permits re-use and customization of compliant process fragments.
5. A formally grounded behavioral model for service compositions and end-to-end business processes to verify the compliance properties of composed services.
6. Monitoring facilities for tracking and validating compliance concerns that can be verified at run-time.

4.1 Auditing Business-process driven SOAs

To provide the ability to establish control and documentation, reduce risk and error potential, in cases where service-enabled processes impact financial reporting (e.g., in end-to-end sales cycles, payment cycles or production cycles), SOAs should be continuously audited. SOA auditing implies auditing business process and relies on an auditing strategy to evaluate the effectiveness of (internal) accounting control systems, which are needed to ensure that business processes execute according to predefined regulatory policies. By checking accounting control systems, risks can be mitigated while safeguarding service-driven processes and increasing their reliability.

Auditors rely on internal control systems as they provide audit evidence that helps reduce substantive testing. In addition, and perhaps more importantly, auditing the internal control systems of processes within or between organizations is a required practice. An auditing strategy should focus on those fragments of a business process that are exposed to the risk of control weaknesses, while fewer efforts need to be spent on those process fragments (and services on which they rely) with strong controls. These items become candidates for immediate evaluation and, where necessary, remediation. For example, handling salaries might be deemed a low-risk item since they are tightly controlled by a small group of people. Revenue recognition, on the other hand, might be deemed high risk because of loosely defined recognition procedures. This strategy becomes particularly significant in large, business-critical SOA-applications. According to the standard control definition given by ISA 315 [3], control activities performed on business processes (and therefore part of any SOA-based solution) may fall under the following five classes:

1. Performance reviews: reviews and analyses of actual performance versus budgets, forecasts, and prior period performance; relating different sets of data (operating or financial) to one another, together with analyses of the relationships and investigative and corrective actions; comparing internal data with external sources of information; and review of functional or activity performance.
2. Information processing control procedures: encompass application controls, which apply to the processing of individual business processes. These controls help ensure that all transactions occurred are authorized, and are completely and accurately logged and processed.
3. Physical controls: encompass the network-level security of service end-points, including adequate safeguards such as secured access/control to services; measures against data availability threats (e.g., XML attacks), and data integrity.
4. Segregation of duties: intended to reduce the opportunities to allow any person to be in a position to both perpetrate and conceal errors or fraud in the normal course of the persons duties.
5. Authorization: accounting controls need to check procedures of reviewing and approving specific operations or transactions, e.g., approving the invocation of purchase orders, or change orders.

To address the above business process control activities, a service auditing methodology should accommodate the following auditing SOA tenets that are derived from intersecting core SOA with basic auditing principles [4], [3]: independent auditing by possibly using an independent auditor (human or automated); policing the SOA behavior by monitoring events or information produced by the services/processes, monitoring instances of business processes, viewing process instance statistics, and so on; real-time reporting by disclosing in real-time material events such as significant write-downs or bad debt recognition;

logging execution trails; and performing continuous auditing of business processes.

4.2 Dealing with the Effects of Business Process Changes

Changes that characterize business processes may have deep effects [5] and require that a business process be redefined and realigned within an entire process supplychain (including business partners, suppliers and customers). This may eventually lead to modification and alignment of business processes and calls for change oriented methodologies to provide a sound foundation for deep service changes in an orderly fashion that allow services to be appropriately (re)-configured, aligned and controlled as changes occur [5]. A business process change-cycle may be subdivided in different phases as described in the following.

The initial phase in a business process change-cycle focuses on identifying the need for change and scoping its extent. One of the major elements of this phase is understanding the causes of the need for change and their potential implications. For instance, compliance to regulations is major force for change. Regulatory requirements such as HIPAA and Sarbanes-Oxley provide strict guidelines that ensure companies are in control of internal, private, public, and confidential information, and auditing standards such as SAS 70 serve as a baseline for regulatory compliance by verifying that third-party providers meet those needs. All of this may lead to the transformation of services within a business process value chain. Here, the affected services-in-scope need to be identified. These assist in understanding the nature of services-in-scope and related services and provide a baseline for comparative purposes and determination of expected productivity, cost and service level improvements.

The second phase, called service change analysis, focuses on the actual analysis, redesign or improvement of the existing services. The ultimate objective of service change analysis is to provide an in-depth understanding of the functionality, scope, reuse, and granularity of services that are identified for change. To achieve its objective, the analysis phase encourages a more radical view of process (re)-design and supports the re-engineering of services. Its main objective is the reuse (or repurposing) of existing service functionality in to meet the demands of change. The problem lies in determining the difference between existing and future service functionality.

As service changes may spill over to other services in a supply-chain, one of the determining factors in service change analysis is being able to recognize the scope of changes and functionality that is essentially self-sufficient for the purposes of a service-in-scope (service under change). When dealing with deep service changes, problems of overlapping or conflicting functionality several types of problems need to be addressed [6], [5]:

1. Service flow problems: Typical problems include problems with the logical completeness of a service upgrade, problems with sequencing and duplication of activities, decision-making problems and lack of service measures.

2. Service control problems: Service controls define or constrain how a service is performed. These include problems where a service-in-scope ignores organizational policies or specific business rules and problems where external services require information that a service-in-scope cannot provide.

3. Conflicting services functionality (including bottlenecks / constraints in the service value stream): The functionality of a service-in-scope may conflict with functionality in related services. Conflicts also include problems where a service-in-scope is not aligned to business strategy, where a service may pursue a strategy that is in conflict with is incompatible with the value chain of which it is a part, and cases where the introduction of a new policy or regulation would make it impossible for the service-in-scope to function.

During the service change analysis standard continuous process improvement practices such as Six Sigma DMAIC practices or Lean Kaizen [7] should be employed. These determine the services changes and define the new services and standards of performance to measure, analyze, control and systematically improve processes by eliminating potential defects.

During the third and final phase, all of the new services are aligned, integrated, simulated and tested and then, when ready, the new services are put into production and managed. To achieve this a services integration model [1] is created to facilitate the implementation of the service integration strategy. This strategy includes such subjects as service design models, policies, SOA governance options, and, organizational and industry best practices and conventions. All these need to be taken into account when designing integrated end-to-end services that span organizational boundaries.

4.3 High-level Languages for Compliance-based Applications

Research is required in high-level declarative concepts for the specification of services languages and service-based applications that allow lay and experienced users and other stakeholders to express their views and requests in terms of what needs to be achieved rather than on how to achieve it. One direction which could be followed is expressing the requests of the stakeholders at the requirement or goal level, where a goal expresses the problem space with the core of the business process captured through high-level goals and a set of plans attached to a given goal, which represent a collection of different strategies and operating tactics. Stakeholders must be able to declare their high-level requirements in a natural and intuitive manner. For instance, a user may be able to specify that all financial business processes should comply to SOX section-409 by reporting in real-time all events that could affect financial results.

Preliminary research work on developing a service request language for XML based Web services in electronic marketplaces has been reported in [8]. This experimental service request language contains a set of appropriate constructs for expressing requests and constraints over requests as well as scheduling operators. User interaction can be perceived as a series of plans that potentially satisfy a request. This approach can be extended and combined with traditional business-process modeling and constraint-specific request language constructs to create executable business process specifications out of user formulated requests, such as compliance requirements.

Preferences and QoS are constraints could potentially be included in a user request. Such requirements must also be able to describe annotations for processes or process elements containing descriptions of behavioral, QoS or SLA features, regulations and policies. Previous work in this area has been reported in [9] where the authors use QoWL an XML-based language that comprises a subset of Business Execution Process Language (BPEL) and a set of QoS extensions for specification of QoS requirements. Constraints and preferences were studied in the area of CSP (Constraint Solving Problem) in [10] where temporal reasoning mechanisms for preferences are provided.

4.4 Compliance-aware Service Composition and Reuse Patterns

Business processes and the service compositions realizing those processes can be created faster and at lower cost if compliance-aware business process-fragments are reused. This approach requires the separation and unique identification of reusable content and its encapsulation in business process fragments (i.e. building blocks such as service patterns or templates) to rapidly tailor service compositions as users or individual application needs demand. Service patterns are a set of repeatable and parameterisable service compositions (and business sub-processes) based on best practices facilitating application and systems delivery and development. The reusable customized and/or differentiated service patterns can be offered by service providers to their customers. This can help guide users in quickly assembling and deploying optimized engagement models and problem solutions. For example, subprocess templates can be defined during modeling time of service compositions to enable faster development of compliant business processes. In addition, such templates can be continually extended with concrete parameter values to incorporate additional requirements (e.g., compliance specialization) and can be stored again as reusable units of functionality.

The ability to discover and compose templates and the ability to parameterize them in order to maintain compliance of the service composition (e.g. a BPEL process) will provide solutions for improving reusability of service compositions, which is clearly a need not addressed by the existing SOA technology landscape.

Some recent research activities address the issue of service composition reuse and specialization as described above. For example, [11] provides a higher level of abstraction for higher reuse through high-level patterns. The approach lets developers write patterns in terms of high-level functionalities. [12] introduces the concept of abstract composite Web service that can be specialized to particular concrete compositions and can be reused in the construction of larger or extended compositions, while [13] proposes a technique that provides users with a context-aware service selection by recommending combinations of services that are most appropriate in a given context. These approaches lack the support for compliance assurance and do not enable adequately the reusability of service composition artifacts that comply to business requirements.

4.5 Compliance-aware Behavior Specification and Checking

Techniques to automatically check the compliance of process models against compliance rules are particularly important for compliance-aware business processes. In addition to business process models, business protocols - which specify the external messaging behavior of services (viz. the rules that govern the service interaction between service providers and clients) - can be also be affected due to changes in policies and regulations and thus require compliance checking.

For compiance-aware business processes we need to ensure that a non-functional aspects and compliance may also be specified by the way of abstract protocols such as trust negotiation protocols, which can then be implemented by business compliant protocols. Dynamic service composition could then ensure that these non-functional aspects are correctly dealt with avoiding behavior anomalies or unexpected uses.

Research work which is interesting for such activities can be found in [14] which presents a method to improve the reliability and minimize the risk of failure of business processes from a compliance perspective. The proposed method allows separate modeling of both process models and compliance concerns. Business process models expressed in BPEL are transformed into pi-calculus and then into finite state machines and compliance rules are translated into linear temporal logic. In this way, process models can be verified against these compliance rules by means of model checking technology.

In the area of business protocols [15] points out the necessity of services including specification of their external behavior such as timed Web service protocols. Such a specification can be used to decide whether a service can be used in some dynamic service composition as part of a business process. Moreover, such a specification can be extended with non-functional requirements, for example by annotating business protocols with privacy policies [16].

4.6 Compliance-aware Service Monitoring

In SOA solutions, a services management and monitoring infrastructure provides comprehensive ways of understanding exactly what is involved in a business process so it can cross organizational boundaries and function as an integral element in an end-to-end process chain. It also provides the means of auditing business processes that cross organizational boundaries. What is required is monitoring techniques and algorithms to validate the compliance concerns at runtime and to provide remedial mechanisms in case of policy violations.

Existing auditing solutions and tools are hopelessly outdated and are not applicable to SOA solutions [[17]. These are tightly coupled to the controlled application, and assume that applications are homogenous and monolithic in nature. In particular, existing Computer Assisted Audit Techniques (CAATs), provide merely support for document management, financial data-analysis (e.g. Unit 4 Account Analyser) and standard flowcharting techniques. In addition, some expert systems, simulation and mathematical systems supporting auditing have been proposed, however, they concentrate on quantitative analysis, treat control processes as black boxes, and, are typically based on unrealistic and rather restrictive assumptions. On the other hand, existing methods and tools to manage and monitor service-enabled processes, notably Business Process Management and Business Process Activity tools, including the ARIS Process Performance Manager and HPs Business Process Insight, fall short in providing sufficient support for auditing SOAs. In particular, BPM tools merely focus on business performance monitoring and continuous evaluation of process execution against service level objectives, depicting information about issues like bottlenecks, throughput and resource utilization in a graphical manner.

Some already existing research results can form a sound basis for addressing the requirements of this theme. Run-time Web service monitoring is essential for real world service-oriented systems. It allows system stakeholders to detect anomalous situations and maintain high level of QoS during system lifecycle. To address such requirements [18] proposes a framework and a tool for automatically deriving Web service monitors from high-level requirements descriptions. Other approaches concentrate on capturing and monitoring negotiations that incorporate security policies and policy models that facilitate service lifecycle management [19].

5. Summary

Business processes form the foundation for all organizations, and as such, are impacted by industry regulations. Where business processes stretch across many cooperating and coordinated systems, possibly crossing organizational boundaries, business process-driven SOAs help deliver control over business processes, fostering standardization across a company or an end-to-end process chain and compliance with regulations, policies, and best practices. Compliance regulations, such as HIPAA, Basel II, Sarbanes-Oxley and others require all organizations to review their business processes and ensure that they meet the compliance standards set forth in the legislation. Therefore, SOAs should play a crucial role in corporate governance, allowing management to ascertain that internal control measures that govern their key business processes can be checked, tested, and potentially certified with their underlying Web services.

The challenges of compliant business processes and regulation compliant-SOAs constitute a vibrant area of service research, which has so far received only limited attention and has never been addressed to its entirety. For a holistic approach to compliant business process management (one that covers the entire compliance life-cycle from design time checking to run-time monitoring and adaptation of services), several important research problems need to be addressed. These include: advanced mechanisms for auditing SOAs, a sound methodology to manage compliance-centric business processes, a more "human-centric" approach to compliance-driven service development, re-use and customization of compliant process fragments, formal verification of the compliance properties of composed services, and, finally monitoring facilities for tracking and validating compliance concerns at run-time.

References

1. Papazoglou, M.P. (2007) Web Service: Principles and technology. PrenticeHall.
2. Rezaee Z. (207) Corporate Governance Post-Sarbanes-Oxley: Regulations, requirements and integrated processes. John Wiley & Sons.
3. International Federation of Accountants. (2006) Handbook of international auditing, assurance and ethics pronouncements, John Wiley & Sons.
4. R. Hayes et al. Principles of Auditing: An introduction to international standards on auditing. Prentice Hall/Financial Times.
5. Papazoglou M.P. (2008) The Challenges of service evolution. Proceedings Advanced Information Systems Engineering Conference: CAISE 2008, Springer-Verlag, Montpellier, France.
6. Harmon, P. (2007) Business process change. Morgan Kaufmann.
7. Martin. (2007) J. Lean Six Sigma for supply chain management. McGraw-Hill.
8. Lazovik A., Aiello M., Papazoglou M. P. (2006) Planning and monitoring the execution of web service requests. J of Digital Libraries, 6(3).
9. Brandic I., Pilana S., Benkner S. (2006) Amadeus: A holistic service-oriented environment for Gridworkflows, Proceedings 4th IEEE International Conference on Grid and Cooperative Computing.
10. Khatib L. et al. (2001) Temporal constraint reasoning with preferences. 17th International Joint Conference on Artificial Intelligence: IJCAI, Seattle, Washington, USA.
11. Melloul L., Fox A. (2004) Reusable functional composition patterns for web services. IEEE International Conference on Web Services: ICWS'04.

12. Bova R., Benbernou S., Hassas S. (2006) An immune system-Iinspired approach for composite web services reuse. Proceeding of ECAI 06 - 4th International Workshop on Artificial Intelligence for Service Composition.
13. Bova R., e. al. On embedding task memory in services composition frameworks, IEEE International Conference on Web Services: ICWE 07.
14. Liu Y., Muelle S., Xu K. (2008) A static compliance-checking framework for business process models. IBM Systems Journal, 47(1).
15. Benatallah B., et. al. (2005) On temporal abstractions of web services protocols. Proceedings Advanced Information Systems Engineering Conference: CAISE 2005, Springer-Verlag, Porto, Portugal.
16. Guermouche N., et al., (2007) Privacy-aware web service protocol replaceability. IEEE International Conference on Web Services: ICWS07.
17. Murthy U.S., Groomer S.M. (2004) A continuous auditing web services model for XMLbased accounting systems. Accounting Information Systems, Elsevier, 5(2).
18. Robinson W.N. (2003) Monitoring web service requirements. Proceedings of the IEEE International Requirements Engineering Conference, IEEE Computer Society.
19. Skogsrud H. , Benatallah B., Casati F. (2003) Model-driven trust negotiation for web services.IEEE Internet Computing 7(6).

Business Process Design: Towards Service-Based Green Information Systems

Barbara Pernici, Danilo Ardagna, Cinzia Cappiello

Politecnico di Milano, piazza Leonardo da Vinci 32, Milano, Italy

Contact author: barbara.pernici@polimi.it

Abstract: This paper discusses the impact of energy consumption on information systems and business processes design. The goal is the development of context-aware and sustainable information systems where energy consumption reduction is considered at the technological level, on the basis of adaptable technology, on the governance level, with the design of context-aware processes and data, and at the strategic level. The adoption of a service-oriented approach and the interconnection among the different levels are discussed.

1. Introduction

Climate debate and Sustainable Growth concern over energy use have thrown the spotlight on power consumed by Information Technology (IT). Since information management has become pervasive in modern society, the impact of IT on energy budget is becoming more and more significant. The growth in the number of servers and the increasing complexity of the network infrastructure has caused an enormous spike in electricity usage. Nowadays, service centers alone consume 1.5% of the power produced in the US, and are projected to reach 4.5% within 5 years. This has driven efforts to reduce the power consumed by service centers and at the device level. Another issue related to energy consumption which is influencing IT decisions in many countries has been the introduction of carbon taxes connected with CO_2 emissions and the carbon credits debate. There is a strong need for new instruments able to analyze the impact of IT decisions and enterprise business processes on energy and costs and to set an active control on Information Systems (IS) on the basis of the energy driver.

In a recent paper, (Murugesan 2008) analyzes the environmental impact of IT along four dimensions: design, use, manufacturing, and disposal of IT systems. This paper analyzes mainly the first two dimensions: design of Information Systems under an energy consumption perspective, focusing on service and information management, and use of Information Systems, focusing mainly on the reduction of the resources needed for processing information and for information storage after its elaboration.

Please use the following format when citing this chapter:

Pernici, B., Ardagna, D. and Cappiello, C., 2008, in IFIP International Federation for Information Processing, Volume 280; *E-Government; ICT Professionalism and Competences; Service Science*; Antonino Mazzeo, Roberto Bellini, Gianmario Motta; (Boston: Springer), pp. 195–203.

Several research directions are emerging in the literature to improve the quality of Information Systems. Software as a service suggests economies of scale and, in recent years, large service centers have been setup to provide computational capacity on demand to many customers who share a pool of IT resources. With the development of the Service Oriented Architecture (SOA), multiple service providers can offer functionally equivalent web services which may differ for their offered Quality of Service (QoS). Virtualization technology can be exploited to improve the efficiency of use of hardware infrastructures, increasing the average percentage utilization of the systems and allowing the dynamic reconfiguration of physical infrastructures.

Nowadays, IT systems are required to provide high availability, reliability, and performance. Increased business continuity requirements, which necessitate the replication of data to protect against system failures, and the growing trend to leverage a great variety of information for business operations, are driving customers to store more data than in the past. IDC predicts storage annual growth around 60%. Redundancy improves systems' QoS, but may introduce energy inefficiencies.

In our work, we focus on the point that energy efficiency should be given a very relevant role in Information Systems design. In fact, advances in autonomic and self-healing service-based systems enable a potential reduction of system redundancy, and energy optimization related to data management is more and more challenging.

The goal of the paper is to discuss a systematic set of theoretical approaches and methods and tools towards the implementation of "energy-proportional" Information Systems, i.e. to consume energy according to the amount of work performed, contrary to the current state of the art, in which systems are mainly under-utilized and perform many non-essential tasks. Our focus is mainly towards a green approach to the use of information and application in Information Systems, at a software and management level, rather that on the development on the underlying hardware infrastructure. The aim is to reduce redundant components by designing systems able to react dynamically to variable operating conditions and maximize the use of resources with minimal energy consumption, through their self-reconfiguration. Current work in sustainable and power aware computing suggests designing systems with a trade off between QoS and energy consumption.

An information system approach allows considering all components which are needed for information management in an organization in a global framework. We will aim to develop an "IS purifier" approach, in analogy to what is being done for cleaning water for a sustainable environment. The approach will be based on a triple perspective approach to reduce and streamlining energy consumption in Information Systems: a) IS green governance to support strategic decisions in developing green Information Systems and to evaluate the impact on energy consumption and CO_2 emissions, b) IS green control to evaluate, optimize, and govern services and data both at an application and at an infrastructural level with emphasis on energy efficiency, and c) specific techniques to support   the purification of parts of the system (e.g., service and data redundancy elimination) when critical situations arise that might have a deep impact on energy consumption.

2. Related work

Green computing is a new discipline and practice of using computing resources with a focus on the impact of IT on the environment. Initiatives have been taken in order to reduce the use of hazardous materials, maximize energy efficiency, and recycling products and materials. Green computing has been started in 1992 with the foundation of the Energy Star program and currently is sustained both by government regulations (e.g., EU directives 2002/95/EC on the reduction on hazardous substances, 2002/96/EC on waste of electronic equipment) and by the industry (e.g. EPEAT criteria for the evaluation of products by the Green Electronic Council, or the IBM Big Green project on the energy efficiency of data centers).

At the governance layer, literature contributions are by (Jokinen 1998), which examines the relationship between the information society and sustainable development on theoretical and conceptual levels, and (Cohen 1998) which focuses on e-commerce and environmental sustainability. Though no definitive conclusions are drawn, these papers provide a starting point and raise green IT issues at an early stage. (Yi 2007) provides a review of the state of the art of projects, literature, and products addressing how e-business/ICT affects the environment. They mention ISA, an assessment tool to examine approaches and activities to evaluate the implications of information society technologies (in the EU 5th Framework Pro-gram), and a few scenarios, criteria and indicators as tools for identifying environmental impacts inherent in the information society. (Williams 2008) advocates the need for creating an ecosystem map, introducing the concept, to be developed, of Key green performance indicators. (Borup 2007) discusses the increasing focus on foresight exercises as a tool in public governance of research and industrial innovation systems. Technology foresight, as a systematic analysis and discussion about possible technology futures, gives evidence to Green technology foresight (GTF), or environmentally oriented technology foresight. Environment issues and thoughts about sustainability are if not high on, then at least visible, on the agenda in society in general. This has created a new area of relevance and legitimacy for techno-scientific development and research and new opportunities and markets for environment technology are gaining importance. An integration of science and technology policy with environment policy seems more relevant and obvious than earlier. These things are reflected in the appearance of green technology foresight and also in the inclusion of environment aspects in more general technology foresight activities.

A prospective simulation study of a project commissioned by the EU Institute for Prospective Technological Studies models all known relevant ICT effects using a system dynamics approach in combination with scenario techniques and expert consultations. The results offer debate on how the chosen environmental indicators will have very variable absolute values in 2020, which will depend on many uncertain model parameters. This paper contributes to the general understanding of the environmental impacts of ICT and provides a useful basis for policy-making in the fields of ICT and environment. Scenarios are still qualitative planning and communication tools, but a need arises for predictive management tools. The life cycle assessment (LCA) tool, known as life-cycle analysis, allows for estimating the total environmental impact of a given product or service throughout its lifespan. LCA, as an extended economic or environmental input–output life cycle assessment, has been the most common method applied so far, since awareness and understanding of governance issues are still rather un-studied. An artificial neural network approach embedded in a predictive and empirical model is reviewed as a tool for companies to analyze how their e-business operations influence the environment, based on indicators to be chosen to represent e-business/ICT factors and geo-environmental performance.

At the technological layer, energy consumption in computing devices has received great attention by the research community. Much work has been done in order to achieve power reduction in mobile systems (both at device and network level (Kremer 2001)) to extend battery life, while low power techniques are now progressively introduced in server environments. All major industrial players are taking a position in the green IT area (see for instance (Williams 2008) from Microsoft, (Barroso 2007) from Google, and the IBM Big Green Project launched in May 2007. In academic research, to reduce energy consumption, autonomic techniques have been developed to manage workload fluctuations (Chase 2001) and to determine optimum trade-offs between performance and energy costs by switching servers on and off and by implementing DVS mechanisms (i.e., reduction of CPU frequency of operation of new servers) (Ardagna 2007c, Quin 2007, Kusic 2006). Overall, the development of energy-proportional computing systems is advocated (Barroso 2007), since in current implementations the energy consumption vs. performed work dependency is highly non-linear.

In the Software as a Service area, research has been performed on the maximization of the QoS for end users. First solutions proposed greedy approaches (Maamar 2003) which select one at a time, the best candidate service suitable for the execution of business process activities. (Zeng 2004, Ardagna 2007b, Canfora 2005, Yu 2007) propose more sophisticated techniques based on integer programming, genetic algorithms or heuristics for the solution of the problem. In the Software as a Service area, energy consumption has not been considered yet. Further, a gap exists between the problem of maximization of QoS for end users and the optimum trade-off between performance and energy determined at the technological layer. The aim of this research is to fill this gap by privileging energy considerations and by implementing run-time optimum allocation polices at the technological layer and IS-control modules. The adoption of integrated run-time mechanisms is advocated also in (Feng 2008). Self-* properties for systems as introduced by (Kephart 2003), provide the ability of creating Self-CHOP systems, i.e., Self Configuring, Self Healing, Self Optimizing, Self Protecting systems. Examples of applications are in the areas of Self Adaptive Middleware, Self Healing Databases, Autonomic Server Monitoring, and mobile Information Systems (Penici 2006). While currently this approach is focusing on middleware technology for infra-structure management, such an approach provides the basis for creating systems which change their way of working according to internal and external conditions, and set the basis for further investigation for a comprehensive approach towards the development of green IT for Information Systems.

Concerning data management, data deduplication (Elmagarmid 2007) is a method of reducing storage requirements by eliminating redundant data. In a backup and recovery system, gigabytes of information will be stored over and over again at each backup, creating several copies of data that might change only incrementally over time. With data deduplication, the basic idea is to store only data changes on storage devices, while redundant data is replaced with a pointer to the unique data copy. Current technology has applied data deduplication for the management of system backup enabling up to 300:1 data reduction for backup and storage applications (McGillicuddy 2007). The starting point for data dedupliction is the identification of the redundancies that is the recognition of representations of the same object in different sources (Newcombe 1962). This problem has been known for more than decades as the record linkage or the record matching problem. This research can contribute to a comprehensive green IT approach for Information Systems to support the identification of redundancies in stored files by considering the metadata that describe them and thus by considering semi-structured data. Anyway, data deduplication has to be performed by considering only relevant and useful data. The evaluation of data relevance is an open issue in the literature. Many times relevance is judged by considering subjective evaluations. Previous work just provides a set of guidelines based on a few of quantitative and qualitative parameters. The identification of significant qualitative and quantitative parameters for relevance assessment is needed, in particular considering time aspects for data objects that are not temporally valid or not frequently used.

3. Design of green Information Systems and service-based approaches

In order to evaluate the impact of use of energy and to design new energy efficient Information Systems, innovation is needed both at the strategic, governance, and technology levels (see figure below).

An integrated approach for energy management of systems supporting both applications and data is advocated. A service-oriented approach to application development offers a flexible support for application execution. In forthcoming service technology, adaptivity becomes a major asset, and sets the basis for developing flexible systems which are able to react to variable operation conditions (S-Cube Network, 2008).

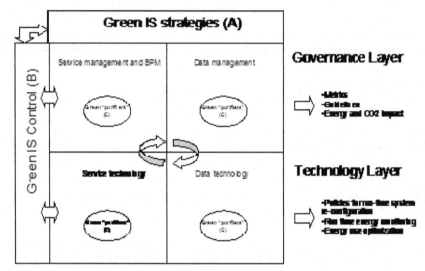

Fig. 1. An integrated approach to green Information Systems

At the strategic level, Green IS strategies have to be developed, considering the context of operation of the system, the main business goals, and the general characteristics of the underlying infrastructure. Such strategic level is needed to define the requirements and constraints for a green IS approach in IT systems.

The IT system provides the infrastructure for running the information system and can be considered as composed by a Governance layer and a Technology layer.

In considering services, we address both services provided inside organizations and external services, as well as the current trend towards out-sourcing and using software as a service.

While existing research is currently focusing on the infrastructure level for service technology, such as in computer centres, and on hardware technology, we propose the development of new original methods for reducing unwanted activities and data towards a "purifying" approach. The general idea is that of identifying improper use of resources in the system and sup-porting their reduction. The proposed approach can be based on the development of research in adaptive, self-healing, and self-managing systems to reduce the energy consumption, also considering external usage and environmental factors. In this sense, we propose the development of research activities towards the realization of "green purifiers" for each of the four components (service governance, data governance, service technology, data technology).

In particular, at the service governance level, research has to focus on new techniques to analyze processes under a Green IT perspective. While Business Process Management technology focuses on process performance and mining, the focus of the research in this area will be (i) on the analysis of the process structure and intermediate data exchanges to reduce the generation of output which is not used within the process or in other processes, (ii) to analyze the energy consumption parameters to support process scheduling when resources are available or less energy is needed, instead of acquiring further computing resources for their execution.

A self-approach as proposed in the service engineering area (Kephart and Chess 2003) has to be investigated, in particular to adapt systems to variable operating conditions and to different phases of the life-cycle of running and executed applications and services. Frameworks for adapting service-based business processes such as the PAWS framework (Ardagna et al. 2007) can be adopted to realize context-aware and sustainable Information Systems.

However, such components cannot be used in isolation and have clear potential interrelations. The monitoring, analysis, and control of the use of such technological components have to be supported by research towards the development of a Green IS Control system, which will provide filtering and decision support functionalities to achieve the goals defined in the Green IS strategies. Research on Green IS strategies will focus on developing a comprehensive model to analyze the energy consumption impact of Information Systems, and for developing methodological guidelines to improve it.

4. Concluding Remarks

The present paper has presented a global approach to designing sustainable information systems, with a particular focus on service-based business processes.

A context-aware and "purifier-based" approach to Information Systems has been proposed, which has to be taken into consideration in the process design phases to result applicable during system operation.

References

1. S. Abiteboul. Issues in Monitoring Web Data. Proc. of the 13th Int. Conf. on Database and Expert Systems Applications, 2002, France. LNCS, 2453. Berlin: Springer, 1-8.

2. D. Ardagna, M. Comuzzi, E. Mussi, P. Plebani, B. Pernici. PAWS: a framework for processes with adaptive Web services. IEEE Software. 24(6), 39-46, 2007

3. D. Ardagna and B. Pernici. Adaptive service composition in flexible processes. IEEE Trans. on Software Engineering, June 2007.

4. D. Ardagna, M. Trubian, and L. Zhang. SLA based resource allocation policies in autonomic environments. Journal of Parallel and Distributed Computing, 67(3):259–270, 2007.

5. L. A. Barroso, U. Hölzle. The Case for Energy-Proportional Computing, IEEE Computer, vol. 40, 2007.

6. M. Borup. Green Technology Foresight as Instrument in Governance for Sustainability. Proceedings of the 2003 Berlin Conference on the Hu-man Dimensions of Global Environmental Change, 386 - 408.

7. G. Canfora, M. Penta, R. Esposito, and M. L. Villani. QoS-Aware Re-planning of Composite Web Services. In ICWS 2005 Proc., 2005. Orlando.

8. J. S. Chase and D. C. Anderson. Managing Energy and Server Re-sources in Hosting Centers. In ACM Symposium on Operating Systems principles, 2001.

9. N. Cohen. Greening the Internet: ten ways e-commerce could affect the environment and what we can do. Environ Qual. Manag. 9 (1), 1-16, 1998.

10. A. K. Elmagarmid, P. G. Ipeirotis, and V. S. Verykios. Duplicate record detection: A survey. IEEE Trans. Knowl. Data Eng., 19(1):1–16, 2007.

11. W. Feng, X. Feng, R. Ge. Green Supercomputing Comes of Age. IT Professional, 10(1), 17-23, 2008.

12. M. A. Hernandez, S. J. Stolfo. Real-world data is dirty: Data cleansing and the merge/purge a problem. Data Min. Knowl. Discov., 2(1):9–37, 1998.

13. Hodge, G.M. Best practises for digital archiving, D-Lib, January 2000.

14. P. Jokinen, P. Malaska, J. Kaivo-Oja. The environment in an "Informa-tion society": a transition stage towards more sustainable development? Futures 30 (6), 485-498, 1998.

15. J. O. Kephart, D. M. Chess. The Vision of Autonomic Computing. IEEE Computer, 36 (1), 41-50, 2003.

16. J. Kephart, H. Chan, R. Das, D. Levine, G. Tesauro, F. Rawson, and C. Lefurgy. Coordinating Multiple Autonomic Managers to Achieve Speci-fied Power-performance Tradeoffs. In ICAC Proc., June 2007.

17. U. Kremer, J. Hicks, J. M. Rehg. A Compilation Framework for Power and Energy Management on Mobile Computers. In LCPC Proc., 115-131, 2001.

18. D. Kusic and N. Kandasamy. Risk-Aware Limited Lookahead Control for Dynamic Resource Provisioning in Enterprise Computing Systems. In ICSOC 2004 Proc., 2004.

19. Z. Maamar, Q.Z. Sheng, B. Benatallah. Interleaving Web Services Composition and Execution Using Software Agents and Delegation. In WSABE Proc, 2003.

20. S. McGillicuddy. Data deduplication technology of growing interest to SMBs,http://searchcio-midmar-ket.techtarget.com/news/article/0,289142,sid183_gci1265307,00.html, 2007.
21. V. Metha. A Holistic Solution to the IT Energy Crisis. http://www.greenercomputing.com/reviews_third.cfm?NewsID=36321, 2007.
22. S. Murugesan, Harnessing green IT: Principles and practice. IEEE IT Professional 10(1), 24-33, 2008.
23. H.B. Newcombe and J.M. Kennedy. Record Linkage: Making Maxi-mum Use of the Discriminating Power of Identifying Information. Comm. of the ACM, 5 , 563-566, 1962.
24. B. Pernici (ed). Mobile Information Systems Infrastructure and Design for Adaptivity and Flexibility, Springer 2006
25. S-Cube Network, http://www.s-cube-network.eu/, 2008
26. J. Williams, Joseph, L. Curtis. Green: The New Computing Coat of Arms? IT Professional, 10(1), 12-16, Jan.-Feb. 2008.
27. L. Yi, H. R. Thomas. A review of research on the environmental impact of e-business and ICT. Environment International 33(6): 841-849, August 2007.
28. T. Yu, Y. Zhang, and K.-J. Lin. Efficient algorithms for web services selection with end-to-end QoS constraints. ACM Trans. Web, 1(1):1–26, 2007.
29. L. Zeng, B. Benatallah, M. Dumas, J. Kalagnamam, and H. Chang. QoS-aware middleware for Web services composition. IEEE Trans. on Software Engineering, 30(5), May 2004.

SIFET-CBA Project

Mario A. Bochicchio, Antonella Longo, Federica Longo, Antonio Bernardo

Università del Salento, Italy, {mario.bochicchio, antonella.longo, federica.longo, antonio.bernardo }@unile.it

Abstract: Innovating the Public Administration is not just the union of various tasks (innovating institutions, reengineering administrative processes and using innovative technologies) performed in isolation, because of the additional complexity coming from their coupling. Conceptual modelling techniques and rapid prototyping tools can help public managers and administrators to better understand the reciprocal dependencies between the various tasks and to bridge the gap between the different cultures and languages (juridical, organizational, managerial, information technology, ...) typical of the e-Government.

Keywords: conceptual modeling, system modeling, process innovation

1. Introduction

In recent years the diffusion of communication networks and distributed applications allowed the development of new interaction paradigms in Public Administration, under the collective name of e-Government, meant also as a way to organize public Administration for better serving citizens and enterprises on a comprehensive scale. As a consequence, the basic outline of an e-government vision has emerged and governments have taken promising steps to deploy e-government services both in USA and in Europe [1]. Much remains to be done if this vision is to be broadly realized, to create innovative services within a coherent system of juridical and economical rules based on new technologies and concepts.

Innovating the Public Administration, in fact, is not just the union of various tasks (innovating institutions, reengineering administrative processes and using innovative technologies) performed in isolation, because of the additional complexity coming from their coupling [1]. The crucial point is to foster the consciousness of the holistic approach to integrate and extend models, design methodologies and techniques to face the new e-government challenges. This paper is focused on the innovation in Local Public Administrations and small-medium public utilities (LPAs in the following), to give an integrated and trans-disciplinary answer to the following questions:

Please use the following format when citing this chapter:

Bochicchio, M.A., et al., 2008, in IFIP International Federation for Information Processing, Volume 280; *E-Government; ICT Professionalism and Competences; Service Science;* Antonino Mazzeo, Roberto Bellini, Gianmario Motta; (Boston: Springer), pp. 205–217.

1. how to foster an effective e-gov. approach in the current context of "institutional uncertainty" about the role of the LPAs toward the citizen's community?
2. in the current panorama, what new options are imposed and what new tools and methodologies are given to LPAs to achieve a better performance and to improve their relationship with citizens?

In particular, referring to the latter question, the paper aims at two main goals:

a) how to involve the managers of LPAs in reshaping the organizational and operational structure of the same LPAs, adopting the ICT to improve their efficiency and effectiveness;

b) how to bridge the gap between the various "cultures" and languages (juridical, managerial, organizational, technological, …) needed in the new e-gov. scenario.

We decided to orient our approach to Local Administrations because of their very poor performance in several key sectors: in Italy, for example, the official evasion figure of local taxation is around 30% while the fiscal contentious between citizens and LPA has reached a critical level [5]. Moreover, small and medium LPAs are often overwhelmed by outdated managers and bureaucratic employees culturally unable to manage the complexity of the new institutional and technological situation.

Among other LPAs, local public utilities are very problematic, like some Land Reclamation and Drainage Authorities of Apulia, that are in compulsory administration from 2004, because considered unable to properly manage the funding process (based on taxation) and to demonstrate the direct benefits produced to citizens. In the opinion of the authors, this "ineptitude" is directly related to the lack of (managerial, methodological, operational, juridical, …) methodologies, tools and best practices to prefigure how normative and technological innovation can bridge the gap between the "paper based" government and the e-government

In the paper we propose an applied-research experience coming from the collaboration among the University of Salento and the Land Reclamation Authority of Arneo in the South-East of Apulia (Italy), with the aim at supporting the local utility to regain its role by increasing its performance and reducing the normative and informative asymmetries in taxation.

The paper is structured as follows. In Section 2, we present the context and the motivations at the root of our research. Section 3 discusses the reference framework we adopt and the main related tools. In Section 4 we present some results we achieved applying this framework to the Land Reclamation Authority of Arneo. Section 5 concludes the paper and depicts some further research developments.

2. Context

In the perspective of the institutional dimension of technology innovation, the unclear distinction, widespread in the European legal tradition, between law and regulations creates uncertainty [6]. In fact, in the Law the decisional process takes place as authoritative form in the circle of command, with informal and uncontrollable behaviours. The result is a "mono-directional construction" aimed at reaching specific goals. The regulation, instead, is characterized by its practice, so it has conditional and "multidirectional" nature. It is based on the "what if" principle, with hypothetical not executive clarifications and it depends on the position of the single actor.

The use of ICT can produce radical improvements in administrative procedures, if it is supported by the optimization of the corresponding process. The normative techniques of regulation and simplification pursue the goal of *"regulation in simplification"* [8], which means:

- eliminating useless procedural steps unnecessary to decision making;
- reducing functional interferences between procedures regulated by different norms, unifying them in a unique procedural flow with one regulation;
- rationalizing the communication processes among the figures involved in decisions and creating a unique and consistent interface with the citizen;
- promoting the widespread access to decisions and their effects.
- The user centered approach in designing e-services and on-line applications is the corresponding facet in the software development community.

Actually, providing citizens with e-services is a hot research topic, and in particular researchers focus their attention on the implementation of a single point of access to public services and information, the development of integrated platforms, which will allow the public sector to provide citizens, businesses and other public authorities with information and public services structures. Examples of research and business applications and methods for integrating heterogeneous legacy information systems are extensively described in [3]. Nevertheless, the scenario is not homogeneous, and from an informal survey of the current context in the Southeast of Italy, we found:

- inconsistent and uncoordinated organizational growth with hundreds of processes overlapping in the years, with outdated organization solutions;

- incompatible ICT solutions and a correspondent inefficient usage of ICT
- lack of horizontal and vertical communication in the institutional structure.
- Other considerations related to the local taxes' management process contribute to better understand the poor quality of data owned by the Local Administration. In summary, our experience is that:
- Several sources may provide data to the system with different quality, according to the source (manual data input, data copied from system to system, etc.);

- Data is often duplicated either due to the poor definition of the business logic (or bad bureaucratic processes) or to technical reasons, or simply for convenience.
- The semantic relationships among information don't exist, making it difficult to enforce the integrity constraints and to guarantee the data correctness.

3. UWA+, methodology and tools

The holistic approach in e-government creates new processes and scenarios, as they are highly knowledge intensive and they rely on the strict interaction between people and information technologies (IT in the following). These points imply that IT must reach the "heart" (the decisional level) of the administrative work, and not only its "hands" (the operational level). So the management of legal/administrative knowledge becomes a decisive driver in the administration. At the same time, designing governmental applications and services touches two issues: coupling concepts and systems and making use of standards. So, a right innovation methodology must combine Legal Drafting and engineering techniques, to develop normative and technological tools in an integrated fashion to reduce the gap of the normative asymmetry, cause of the informative asymmetry and of many inefficiencies.

Before the last Italian Constitutional reform (Law n. 3/2001) in LPAs the technological innovation (see [10]) has consisted of two alternative models: *insourcing* or *outsourcing* of ICT services [12]. The first approach has been subjected to unmodified informal behaviors and to authoritative bureaucratic formalism. In the latter case externalisation has made providers de-facto owners of data and knowledge, acquiring dominant position in IT innovation. In both cases LPAs have lacked any independent position in the adoption of new technologies and they have used (or have been used by) unidirectional approaches with no care about the delivery and the economic exploitation of information asset.

Nowadays LPAs, to exploit the autonomy, must "know themselves",: they must be conscious of their experiencies heritage, of their procedures and functionalities for delivering services, of their ability in understanding citizens needs, of their performance, just to be able to decide to change. Methodologies like UWA+ [13], extensively based on conceptual modeling techniques, can be very important to help LPAs to better define their internal structure, their processes and their information systems, and to manage and evolve it.

In this scenario, public utilities (LPAs in general) are very different from private ones because of the juridical nature of the relationship between citizens and the utilities: the services offered from the utilities are not an option for citizens, that are "forced" to pay for the received services. The form of the contribution is the same of a local tax, but in the new perspective of the constitutional reform. As a consequence, is not an option for the public utilities to correctly inform citizens about all aspects (both qualitative and quantitative) of the offered services.

This requires, the creation of an effective local taxation system, involving both legal and technological aspects, where fiscal questions are faced from different perspectives, in homogeneous legal and informative "environment", with the support of two complementary instruments called:

- TUnifET (*Testo Unificato delle Entrate Tributarie*, that is the Unified Sheet of Fiscal Incomes)

- SIFET (*Sistema Informativo della Fiscalità e dei Tributi*, that is the Fiscal Information System of the public utility).
- The description of the TUnifET, also reported in [14] for a similar case of study, is out of the scope of this paper.
- The creation of the SIFET for the CBA case of study is reported in the next subsection.

3.1 SIFET

In order to know itself and its territory and to achieve the tools and the abilities to measure its performance, the CBA must be conscious about the information and knowledge heritage owned inside, eventually completing and complementing it with external sources. The goal is to expose information owned inside, asking citizens and enterprises to complete and update it. New technologies (Internet, mobile, etc.) are very effective for this task, because they support the development of real-time/near-real-time services. To enable this instant access/instant response to take place, a blending of Ubiquitous Web applications with data from legacy archives and Information systems is needed, requiring design methodologies borrowed from both database and hypermedia communities.

With reference to taxation process operated by the CBA, the main goal has been the design and the implementation of the *Office of Incomes,* a center of real time incomes aggregation, to give CBA the chance to know its actual entrances and to plan the budget on "certified" data. The system for managing and facilitating the heterogeneous data transformation and integration is based on techniques of database integration design, while the design of the Web application for the citizen-side management of taxes is based on UWA+ framework [13] and on tools of fast prototyping [2]. The framework integrates a conceptual modeling methodology for designing web applications (UWA), with a tool for measuring KPIs (the HIGO grid) and with methods for integrating heterogeneous data sources. The user centred design methodology and the implementation of prototypes, generally recognized as very effective in improving the end user acceptance of the applications, aims to actively involve the CBA managers in the design of the SIFET. Data integration is constantly monitored by the Income Office, according to citizens' requests in the TunifET regulatory design. Beside, through the SIFET, citizens are initiated to use multichannel communication techniques with the Administration, in order to make the informative certainty easier, which is a necessary condition to reach the income certainty, vital for the Public Utility.

4. Validating the approach: the SIFET-CBA project

The Italian *land reclamation and drainage authorities* (consorzi di bonifica) are local public organizations, which main tasks are:

designing, implementing and maintaining public works concerning plumbing, drainage and land reclamation

improving the management of waters for different purposes (irrigation, dam , drainage management, ...)

Authority's operational expenses are split among the estates' owners of the area, according to the benefits achieved (or achievable) from the works made and maintained by the Authority. Yearly, the Authority requires each owner to pay for an amount determined by:

Estate's Land Register data of each owner;

Hydraulic technical land indexes (permeability, average slope, ...) of each land parcel;

Authority's maintained works' usage

The *Consorzio di Bonifica dell'Arneo* (CBA in the following, literarily: Land Reclamation and Drainage Authority of Arneo), is a public organization based in Nardò, in the South-East part of Italy. It employs 68 people, manages 250.000 hectares and 200.000 estates in Salento area, and yearly issues 180.000 notices for about 15 M€/year, but in the last operation year (2004) 95% of them were claimed with open questions of law.

So the aim of the project has been to support CBA in reducing the information asymmetry between the Authority and land owners through an extensive use of new technologies.

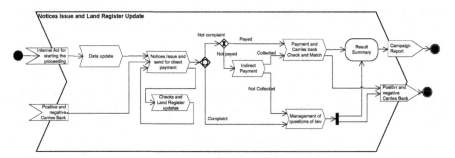

Fig. 1. Notices Issue and Land Register Update Process overview

In order to allow management to evaluate the impact of their choices in the egov scenario, we shared the UWA+ framework main outcomes and implemented a working prototype. Thus a further result has been the formalization of the AS-IS and TO-BE process of notice issue and collection and the definition of KPIs according to the different stakeholders in order to evaluate the performances in relation to the different choices.

Today in CBA the process starts with a request from the Authority board to the EDP Manager to issue payment notices (Figure 1). The first step is the calculation of the due amount for each estate insisting on the pertinent area; since necessary info is on paper, EDP workers manually update info into an AS400 system. This data are

contained in a document called Parcel Sheet, about the cadastral income, the land income, technical indicators about the works intensity, the hydraulic behaviour index, the land stock index

about hydraulic works related to the estate, which, if well maintained by the Authority, improve the estate value

about owner's personal data, payments, refunds and sanctions.

Then payment notices are printed and directly sent to each owner, to be paid within a deadline. The not-paid notices are collected by to a debt collector for indirect payment.

Payments and carries back are matched with collected payments notices and positive or negative differences are notified to owners.

An office counter is always available to receive complaints and update the estate' status in the Land Register during the direct and indirect issue and collection period.

For lack of space, we only show diagrams of the sub process about notice issue for the direct payment. Figure 3 displays the AS –IS assembly line diagram. It is made up with the activity diagram in the upper part, showing actors performing the different activities, the automated activities (with the computer icon), and the involved information resources in the lower part . The two are connected through read/write data links with the related activities (the black points show read data , white points are information written during the activity).

	Cost	Quality	Time
Manager	∠Number of employees ∠Mean cost of directly collected notice ∠Mean cost of payments via debt collector	∠Complained notices rate ∠Correct notices rate	∠Mean time for a Complained Proceeding ∠Mean Time for a proceeding
Land's Owner	∠ Mean time spent in queue	∠Understandability Payment notice ∠Number of requested information ∠Operations complexity	∠Punctuality ∠Mean time for an answer
Worker	∠System availability ∠Satisfaction level ∠Complain rate	∠Data Entry complexity ∠Number of integration requests	∠Mean time for a check ∠Mean time for data entry ∠Mean time for system transaction

Fig. 2. Stakeholders KPIs according to HIGO approach

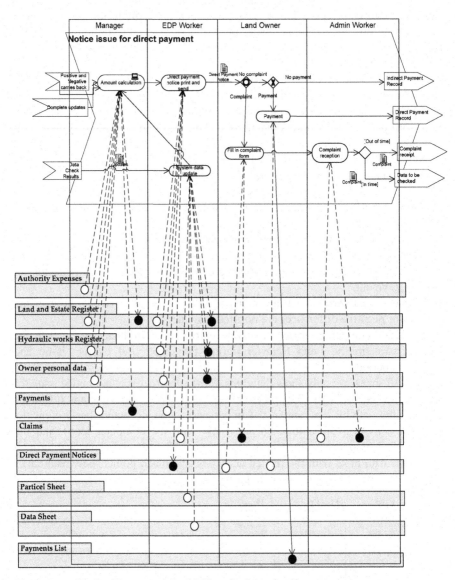

Fig. 3. Assembly line diagram of the AS IS notice issue for direct payment process

According to Higo grid, KPIs have been defined in the categories of Cost, Quality and Time for each stakeholder, worker, land's owner and manager, as shown in Figure 2.

Table 1. Target objectives for Manager's KPIs

Manager Indicators		To-Be Objective
Category	**Indicator**	
Cost	Number of Employees (FTE)	Reduce the work load per employee by 30%
	Mean cost of directly collected notice	Reduce the front end work hours by 50%.
	Mean cost of a notice via debt collector	Reduce the front end work hours by 50%
Time	Mean Time for a proceeding	The whole mean time must be reduced by 50%
	Mean time for a Complained Proceeding	Reduce the time for a practice by 30%,.
Quality	Correct notices rate	Improve notices correctness by 80%
	Complained notices rate	Reduce the complained notice rate by 50%

In order to improve the process efficiency and the relationship quality with customers, the new target values have been defined, and a new process has been designed, supported by Web tools. As an example Table 1 shows KPIs target values for the Manager's stakeholder,

The new process aims at balancing the information asymmetry towards the user, let him be the manager of his information, update his data and provide land's owner with motivations of his notice amount.

Figure 4 shows the Assembly line diagram of the TO-BE notice issue for direct payment process. It has been designed to meet the following goals:

- to provide customers with an always and everywhere available counter in order to reduce litigations related to not updated data
- to provide customers with a tool enabling them to manage their information and payments
- to update the Land Register, which must be accessible in real time for calculation and checks

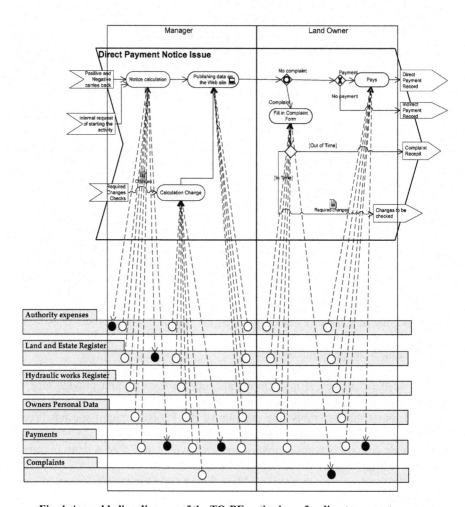

Fig. 4. Assembly line diagram of the TO-BE notice issue for direct payment process

The conceptual model of the Web application has been designed using UWA approach. In Figure 5 the hyperbase in the large is displayed, showing the main information entity types and their semantic relationships. Entity types are straight related with the information resources in the assembly lines. Figure 6 shows the hyperbase in the small of the Building entity type where attributes are straight related with the data model, necessary to implement the prototype using a fast prototyping tool.

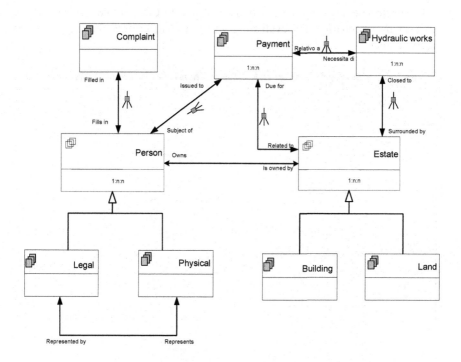

Fig. 5. Hyperbase in the large of the Web Application supporting the Notice issue and payment process

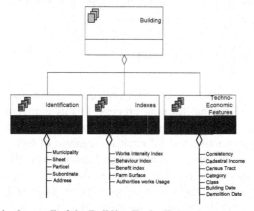

Fig. 6. Hyperbase in the small of the Building Entity Type

The result is shown in Figure 7: the screenshot displays the land owner personal web page, with his personal information, his buildings, his lands, the notices to be paid online and the ones already sent to the debt collector.

The prototype has been discussed and tested with CBA employees, simulating different user scenarios and evaluating with the management the impact of the diverse choices.

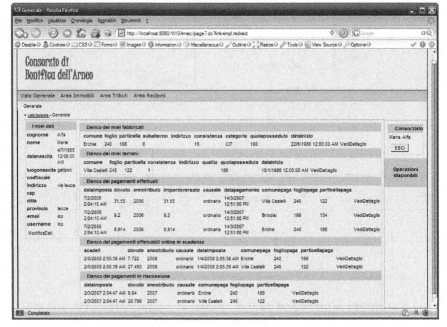

Fig. 7. A screenshot of the Web Application supporting the notice issue process.

5. Conclusions and further works

The interdisciplinary experience of CBA project has promoted the institutional, normative and organizational learning process. In this e-government experience CBA has not been "buyer of innovation", but "author and actor of institutional innovation" in the normative and informative scenario of technology usage. So, instead of bearing the increase of knowledge, learning, discipline and adaptation costs, the CBA finds out the relativity of the e-government impact in an ongoing transforming context, like the Constitutional Italian one, and, in the specific sample of local taxation, it combines innovation and the reconstruction of trust in the relationship with citizens, on the ground of information circulation and availability. The results concern

The definition of clear lexicon and semantic in the regulations with taxpayer's relationship

Positive financial benefits without additional costs

The elimination of unwanted effects, like fiscal trial

- The main advantages perceived by CBA's board have been:
- learning by doing for employees involved in the project, and knowledge transfer from the project team to the rest of employees;

- better aptitude to innovation;
- savings and reorganization of local taxation.

We are planning to extend the empirical validation of the model and the tools in order to tune and customize them to different contexts and sizes. Moreover this experience of holistic model can be extended from the local taxation to other functions in the LPA, having already verified the citizens' goodwill to pay according to indicators of regulation and reorganization of informative processes.

6. References

1. Lenk k., Traunmüller R., Electronic Government: Where Are We Heading?, in Traunmüller R., Lenk K. (Eds), EGOV 2002, LNCS 2456, pp. 1-9, 2002, Springer-Verlag, Heidelberg 2002.
2. UWA (Ubiquitous Web Applications) Project: http://www.uwaproject.org.
3. Bochicchio M. A., Longo A.: "An Effective Approach to Reduce the "Avalanche Effect" in the Management of Fiscal Data in Local Public Administration. ICSM 2002: 560- 567
4. Bochicchio M., Longo A.: "Data Cleansing for Fiscal Services: the Taviano Project", in ICEIS 2003, Angers, April 2003
5. Ministero dell'Interno, *Analisi Gestionale e Finanziaria degli Enti Locali* (Ufficio Studi della Direzione Centrale della Finanza Locale), Settembre 2002.
6. Graham G.A., *Regulatory Administration*, in Graham G.A., Reining jr. H.F. (eds.), *Regulatory administration*, Wiley and Sons, New York, 1943, 16
7. Dipartimento della Funzione Pubblica, *Proposte per il cambiamento nelle pubbliche amministrazioni*, Rubettino, Soveria Mannelli, 2002
8. OECD, Regulatory quality and public sector reform, Puma/reg (97), 1, Paris, 1997
9. Salmon P., *Decentralization as an Incentive Scheme*, in Oxford Review of Economic Policy, vol. 3, n. 2, 1987, pp. 24-43
10. Morgan G. *Images*, Trad. italiana, Franco Angeli, Milano. 1995
11. Giarda P., Le regole del federalismo fiscale nell'articolo 119: un economista di fronte alal nuova Costituzione, JEL Classification. H7, Working Papers No. 115/2001, Jan. 2002, 11
12. Natalini A., *Le semplificazioni amministrative*, Il Mulino, Bologna, 2002
13. Bochicchio M. A., Longo A., UWA+: bridging Web systems design and Business process modeling, workshop on "Hypermedia Development & Web Engineering Principles and Techniques: Put   them   in   use.",   HT04, http://www.ht04.org/workshops/WebEngineering/HT04WE_Bochicchio.pdf
14. A. Longo, M. Bochicchio, M. Carducci, "Reducing Normative and Informative Asymmetries In Fiscal Management for Local Administration", in "Digital Communities in a Networked Society e-Commerce, e-Business and e-Government", Ed. R. Suomi, C. Passos, M. Mendes, Kluwier Academic Publishers ISBN 1-4020-7795-5, pp. 13-24.

Reengineering Lead to Cash - Process and Organization

Giorgio Rimini[1], Paolo Roberti[2]

[1]British Telecom, Italy, Giorgio.rimini@bt.com

[2]Business Integration Partners, Italy, Paolo.Roberti@mail-bip.com

Abstract: In the last few years, BT Italy has recorded an important business growth, which has led to a high complexity and a request to improve governance of fulfilment process. This paper presents the BT Italy case study of reengineering the Lead to Cash business processes to reduce time to market and improve customer's satisfaction. The operational levers applied to realize project objectives are business process reengineering, organizational review and tools enhancement. In the process reengineering "Performing process methodology" and Higo framework have been applied. The first part of the paper presents the BT scenario, the second part describes the process reengineering and the organizational interventions. The last paragraph presents the expected benefits and the conclusion of the case study.

Keywords: Business Process reengineering, Centralization of customer request, Business Process Management

1 Introduction

Since last years, the Italian Telecommunication Industry has experienced a growing competition rate. Acquiring a new customer and retaining an existing one is more challenging than before. Operators need to have lean-and-customer-oriented processes to build a competitive advantage.

This paper presents the case study of BT Italy, which has reengineered the Lead to Cash business process to reduce time to market and improve customer's satisfaction. The lead-to-cash process goes from initial contact, to sale, to service delivery, to payment collection. Lead-to-Cash represents in Telecommunication market one of the most significant areas to build customer satisfaction and to acquire competitiveness. Given these conditions, competition is in the way services are produced and delivered rather than in the nature of the service itself. The first paragraph describes the BT Italy as-is scenario, the second illustrates the

Please use the following format when citing this chapter:

Rimini, G. and Roberti, P., 2008, in IFIP International Federation for Information Processing, Volume 280; *E-Government; ICT Professionalism and Competences; Service Science*; Antonino Mazzeo, Roberto Bellini, Gianmario Motta; (Boston: Springer), pp. 219–226.

business process reengineering intervention, and the third presents expected benefits and conclusions.

2. Framework

Service competitiveness is based on process level of performances. In the modern management theory, a process is competitive if it is more profitable, delivers a better quality and service than other ones. In this sense, engineering of service processes represent a critical success factor. A competitive service process should also be sustainable. A process is sustainable if it can maintain competitive performances over time. To be sustainable process performances should be acceptable to the process stakeholder communities. Process stakeholders and performance measurement are integrated in a conceptual grid called Higo[R] [5, 6] that considers performances not only for managers and customers but also for workers. In BT Italy case, Higo concepts have been used to improve lead-to-cash processes in a performing conception. "Performing process methodology" has been applied in this case study and it has been articulated in the following phases:

1. Define process performance
2. Model process flow
3. Design process cockpits

All stakeholders have been involved in the project activities with interviews, analysis etc. People at all levels of organization (operator, manager and director) contributed to the project, with a strong commitment of the CEO and Top Management.

The process reengineering focused on interventions which implied significant outcomes in terms of swiftness of execution and adaptability to existing context, in order to rapidly improve competitiveness and assure sustainability in a long term vision.

3. BT Italy scenario

BT Italy is a major provider in Italy of data, voice and internet services to corporate customers. The competitive advantage has been guaranteed by BT capacity of providing customized solutions to its customers. High-customized offers entail low standardization of processes and increasing degrees of complexity, hardly compatible with an efficient industrialized approach. For those reasons, two-parallel chains have been implemented to activate services: customized chain, for complex products; and standardized. The business growth has led to a high complexity and a complex governance of the lead to cash processes, which have reached industrial volumes but kept craft made processes and product catalogues.

In the last years, several projects had taken place. Nevertheless, they brought mainly limited results due to the focus more on tools than processes, and to the use of approaches that considered top management's views of the problem without a check on operational activities. Therefore, a further initiative started on May 2007. This project, namely Eleven, was run by the support of Business Integration Partners, a consulting firm.

4 The project "Eleven"

The project "Eleven" started on May 2007 with the following objectives:

- Reduce time to market and optimize quality in order to offer a wide range of service customized into comprehensive solutions that exactly fits to customer needs
- Increase operational efficiency and focalize sales team on customer relations and acquisition of new market share.

- "Eleven" is composed by the following steps:

- **Step 1,** focused on diagnosis of the main critical situation and to produce a master plan of the intervention required
- **Step 2,** focused on engineering the to-be solution.

The duration of the project was about 8 months.

The operational levers applied to realize project objectives were: business process reengineering, organizational review and tools enhancement.

Eleven Step 1

The first phase aimed to analyze the as-is scenario by designing all processes, identifying and prioritizing issues, defining intervention areas and plan.

Supported by the lesson learned from previous experiences, it has been considered both Top Management and Business Operators' point of views. A lot of effort was spent to verify continuously the impact of some top-down decisions to the daily operations. More than 100 interviews were done with directors, managers and operators. More than 50 employees contributed actively to it.

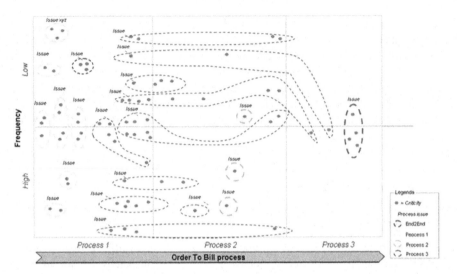

Fig.1. Main issues diagram

Eleven Step 2

The second phase has mainly developed the following streams:

- *Business Process Reengineering*: focalized on *lead to cash* processes which ranges from customer's contract signature to customer's service delivery (*translate order contract*)
- *Information heritage:* order content standardization in terms of owner, utilization of data and tracking form
- *Organizational Review:* creation of a new organizational structure and formalization of the operational responsibilities of single actors involved
- *Business Process Monitoring*: implementation of a monitoring tool to measure process performance

Evolutionary Model

In order to realize project objectives and to guarantee an overall vision of the change roadmap, it has been created a reference Order Management model to be built in BT Italy.

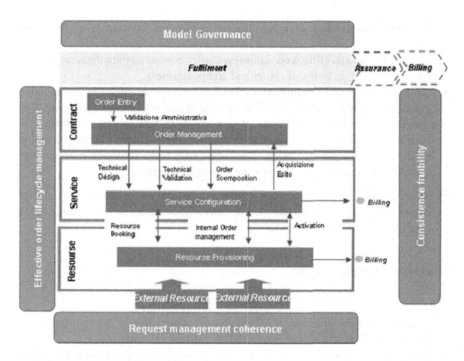

Fig.2. Evolutionary Model

The evolution is delivered by a two-stage approach:

Stage 1: the main focus is processes and organization. In this phase we minimized the impact on IT systems to facilitate the changes adoptions;

Stage 2 the main focus is enhancing IT systems to support activities, to tune processes and to develop a structured order management model based on a workflow management system

Eleven step 2 is aimed to realize evolution stage 1 in terms of processes and organizational intervention.

Business Process Reengineering

The BPR was focused on customized delivery chain and it has provided punctual intervention to the standardized chain for all customer segments.

The customized delivery chain is referred to non-standard product and presented the most significant problems and the principal margin of optimization in terms of efficiency and effectiveness.

The key-elements that have driven BPR are described below:

- **Centralization of customer request:** operational process oriented to the customer total request instead of single product order

- **Structured Activities:** improvement of operational efficiency of the order lifecycle
- **Information availability and solidness**: order content standardization in each phase of process in terms of owner and compulsoriness
- **Parallelizability and simplification**: manual activities automation and deletion of duplication by a deep review of order content and information supplying flow
- **Process Governance**: definition of a new organizational unit dedicated to *Translate Order Contract* process management and punctual tracking of timing and owner of process execution. Translate Order Contract is the process from customer's contract signature to the beginning of contract delivery.

For every single key element, specific interventions have been defined in terms of processes, organization and systems. The intervention brings synergy to the Stage 1 of the Order Management Model.

Organizational Intervention

The most relevant needs in terms of organization were:

- Creation of a new structure, the TOC Room, responsible of the translate order contract activities and able to guarantee the process governance
- Definition of a specialist unit, the *Low Level Design Group,* responsible of low level design customer solution for non standard complex product

Toc Room

The new solution governance is guaranteed by the creation of an organizational unit responsible of the translation of contract in clean orders workable by delivery units. The new structure implies an overall simplification of the as-is scenario, in which the TOC activities were fragmented on 4 different divisions in a best effort approach.

The significant novelty of this intervention consists in the assignment of the punctual responsibility of the Translate Order Contract activities in terms of timing and quality.

Toc Room positioning has been defined balancing need to create synergy with sales division and the requirement of independency of the new structure that would have been able to coordinate sales and delivery activities on customer orders.

The organizational microstructure has been defined by activities classification in terms of required level of responsibility and standardization level.

The TOC Room dimension has been defined in the hypothesis of three in sourcing levels to guarantee a high level of quality, cost control and acceptable timing.

Low Level Design Group

One of the most relevant problem in the as-is scenario was the gap of responsibility in customer solution low level design

This gap implied recycle and partial overlapping of activities and also the increase of time to market.

The Eleven project has defined:

- A task force responsible of this activities
- Engagement rules to involve the LLD Group
- Low level design scope and content
- Dimension and positioning.

Business Process Monitoring

In order to achieve the governability objectives Eleven has developed a performance measurement framework. The BT Italy model is based on HIGO framework. It is based on four performance classes: Time, Quality, Volumes and Economics.

Time: It groups all indicators measuring the time by which activities are completed

Quality: This class monitors the quality of the main activities, suck as order that cannot be completed.

Volumes: This class monitors the volumes of orders either work-in-progress or completed

Economics: This class monitors the immobilized amount of money behind work-in-progress orders or order that cannot be completed.

The model is based on a hierarchy of indicators to allow multi-level analysis from the end-to-end process to the critical activities to be monitored. We have allowed both high level (Top Managers) and operational level (team players manager) monitoring.

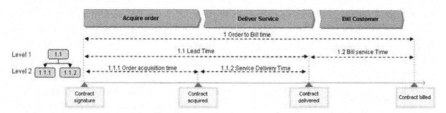

Fig.3. KPIs hierarchy

The figure above shows an example of hierarchy for KPIs of the class Time. We have broken the main process down into activities which are critical to the business performance. Each activity is uniquely associated to an organizational structure. In this way we have been able to measure the players' contribution to the overall process performance.

The model has been developed in a web-based dashboard that allows BT Italy to measure and monitor the order to bill process.

5 Conclusions

The project Eleven is perceived by BT Italy as a successful business process reengineering. The applied methodology and the shared approach have facilitated a spread consensus among employees, which have contributed proactively to project activities.

Main success factors have been:

Collaborative approach, which has led all key players to actively participate on the solution definition, and to share improvement logics and operational choices.

Pragmatism and quick-wins focus, which have led to a wide perception of the project as an effective vehicle to improve operational activities.

Synergic combination of levers, such as organization, processes and tools, to identify the most effective solution matching the evolving needs of the context.

The intervention is expected to improve the process performance by reducing the lead time of the lead to cash chain, increasing operating efficiency and reduce manual activities.

References

1. Bartezzaghi E., Dove va il BPR?, Mondo Digitale, n.2, pp. 27-49, 2002
2. Davenport T.H., The Coming Commmoditization of Processes, Harvard Business Review, June 2005
3. Davenport T.H., Mission Critical: Realizing the Promise of Enterprise Systems, 2000
4. Henry Mintzberg, La progettazione organizzativa, Il Mulino, Bologna, 1996
5. Longo A., Motta G., Designing Business Process for sustainable performance: a model and a method, Business Process Design Workshop, 3d International Conference on Business Process Management, Nancy 5-7 September 2005
6. Motta G., Pignatelli G., Competitività e sostenibilità dei processi gestionali, AICA, Milan, 2007
7. Klein M., Herman G.A., Lee J., O'Donnel E., Malone T.H., "Inventing new business process using a process repository", in Malone T.H., Crowston K., Herman G.A., *Organizing Business Knowledge - the MIT process handbook*, The MIT press, Cambridge Ma., 2003
8. Enhanced Telecom Operation Model (eTOM) The Business Process Framework for the Information and Communication Service Industry, TeleManagement Forum, November 2005
9. Parmenter D., Key Performance Indicators: Developing, Implementing,and Using Winning KPIs, John Wiley & Sons, New Jersey, March 2007.

Business Process Monitoring: BT Italy case study

Giorgio Rimini[1], Paolo Roberti[2]

[1]British Telecom, Italy, Giorgio.rimini@bt.com

[2]Business Integration Partners, Italy, Paolo.Roberti@mail-bip.com

Abstract: This paper presents the case study of BT Italy, which has implemented a performance dashboard to monitor business processes to deliver customer services. Top Management had a punctual view of the business processes, performance, such as Order Acquisition, Order delivery. Nevertheless, it wanted to enhance the end-to-end view to take actions improving the customer experience and reducing the lead time. The project objective has been to build a model to monitor the performance of customer services business processes, such as from customer's service request to service delivery and bill. Higo has been the main framework to define and select key performance indicators. The first part of the paper presents the BT scenario, the second part describes the performance monitoring model and the performance dashboard. The last paragraph presents the expected benefits and the conclusion of the case study.

Keywords: Business Process Management, Key Performance Indicators, Performance dashboard, Higo.

1. Introduction

Competition in the Italian Telco industry is getting stronger. Operators are struggling to acquire new customers and retain existing ones. It is crucial to design business processes to improve the customer experience and to increase revenue productivity. Moreover, Top Management must be able to monitor timely business processes performance and take necessary actions to steer business results.

This paper presents the case study of BT Italy, which has implemented a performance dashboard to monitor business processes to deliver customer services. The first part of the paper presents BT's scenario, the second part describes the performance monitoring model and the performance dashboard. The last paragraph presents the conclusion of the case study.

Please use the following format when citing this chapter:

Rimini, G. and Roberti, P., 2008, in IFIP International Federation for Information Processing, Volume 280; *E-Government; ICT Professionalism and Competences; Service Science*; Antonino Mazzeo, Roberto Bellini, Gianmario Motta; (Boston: Springer), pp. 227–234.

2. Framework

As competition gets stronger, companies struggle to maintain business competitiveness. Management theory suggests that business competitiveness does not come only from pure financial performances, but from a combination of financial, quality and service performance. Performance needs to take in account all company stakeholders, which Edward Freeman defines "Those groups without whose support the organization would cease to exist".

Motta suggests trough the Higo grid to consider the point of view of the three stakeholders: Management, Customer and Worker. This grid fits BT Italy needs to monitor performance better than the Balanced Scorecard which considers mainly the management's point of view.

Below is represented an example of the Higo grid.

	Cost	Flexibility & speed	Quality & satisfaction
Manager	1. Production unit cost 2. Productivity 3. Usage / workload	1. Process duration 2. Activity timeliness 3. Resource flexiblity	1. Spec conformity of service and products 2. Technology dependability
Customer	1. Customer access / acquisition unit cost 2. Customer use cost	1. Response time 2. Response timeliness 3. Vendor flexiblity	1. Expectation conformity of the service 2. Service dependability 3. Customer satisfaction
Worker	1. Execution unit cost 2. Preparation effort	1. Technology response time 2. Technology timeliness 3. Activity & technology flexibility	1. Expectation conformity of work / work environment 2. Technology dependability 3. Employee satisfaction

Fig. 1. Higo Grid

Parmenter (2007) suggest a 12-step model to select and implement KPIs:

1. Senior Team Management commitment
2. Establishing a "winning KPI" project team
3. Establishing a "just do it" culture
4. Setting a holistic KPI development strategy
5. Marketing KPI system
6. Identify organization-wide critical success factors
7. Recording a performance measures in a database
8. Selecting team-level performance measure

9.   Selecting organizational winning KPIs
10. Developing the reporting frameworks at all levels
11. Facilitate the use of winning KPIs
12. Refining KPIs to maintain their relevance

Together Higo grid and the 12-step model have been used to implement a successful performance Dashboard. The following paragraphs present the way these models have been applied to BT Italy context.

3. BT scenario

Since 1995, BT Italy has been a major provider in Italy of data, voice and internet services to corporate customers. Historically it has provided tailored solutions to its customers. Moreover it has been offering a wide product bouquet to create a high value proposition. The company organization reflected the effort to be closer to the customer with six business units facing different customer segments.

Several initiatives took place to improve business processes performance. Top Management had a punctual view of the business processes performance, such as Order Acquisition, Order delivery. Nevertheless, it wanted to enhance end-to-end view to take actions improving the customer experience and reducing the lead time. Therefore, supported by the consulting firm Business Integration Partners, BT Italy started a challenging reengineering project, namely "Eleven", that encompassed all the company and aimed to innovate the way services were delivered and monitored.

4 The business performance monitoring model

The project objective has been to build a model to monitor the performance of customer services business processes, such as from customer's service request to service delivery and bill. For that reason it was important to monitor both completed and work-in-progress orders. In this way management could not only analyze business process performance but also take timely actions impacting on-going orders. Therefore, the model considers the following classes: Time, Quality, Volumes and Economics. The former two classes aim monitoring the lead time and the quality of each activity of the processes. The remaining two classes monitor the work-in-progress orders and the revenues on the Fiscal Year embedded into orders fulfilment. Time and quality classes are calculated for all completed order within a certain period of time. In this way it is possible to break an end-to-end lead time into the lead time of the activities which compose them. Indeed, Volumes and Economics classes are calculated for all work-in-progress orders at the maximum date of a certain period of time. Unlike HIGO, the model does not monitor the costs related to the process, mainly FTEs (Full Time Equivalent) and fixed costs, but the revenues immobilized into work-in-progress orders. By knowing the revenues on the fiscal year of these orders, the Top Management can better prioritize actions. Such as, pushing orders that worth the most.

As Parmenter recommends, the model aims giving both a high level and operational level views of the process performance. These depend on the user's level, which could be either a top manager or a process team member. Therefore, we have created a hierarchy of indicators allowing multi-level analysis ranging from the end-to-end process to the critical activities to be monitored.

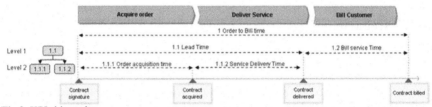

Fig.2. KPIs hierarchy

The figure above shows an example of hierarchy for KPIs of the class Time. The main process has been broken down into activities which are critical to the business performance. Each activity is uniquely associated to an organizational structure. In this way it is possible to measure each process player's contribution to the overall process performance.

Below are shown the drivers to select indicators:

- Relevance to the customer
- Relevance to the Top Management
- Availability of needed data to calculate the indicator. In this way it has been minimized the impact on the current IT systems of BT Italy.

The latter but not the least driver has been the feedback from future users. More than fifty one-to-one meetings were held to share the model with both the top management and the main team managers. The model considers the performance monitoring needs of different business unit directors. In this way it has gained a spread consensus.

The model includes a total of 68 indicators divided into three levels (18 are first level indicators). Below are shown some indicators:

Table.1. KPI

Time	Quality	Volumes	Economics
• Order to Bill time • % of delivered-on-time orders • Order to delivery time	• % of delivered orders without de-validation • # of de-validations • # undeliverable orders	• # of work-in-progress orders • # of work-in-progress-and-late orders	• Total Revenues on the fiscal year • Total revenues on the FY on process X

The model adds further information to some indicators, such as aging, process phase, and responsibility. Therefore, the user can make specific orders' analysis. For example, work-in-progress orders that are more than 90 days late, revenues immobilized in orders of phase 1 or in undeliverable order due to client's responsibility. Since there are different processes depending on products category, there are indicators measuring the same performance but with different calculation formulas.

5. The performance dashboard

The objective was to provide a user friendly interface with the following features:
- Allowing at-first-sight performance analysis. Top managers wanted to have all information they need to figure out the process performance. This just in a web page without scrolling;
- Allowing targeted analysis. Users should be able to analyze process performance by measuring indicators for specific dimensions. Such has clients, products, etc;

- Supporting management decision making. Managers should be able to identify orders with the worst performance. Moreover they should know whom to contact to deal with;
- Allowing users to drill indicators down to specific orders or to the next hierarchical level.

Within a period of three months, a web-based application has been delivered. It allows measuring and monitoring the indicators defined on the model described above. The same sharing approach as for the model was applied. Therefore, the dashboard is a result of several one-to-one meetings with directors and process owners. There are no access profiles. So, all users from different business units see the same indicators. Hence, every manager is aware of the contribution to the overall process.

The dashboard home page has four sections, one for each performance class indicator. The sections fit into the PC screen without scrolling. Also it shows the relevant indicators and other information, such as trends, to monitor process performance. To make the monitoring as visual as possible, we used objects such as tachymeter and charts, mainly bar and pie charts. Tachymeters have red or green areas. By looking at the area colour, the user can immediately understand whether the performance is negative or positive. Others indicators are represented with charts. For example, volumes of work-in-progress orders are represented trough a pie chart. Its slices show the volumes of the three main sub-process of the Order To Bill process. In this way user can immediately understand which the overloaded sub-process is.

To facilitate performance analysis and decision making, all these objects are mouse-scroll-over sensitive. By clicking on a specific bar or pie slice, the user can open a report showing only orders behind the selected object part. In this way, users can immediately focus their analysis on specific indicators value. For example, they can monitor the aging of late orders (which is represented by a bar charts with 5 age ranges) and analyze orders that are more the 90 days late.

The way users can see indicators and drill them down to next indicator's hierarchy it is similar to web site navigation. At the head of each page there is a bar with all the dimensions that the user can select to make a targeted analysis. Every time it is possible to visualize selected indicators filtering by one or more dimensions. To meet different business unit directors' needs without creating different profiles, the following analysis dimensions have been implemented: period of time (from, to), client, product name, product category, order type (new, modify, etc), business unit. For example, business unit director can monitor the performance of its business unit by selecting it by a drop-down list.

The selected software to develop the dashboard has been Pentaho suite, which is an open source application. It better fits all the project needs that can be summarized by the following drivers:

- Low license costs. It has no license costs.
- Low impact on current systems architecture. It does not need a complex integration with source systems.

- Availability of "*off the shelf*" features (reporting and KPIs analysis). It has rich libraries of graphical objects and reports to better show indicators.
- Short Time to Delivery. The Dashboard has been delivered in three months including a tuning phase in which some new features had been added.

Below is represented the application architecture:

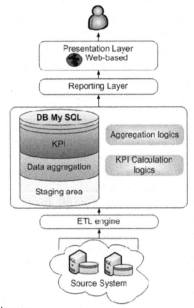

Fig. 3. Monitoring tool architecture

The dashboard is integrated with two source systems. It receives data that are loaded by an ETL engine. An OLAP application calculates indicators that are shown through a web-based application, which is accessible within BT intranet.

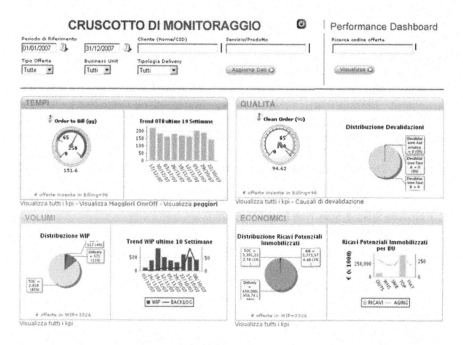

Fig. 4. Performance dashboard home page

The figure above shows the tool home page which allows monitoring the performance of the main indicators for each class.

6 Conclusions

HIGO framework had been useful to define and select KPIs to monitor business processes of BT Italy. By making some adjustments it has allowed the definition of several indicator which BT Italy is monitoring trough a user friendly interface. The deployed performance dashboard helps both top and operational managers to monitor performance and take day-by-day action to improve customer experience. In the future, BT Italy wishes to extend the performance monitoring to the moment the customer has the first touch point with BT and to the moment BT receives the payment from the customer.

References

1. Inform-IT, Foundations of IT Service Management Based on ITIL® V3, Jayne Wilkinson, September 2007
2. Kaplan R. S., Norton D.P., Balanced Scorecard, Harvard Business School Press, Boston, Ma, 1996
3. Kaplan R. S., Norton D.P., The Balanced Scorecard - Measures that Drive Performance Kaplan e Norton, Harvard Business Review,1992
4. Longo A., Motta G., "Designing Business Process for sustainable performance: a model and a method", Business Process Design Workshop, 3d International Conference on Business Process Management, Nancy 5-7 September 2005
5. Motta G., "Il metodo dei KPI" in Bracchi G., Francalanci C., Sistemi Informativi e impresa digitale, McGrawHill, Milano 2005
6. Motta G., Pignatelli G., Competitività e sostenibilità dei processi gestionali, AICA, Milan, 2007
7. Parmenter D., Key Performance Indicators: Developing, Implementing, and Using Wining KPIs, John Wiley & Sons, New Jersey, March 2007.

Dealing with Availability in an international Service Management scenario

Flavio Gaj[1], **Giovanni Umberto Germani**[2]

[1] Head of ICT Operating Processes & Quality of UniCredit S.p.A, Milan, Italy
[2] Department of Computer Engineering and Systems Science, University of Pavia, Italy

Abstract: In today's global economy context, since companies rely heavily on their information systems to delivery services to their Customers, any downtime can have serious impacts on their business. At the same time, the traditional approach of measuring the availability of only systems and components is no longer sufficient and must give way to a more comprehensive measurement that takes account of the whole service delivery chain. In this paper we present the method used by an international ICT service provider as UniCredit Group, to monitor and improve the availability of its services.

1 Introduction

In today's global economy context, organizations of every kind and in all parts of the world have become increasingly dependent on their IT systems. E-commerce made it possible to conduct business 24 hours a day, 7 days a week. New, powerful applications allow businesses and institutions to introduce unprecedented levels of computerization into their daily operations, to the point that nowadays we all depend on reliable access to computer systems at all times.

This need has dramatically increased the importance of systems availability. Since companies and organizations rely heavily on computer systems to conduct their business, any downtime can seriously cripple their business. More than just lost productivity, downtime has come to mean lost revenues and even weakened market position. At the very least, IT downtime can severely impact a business' operations and increase cost enormously.

Availability means that a system is on-line and ready for access [1]. A variety of factors can take a system off-line, ranging from planned downtime for maintenance to catastrophic failure. The goals of high availability solutions are to minimize this downtime and/or to minimize the time needed to recover from an outage. Exactly how much downtime can be tolerated will dictate the comprehensiveness, complexity and cost of the solution.

High availability is a convenient label, but its meaning is often misunderstood. High availability is not a specific technology nor a quantifiable attribute. Rather, it

Please use the following format when citing this chapter:

Gaj, F. and Germani, G.U., 2008, in IFIP International Federation for Information Processing, Volume 280; *E-Government; ICT Professionalism and Competences; Service Science*; Antonino Mazzeo, Roberto Bellini, Gianmario Motta; (Boston: Springer), pp. 235–244.

is a goal to be reached, one that has different meanings according to need. A variety of strategies, technologies and services are used to accomplish that goal.

Following the new trend which sees the transition to a Service Oriented Economy [2], the simple concept of availability of IT systems (the accessibility of a system resource in a timely manner, i.e. the measurement of a system's uptime) is no longer sufficient and should be extended to a wider concept of *Services Availability*.

2. Approaching Service Availability

Let *UT* be the Up-Time, i.e. the time interval in which the service[1] is running in the desired Operating Window *OW*, then in its most elementary form, service availability *A* is defined as:

$$A = \frac{UT}{OW} \times 100 \tag{1}$$

In assessing service availability in a real, complex ICT scenario, the designer has to find the right balance between:
- Costs of measures.
- The significance of the parameters.
- The effectiveness of the measure as a mean of communication between Customers and Supplier, and as an analysis tool of downtimes aimed at improving the service quality.

A first element of complexity is due to the fact that sometimes an incident may impact only a portion of a service, causing the temporary unavailability of some features, while others remain usable by the Customer. In these circumstances, the designer must face one of the following alternatives:
1. Define as a "Service" each atomic set of functionalities, and measure the availability for each of them (at the most detailed level, the single physical transaction).
2. Define as a "Service" a comprehensive set of functionalities, and weigh the downtime of a limited portion of functionalities with a corrective factor ranging from 0 to 1.

The pros and cons of the two solutions are self-explanatory. In the first case the associated costs may be high, but the information is so detailed and analytic that no misunderstanding may arise. In the second case the costs are lower, (the indicator is only one), but the algorithm may lead to conclusions that someone

---

[1] In defining what a Service is, we embraced an "end-to-end approach", looking at services as Customers do. [3]

may consider to be arbitrary. Our method follows the middle road between these two approaches, as explained in next section.

3 Measuring Service Availability in a Complex Context

In measuring service availability, we use a granularity which takes into consideration a comprehensive and exhaustive set of functionalities, without descending to the level of detail of single transactions. Furthermore, we choose a set of functionalities that has the ability to be significant for the main counterpart (the Customer).

In our model each Service is split into the relative SubServices, in turn divided into a set of Components. A weight is assigned to each SubService/Component, modeling its importance compared to the Service/SubService to which it belongs.

Table 1. An example of Service breakdown structure

SERVICE	SUBSERVICE	SUBSERVICE COMPONENT	COMPONENT WEIGHT vs SUBSERVICE	SUBSERVICE WEIGHT vs SERVICE
				100
			100	
		Cash pooling	5	
		Conditions	15	
		Current Accounts	40	
	Deposit and Current Accounts	Customer documents	5	20
		Printing of statements and communication to the customer	15	
		Saving Accounts	10	
Current Accounts and Deposit		Teller/Relationship manager to do list	10	
			100	
	Other component	Archive of Teller's journal	40	20
		Suspended items	60	
	Safe boxes		100	20
		Safe Boxes	100	
	Transfer Payments, Collection		100	20
		Cheques	100	
	Corona		100	20
		Nostro/Loro Accounts Reconciliation	100	

When an incident occurs, the following data are collected:
- Start/End time (*Duration*)
- Incident cause (code/sub-code, for eventual analysis)
- Incident Description
- Service/SubService/SubService Component impacted
- Weight for each SubService Component

Let i be the number of incidents happened into the Operating Window OW, then the daily availability A is:

$$A = \frac{OW - \sum_1^i Duration_i \times SSWeight_i \times SSCWeight_i}{OW} \qquad (2)$$

where *SSWeight* represents the weight of the SubService vs Service and *SSCWeight* is the weight of the SubService Component vs SubService.

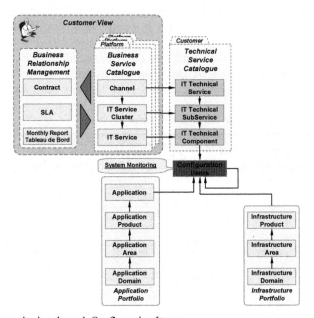

Fig. 1. Service monitoring through Configuration Items

Our approach provides a continuous monitoring of the service status through the use of Configuration Items. A Configuration Item (CI) is a component (IT Infrastructure element) that can be handled individually (i.e. computers, routers, servers, software...) [3]; furthermore, for each component we consider two reliability parameters, well known in the manufacturing industry and literature: MTBF and MTTR[2] [4].

A service is up and running if a number of CIs are up and running together and simultaneously. The number of CIs for complex services may be very high (20-30

---

[2] For the purpose of this document we define MTTR as the whole time needed to manage the incident, including factors that do not belong to the classic definition of MTTR, such as: the way in which the fault is detected, the contractual agreement with the servicing contractor; furthermore we consider any eventual set-up time necessary after the restoring of the device (*Tsetup*).

elements, depending on the level of details of the analysis). We will define this ensemble of components *Service Chain*. The service chain has to be entirely up and running to be able to deliver the whole service.

When dealing with service availability, a common objection is that the problem does not exist because a proper architecture is redundant, and a fault results in the takeover of the redundant component without service downtime.

This is generally true. It is also true; however, that in our experience the occurrence of hardware faults has a very low probability. When they seldom happen, if the redundancy works properly and the switching mechanisms are efficient, the faulty component is isolated and the operation goes on based on the redundant component. They are formally recorded for statistical reasons, but the down-time is set to zero, as they don't impact the continuity of the service. Sometimes the eventual operation to restore the faulty component may jeopardize the Service, although these operations are scheduled (whenever possible) outside the operating window. If a downtime is required or caused, the event is recorded as a fault.

On the other side, software and microcode faults have a dramatically higher probability of occurrence. In these cases obviously the redundancy does not work. The software/firmware controls virtually every functionality at the most detailed level of IT devices, with millions and millions of Lines of Code (LOCs) in any business environment of medium or even low complexity. From a purely theoretical point of view, software errors should decrease over time, because an error, once happened and correctly fixed, does not happen again: this is true. Nevertheless, IT industry is very dynamic and the never-ending innovation and increasing competition push vendors to launch on the market new products, new versions and new releases in more and more smaller time intervals. These bring to the users new functionalities and opportunities, but also new bugs. It is the common opinion that this trend will increase in the next coming years. [5]

For these reasons, it is reasonable, although not fully theoretically correct, to use MTBF and MTTR as parameters representing software reliability. Based on the above assumptions, the theoretic availability *ATring* of a single ring of the service chain is:

$$ATring = \left(1 - \frac{MTTR_{\min} + Tsetup_{\min}}{MTBF_{year} \times 365 \times 24 \times 60}\right) \times 100 \tag{3}$$

The formula is related to operating window "24x7", but in reality the *OW* may be narrower and we may face different situations. Let's define *AEmx* as the resulting effective maximum availability in different hypothesis.

1. The fault probability is fully random vs operating window. In this case the downtime is proportional to operating window.
2. The faults happen only in the operating window. The whole downtime calculated for the window 24x7 falls in a shorter window, so decreasing the resulting availability.

We experienced that some faults are really random (e.g. power supply failure), while other are for sure depending on the fact that the devices are really working. These second type of faults more likely fall in the operating window. Let $ATmx$ be the theoretical maximum availability of the service chain considering faults as random events, then the effective maximum availability may be calculated by following formula:

$$AEmx = \frac{OW_{year} - ((1 - ATmx) \times 365 \times 24 \times 60) \times Percentage_{OW}}{OW_{year}} \qquad (4)$$

where $Percentage_{OW}$ represents the estimation of the percentage of the faults assumed to fall within the operating window. The table below shows the resulting availability in some hypothesis of percentage of faults falling into operating window, in some of the more significant operating windows (we consider the service chain of a typical Web application, with an estimated $ATmx$ of 99,1914%). The percentage of faults in window is assumed to be higher as the window is wider. If we assume, for example, 100% in window for Internet Services (20x7), and 40% for Transactions Driven Applications (day window), the expected availability would be round 99%.

This was an example of a very long and complex service chain. Simplifying it and reducing the number of rings can reduce significantly the down times due to infrastructures. Some trends in infrastructure help in reducing the number of rings: for example virtualization allows basing a number of instances on the same processor. Assuming that the MTBF of a more powerful processor complex is the same of smaller processor complex, we reduce the probability to have a hardware failure in the time frame under consideration.

Table 2. Service availability with different $Percentage_{OW}$

Operating Window			Year Window [m]	Percentage of faults in OW					
h/d	d/w	w/y							
1	2	3	4	0%	20%	40%	60%	90%	100%
11	5	52	171.600	100,00%	99,50%	99,01%	98,51%	97,77%	97,52%
20	7	52	436.800	100,00%	99,81%	99,61%	99,42%	99,12%	99,03%
14,5	5	52	226.200	100,00%	99,62%	99,25%	98,87%	98,31%	98,12%
13	5	52	202.800	100,00%	99,58%	99,16%	98,74%	98,11%	97,90%
18	5	52	280.800	100,00%	99,70%	99,39%	99,09%	98,64%	98,49%
13	5	52	202.800	100,00%	99,58%	99,16%	98,74%	98,11%	97,90%
10	5	52	156.000	100,00%	99,46%	98,91%	98,37%	97,55%	97,28%
12	5	52	187.200	100,00%	99,55%	99,09%	98,64%	97,96%	97,73%
24	7	52	524.160	100,00%	99,84%	99,68%	99,51%	99,27%	99,19%

The downtimes due to application software and operational errors can be calculated on a statistical basis as well, based on the expected number of modifications to running systems. Application software and operation error are man-made mistakes; the incidence of mistakes is higher as high is the change rate, both on the application side and the technology side. The fault reasons listed above must be added to the downtimes estimated by the model.

The impact of application software maintenance in a fast changing business environment may be very high. Short time-to-market can be enemy of stability and availability: exhaustive tests should be balanced with time-to-market case by case.

Technology maintenance is another important source of errors. The number of errors is assumed to be a function of the change rate.

The most important areas to be considered are the following:

Hardware maintenance. Often it's necessary to agree windows of downtime to change/upgrade CPUs, disks control units, or to substitute redundant faulty components that can be substituted at a later time (if possible outside the operating windows, but for sure within the window for 24*365 services).

Software microcode maintenance. In many cases the upgrade of microcode and system software requires the stopping of the devices, with a consequent downtime. For services running "round-the-clock" in these cases the daily availability may severely reduced.

Application software maintenance. In same cases the upgrade of business functionalities or the release of new versions compel the stopping of operations for data migration or rebuilding, and sometimes it may be impossible to do that outside the operating window.

4. UniCredit Group Case Study

Ranking among the top financial groups in Europe, UniCredit has banking operations in 23 countries and international network spanning 50 countries, with about 10.000 branches and approximately 180,000 employees at 31 march 2008. Besides Italy, Germany and Austria, UniCredit operates - in the CEE region - the largest international banking network with about 4.000 branches and outlets and about 80,000 employees. The Group operates in the following countries: Azerbaijan, Bosnia and Herzegovina, Bulgaria, Croatia, the Czech Republic, Estonia, Hungary, Latvia, Lithuania, Kazakhstan, Kyrgyzstan, Poland, Romania, Russia, Serbia, Slovakia, Slovenia, Tajikistan, Turkey and Ukraine. The studies and projects regarding availability (both on cultural side and measurement algorithms and tools) started in 2002, and allowed UniCredit Group to manage effectively its very complex international ICT service providing structure.

UniCredit Group Performance 2007

The following are average values of availability in 2007 for the main services UniCredit Group provided to Customers.

Table 3. UniCredit Group service availability performance (2007)

Service Type	Window	Range of Avg % Availability (1)	Note
Large Workload Banks	11 x 5	99,21 - 99,70	Services to Branch Offices. Large Retail banks of the Group.
Small Workload Banks	11 x 5	99,44 – 99,86	Services to Branch Offices. Smaller specialized banks.
Internet services	20 x 7	99,21 – 99,69	Comparable to Branch Offices Services
ATM/POS	24 x 7	99,57 – 99,80	Included planned maintenance.

(1) Included planned outages

The work done over the year in terms of awareness of persons and tools, and the unrelenting improvement in the day by day activities, led us to improve dramatically the level of quality of the service provided to Customers. The following graph represents our history related to Service availability level, and witnesses how our efforts have been rewarded by high level results.

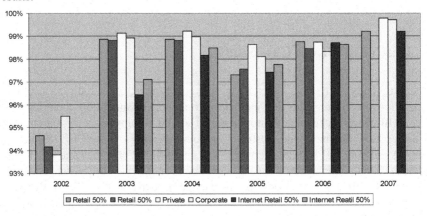

Fig. 2. UniCredit Group service availability trend since 2002

UniCredit Group Positioning

Gartner [6] provide some forecasting and ranking related to availability. We use it as a benchmark for us.

Table 4. UniCredit Group positioning for service availability

Gartner Ranking 2007	Only Unplanned		Planned included		Window	
	h/year	%	h/year	%	h/d	d/w
Best in Class	5	99,94%	12	99,81%	24	7
Outstanding	26	99,70%	50	99,13%	24	7
Very Good	61	99,30%	200	97,02%	24	7
Average (less than)	175	98,00%	250	95,15%	24	7
UniCredit Group						
Retail	UniCredit Group includes Planned downtime.		23	99,21%	11	5
Private			6	99,78%	11	5
Corporate			9	99,70%	11	5
Internet Retail			58	99,21%	20	7

The positioning of Unicredit Group is higher than "Very Good", and in selected services better than "Outstanding".

5. Considerations and Conclusions

The situation described must be a stimulation to adopt and engineer a "continuous improvement" approach.

On one side, to press and to work closely with the supplier to demand a higher products quality. On the other side, to put in place an unrelenting effort to improve application delivery, change management, incident management and problem management processes. The hard reality, in fact, is that in the next coming years a given (possibly high) amount of faults will hit IT Service Providers with growing trends (many devices/products will reach the obsolescence before the maturity and stability). Given that, the ICT management attention must focus on following issues:

1. The structuring and organization (re-engineering) of processes related to: Change Management, Incident Management, Problem Management, Customer/User Communication are the most important critical success factors for an ICT Service Provider in the next coming years. Even though functions are perfects, if the Service is not outstanding the perception of the Customers will be very bad.
2. The technology adoption and upgrade must be carefully evaluated, balancing innovation with technology risks; a "follower" policy in the adoption of new technology can lower risks vs a delay in new products, face to face with an "early adopter" policy that can raise risks vs an earlier market innovation or capacity to process growing traffic volumes. The Customers, i.e. the business should be informed and aware of this balance.
3. The capacity of the organization to face the faults in a proper and timely manner comes not only from structured processes, but mainly from a

"sensitivity/attitude" focused to "recovery the service" (market oriented approach) and not to "solve the problem" (technical approach). Incident should be overcome even with a work-around; definitive solution should come after, opening and managing a problem (asynchronous activities in respect to incident management). In addition, some organizational and procedural actions can help reducing incident duration; in our experience the main areas of improvement are:

- to enable early detection of incidents via probes and monitoring tools;
- to simplify the structure of the service chain (less instances of Operating Systems, Virtualization, …);

- to provide more effective and possibly automatic procedure to 1st level support;
- to provide better procedure for failover of redundant devices;
- to provide more effective restart procedures.

1. The availability percentage, in itself, is meaningless, if not complemented by the approach, the method and the algorithm which it is calculated with. E.g. the old approach of measuring availability of sub-systems and components (mainframe, servers, network…) leads to completely different figures.

2. The availability percentage is aimed, besides being a communication tool to the customers, most of all as a tool to understand what is happening, and to direct the attention of personnel to the most frequent causes of faults. Trends are much more important than the figures itself!

3. At the time being, there are theoretical limits to the target that can be reached; it is important to define them in each own business and operating environment, with the aim to compare the actual performance with reference benchmark. The measure must be focused:

- to improve the ability to react, both for causes "embedded in technology" and in those due to human errors;
- to log and document actions taken, in order to identify possible opportunities for shrinking process times;

- to give elements for technology and organization evolution;
- to acquire and capitalize experience (knowledge management).

References

1. Martin J (1978) Systems Analysis for Data Transmission. Prentice Hall PTR, New York.
2. Sheehan J (2006) Understandig Service Sector Innovation. Communications of the ACM 49, Issue 7:42-49
3. Van Bon J (2007) Foundations of IT Service Management Based on ITIL® V3. Van Haren Publishing
4. Isermann R, Ballé P (1998) Trends in the application of model-based fault detection and diagnosis of technical processes. doi:10.1016/S0967-0661(97)00053-1
5. D'Ambros M, Lanza M (2006) Software Bugs and Evolution: A Visual Approach to Uncover Their Relationship. doi: 10.1109/CSMR.2006.51
6. Scott D (2007) Operation Zero Downtime. Gartner Group report

Service level and Value to Customer as key business drivers: a case studying a leader truck industry

Maximiliano Cascini[1], Manuela Maini[2], Thiago Barroero[3]

[1]Workshop Development Manager, Customer Service, Iveco S.p.a.
maximiliano.cascini@iveco.com

[2]Department of Computer Engineering and Systems Science, University of Pavia, Italy maini.manuela@gmail.com

[3]Department of Computer Engineering and Systems Science University of Pavia, Italy thiagobarroero@gmail.com

Abstract: Since customer satisfaction analysis traditional approaches are out-of-date and do not adequately fit information about customer expectations on services, in this paper we propose a new theoretical approach: the Customer Experience Management. Moreover this paper describes our analysis on the perceived value by customer according to the services that a company supplies. This analysis presents two different approaches: the qualitative and the quantitative one. Therefore we here define innovative way of studying customer satisfaction using both kind of analysis. Basing on the information gathered from the qualitative analysis, we develop a quantitative model to estimate and confirm the causal relations between process Key Performance Indicators. Finally we discuss a case study that demonstrates how we have applied our methodology to a multinational company operating in the automotive industry: Iveco. Specifically the case study focuses on Iveco Customer Service. Our customer value analysis enables management measuring and monitoring return on investments starting from the customer satisfaction and profitability analysis.

Keywords: Service Science, Management and Engineering (SSME), Customer Experience Management (CEM), Value to Customer, Business Intelligence, benchmarking.

1. Introduction

In our service era the value of the service to the customer is a structural driver of business. Therefore we think that a framework that relates the value given to the

Please use the following format when citing this chapter:

Cascini, M., Maini, M. and Barroero, T., 2008, in IFIP International Federation for Information Processing, Volume 280; *E-Government; ICT Professionalism and Competences; Service Science*; Antonino Mazzeo, Roberto Bellini, Gianmario Motta; (Boston: Springer), pp. 245–259.

customer by service operations and the investments and technology spent on developing such service operations should be a key topic in the service science as defined in the well known paper on communication [6]. The value given to customer in service operations is especially critical in those industries where business has a long lasting relation with customers and high loyalty implies higher profitability. This is actually true in durable goods and machinery industries, where the customer care cycle is a structural component of the business and customer frustration may eventually imply churn.

When the business is strongly linked to the value perceived by the customer, as in our case study, tacit knowledge on this value can be considered related to the wishes and expectations that supplier should satisfy. In this case the supplier should understand what is the source of the value perceived by the customer in order to focus investments on it. This view revolutionizes the traditional concept of "Customer Value" and "Customer Satisfaction". Customer value described by a flood of papers is nothing else that the profitability that the customer seen as an asset, generates for the business. Our assumption is that customer value, specifically life time value is nothing else but the end outcome of the ability of the enterprise of satisfying customer expectations. The value perceived by the customers is the cause and life time value is the fact. Similarly, customer satisfaction is a measure that is highly discretionary and might portray what the analyst would like to listen [13,18].

According to this perspective our analysis is based on one of the most innovative approaches on managing customers needs, namely Schmitt's Customer Experience Management (CEM) [19, 20].

CEM suggests new ways of capturing customer satisfaction and loyalty through innovative approaches to the customers and innovative ways of managing information on customers at any level of the organizations. Managing the whole customer experience is the best way for gaining actual satisfaction of customers. CEM implies the ability of enabling feelings of arousal and pleasure in customers. These motivating forces determine purchase choices, which are strongly driven by feelings and not only by material and functional needs of the customers.

2. The analysis framework

The analysis framework includes two analysis stages, respectively qualitative analysis and quantitative analysis.

Qualitative analysis consists of a framework that propose a cause-effect chain that links some input variables (investments) and output variables, that describe customer experience, and finally financial outcomes that describe the business impact of the customer experience.

Quantitative analysis is nothing else than a validation of qualitative analysis. It is based on statistical models that identify and estimate links between variables.

Here below we give a short account of the structure of quantitative and qualitative frameworks.

2.1 Qualitative framework

The qualitative analysis is based on a questionnaire. In this way we have identified KPI (Key Performance Indicators) for each process of the chain. Among the KPI we have focused on those mostly linked to the value perceived by the customer. Every KPI represents different activity supplied by the firm, therefore we have focused on those that enable perceived value to grow up and to outwear. Afterwards we have assumed causal relations between the variables in the chain. For each KPI we have defined metrics, formed by elementary variables, in order to estimate them in the following step of the analysis.

Causal chains are a very innovative approach of representing causal relations between the KPI that describe the activities and the processes of a firm, since they clearly show the directions of the causality. The validity of the information given by the causality chains is strengthened by the numerical results of the Quantitative Model.

Figure 1 represents overall and specific (darker) variables of the service chain.

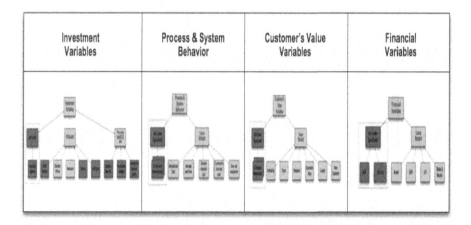

Fig. 1. Customized variables based on the Industry

We here discuss the main features of our case study (trucks):
1. Investment Variables
      HR Educational
      Technology capability

2. Process & System Behavior Variables
        Promise
        TA e TR
        Contact duration
        Customer's incurred cost
3. Customer's value Variables
        Customer's value
        New Customers
        Churn
        Customer Loyalty
        Profitability
4. Financial Variables
        Δ Asset
        Δ LTV
        AGP

Specifically the Value chain in Fig.2. is customized on Iveco after-sale service processes and it represents causal relations between their KPI.

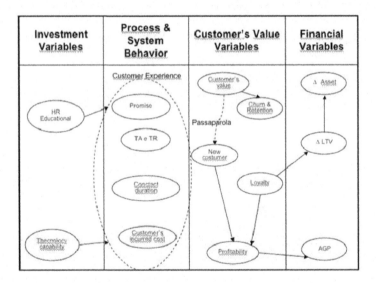

Fig.2. Customized Iveco Value Chain

Starting from this chain quantitative analysis should have to confirm and estimate those causal links that concretely exist and influence the return on the investments that the company has done to capture customer satisfaction and loyalty.

2.2 Quantitative analysis

The quantitative model estimates the causal relations identified by the qualitative analysis.

Interpreting and understanding the quantitative model results from the customer point of view will enable us to affirm which investments really influence customers behaviour and as a result determine rises in customers profitability. Therefore it is clear that such an analysis allows the company to measure return on investments through the analysis of the variables representing customer experience and satisfaction and linking them to the firm supplied activities.

The quantitative model includes two main statistical tools: Granger's causality model [3, 9] and the Latent Variables Structural Equations (LVSE) [21, 23]. These tools have been used in parallel to analyse the historical series of data associated to each variable. The quantitative model is represented in the following Figure 3.

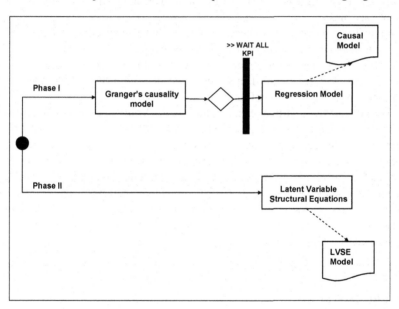

Fig. 3. Quantitative Analysis Model

Granger's causality model has been selected since it greatly deals with time series of data in order to test out whether a causality relation exists between two variables represented through their time series of data. Then we have used the Linear Regression method to estimate the effectiveness of the existing relations [21].

As our main scope, using Granger's causality model [9], we would like to understand if one variable influences an other variable. Especially we are mostly interested in identifying those investment variables that significantly influence the customer perceived value, increasing customer satisfaction. In this way the company can address its investment more accurately toward those activities that boost customer satisfaction.

The analysis methodology makes use of a comparison between the knowledge achieved considering a pair of variables and their relation rather than the piece of information given by each variable individually considered. The strength of the identified relations stands for the capability of a variable to explicate the other one in the pair.

As described our interest is focused on the customer perceived value, which is a variable that cannot be directly observed since it is intangible and immaterial. Whereupon we have introduced also the Latent Variables Structural Equations (LVSE) in the quantitative model [23].

LVSE is a model that allows to study those variables not mentioned in the value chains since they are non-observable but whose influence can be identified analysing their indicators behaviour. Non-observable variables are defined as latent variables.

Value to Customer is the latent variable we have analysed: it is about the value the customers perceive making use of after sales services supplied by Iveco. So, as subsequently deepened, the attention of the study focuses on the Customer Service and the treated series of data come from the Non-Stop Assistance service delivered by Iveco Customer Centre.

The advantages a corporate can gain through "Value to Customer Analysis" are extremely important according to today market dynamics. In fact customers are more and more pretentious and exigent since they can manage lots of information regarding anything they need or they are searching for. Therefore companies need to affected customers. It means that it is not enough thinking only to the supply functional aspects instead companies have to know what are the emotional sides to invest in to render the customer experience extraordinary, unforgettable obtaining customer satisfaction for a longer period measured by the life time value associated to each customer.

3. The case study

Iveco [24] is a multinational company operating in the automotive industry.

Service business accounts the 25% of the whole turnover of the company and it is composed both by Iveco Capital and Customer Service.

Iveco is present with its After Sales Services in America, Europe, Africa and Middle East Asia Pacific with 3.000 service points, 22 spare parts warehouse, 50.000 specialists, 10 millions spare parts orders per year, 300.000 Iveco original spare parts for all the Iveco brands.

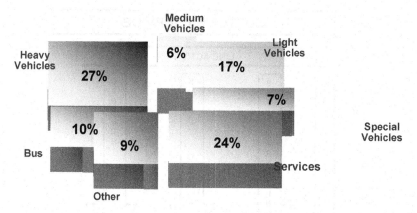

Fig. 4. Iveco Departments

The Iveco "Customer Service" has a network capable of reaching the Iveco customers needs of service all over the world. The Customer Service can be considered as a "company in the company", which is composed both by line activities and staff activities.

Line activities include three main lines:

1. the Sales and marketing line;
2. the Supply Chain line;
3. the Service line.

In general we can say that Sales and marketing and Supply Chain lines deal with spare parts whereas the Service line deals with diagnostic and repair activities.

Firstly we can consider the Sales and marketing line; its scope is to sale original Iveco spare parts, since these parts are the higher guarantee of the brand quality. The sale is driven by focused campaign both on the functional and on the emotional aspects of the product according to the Customer Experience Management principles.

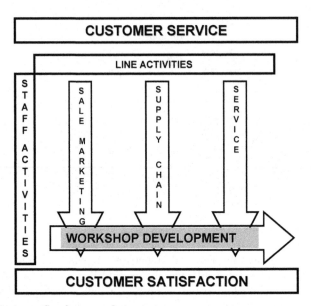

Fig. 5. Iveco Customer Service general structure

A second line is the Supply Chain whose scope is to make available spare parts in good times trough the Iveco workshops network all around the world with monitoring stock levels at a central Iveco warehouses and in the workshops warehouses and then to supply stocks with great managing of times.

The third line is the Service one; its scope is that of granting excellent quality of diagnostic and repairing capability. Therefore Service line deals with:

specializing staff with technical education: Iveco has created a team of specialized mechanics that periodically meet to share solutions to the strangest and most difficult problems (DEEC);

projecting innovative instruments to diagnose failures easier, more precisely and in a shorter time;

building the "telediagnostic" service, as a support of expertise mechanics for those mechanics who reaching trucks in pain can not find a solution to the failure;

defining standardized levels that every international workshop has to perform, such as the schedule for the different interventions.

In addition to the quality of the spare parts, granted by the Sales and marketing line, it is fundamental to emphasize the importance of finding well-trained mechanics since they are able to solve problems in a better way and in a shorter time; in this second case the Service line need to grant to our mechanics a high quality training. It means that the different lines have to interact to deliver the best quality level of service, in this way people is sure that original spare parts are installed by specialized and well trained mechanics. This great interaction between Service and Supply Chain lines assure a high quality level of the service and consequently customer satisfaction rises up. In fact the quickness of repairs will make customer satisfaction to grow up whereas great managing of stocks will increase our dealer satisfaction.

Furthermore Customer Service lines cooperate with some Head Quarters Staff Departments whose activities and projects are oriented to generate customer satisfaction. HQ Staff Departments include Human Resources, Finance, Administration and so on.

Among the HQ staff organisations we will here focus on the activities of Workshop Development whose scope is to manage and organize the service network.

Workshop Development works to find the suitable composition of service network to satisfy customer needs through:

- designing a proper coverage network, equally distributed in the country at an international level;
- monitoring the mechanics training in order to optimize the performances of the assistance, both in terms of efficiency and effectiveness of interventions;

- defining quality standards to ensure the same services in every workshop in the European area;
- managing workshop development. Workshops are the entities that pragmatically enclose every activity of lines. Therefore where and how the workshops are located is fundamental. For example whether they are more or less reachable deeply influences customer satisfaction;
- thinking different kind of services depending on the type of customers; since satisfaction comes from different sources depending on the customers target. For example, whether the market refers to "Daily" (light trucks) rather than to "trucks" (heavy Trucks) the needs of customers are strongly different: truck customers are willing to travel even longer distances to find the best Service Points for their vehicle, instead Daily customers desire higher coverage and specificity of workshops to reach them and solve problems in a shorter time.

These features lead customer oriented Workshop Development management. So we can see that Workshop Development requires compromises in terms of feasibility to fit the needs of different categories of customers. These compromises should be sustainable either for the customer, for the company and for the network.

An example of this trade off is given by the "isocrones": it is a study made by Iveco called TAS that analyses the main vehicles trades and fluxes and defines the minimum presence of workshops on the basis of 45 minutes to get from the Service Network to any points in the main routes in Europe 24H a day 7 days a week.

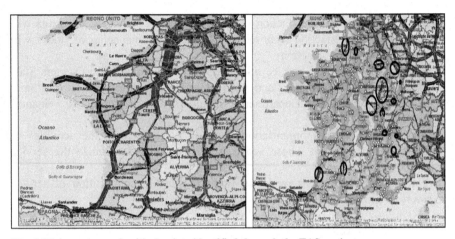

Fig. 6. Main routes and critical points identified through the TAS project

The scope of the TAS (Top Assistant Service) project is to build an adequate structure to deliver a great service level supporting customer into situations of difficulty. Therefore TAS project has as a target to increase the level of Iveco assistance service, allowing both the customer satisfaction and the corporate and workshop profitability to increase.

Iveco Workshop Development also sets and repeatedly monitors the standards for its workshops quality level.

Through these activities the Workshop Development assures excellent level of the customer assistance and simultaneously monitors the profitability achieved through service delivery both for the corporate and the workshops.

So Workshop Development helps Iveco and its service network to manage the trade-off between developing customer satisfaction and making profit.

Iveco delivers the Non-Stop Assistance service through the Customer Centre. The Non-Stop Assistance service is characterised by over 50% of cases resolved within 3 hours after reporting the fault, 80% within 7 hours. This service is valid for the whole truck life and for any model Iveco, under warranty or out of warranty.

The Non-Stop Assistance service is based on the monitored critical items and it aims to improve customer trust facing toward the sensitive problems. Therefore TAS project is aimed at recognising the main European traffic routes and guaranteeing the international customer an Assistance Network with adequate territorial coverage, a higher standard of quality and excellent level of service.

Periodic monitoring of performance standards makes the authorized workshops an element allowing higher quality Service level.

The partnership Iveco with its workshops is fundamental to deliver high performance service level. Since workshops can be considered as an interface between the corporate and the customers, it is very important that Iveco and its

Workshops are linked by a win-win relation of partnership. It means that each side should obtain positive results through the delivered services.

In this way the mission of the Workshop Network is oriented to create, develop and maintain a service network assuring the highest level of service quality to guarantee a profitable partnership with Iveco while satisfying customer expectations. Such a context gives a competitive advantage to Iveco in comparison to the competitors.

The main scope of this study on Iveco Customer Service is to test out whether investments on Customer Relationship Management (CRM) give the expected results.

The analysis allows to understand which elements affect Customer Satisfaction, since we suppose that customer satisfaction is increased through service higher quality level. The causality analysis enables to identify the investment indicators that cause the higher customer profitability.

The analysis is performed using the Quantitative Model that analyses the causality correlations between KPI in the value chain.

Particularly the analysis focuses on the Iveco Non-Stop-Assistance service process and on the activity of the Customer Centre. Every day of the year, 24 hours on 24, in 25 countries in Europe and outside Europe, a team made up of over 80 trained persons is available to solve truck drivers problems.

Through the chassis number of the vehicle, the operator identifies in real-time the truck and its technical characteristics. Then they identify what kind of anomaly affects the truck; so the operator organises the speech, identifying and calling the closest and most suitable workshop to whom to entrust the vehicle. Whether necessary Non-Stop Assistance service provides handling of perishable or dangerous goods. Finally through a series of telephone services Iveco follows the client until the completion repairing of the vehicle.

More precisely the Non-Stop Assistance Service is delivered following specific steps.

First of all an operator receives calls and when needed he opens a dossier grounding the assistance procedure. Each dossier contains a contact history that makes it possible to track all inbound and outbound calls on the same issue.

Depending on the kind of failure he decides which is the best workshop to activate. Iveco scope, according to TAS project, is to activate workshop in no more than 15 minutes and to reach the truck in no more than 45 minutes.

Basing on this stream of activities we have identified the process variables and their causal correlations. We have assumed the investments on Customer Centre technology and on staff training as correlated to the customers perceived value. Therefore the analysis focuses on three main areas of interest, whose variables have been studied.

The areas of interest are:

1. calls: this area refers to Customer Centre performances;
2. staff dimensions: this variable represents the investment on call centre;
3. dossier: theirs KPI refer to the non-stop-assistance service performances.

The selected time series of data symbolizing the Customer Centre activities concern one year of observations.

Calls have been segmented in function of the place of breakdown and of the truck-driver spoken language. Then for each dossier we have analyzed all the information about workshop, failure and assistance management.

In accordance with the hypothesis the analysis expects to confirm that "Value to Customer" is higher whether time to repair is kept the shortest it is possible.

During the analysis we paid attention in taking care of the market target since for different markets there are different customers needs and expectations.

Measured variables compose the metrics for the KPI; so the following variables describe the analysed main processes.

The selected variables regarding Calls process are:

- calls total number;
- missed calls;
- waiting time;
- surrender time.

Each variable has been segmented according to the dimensions of: data (yy-mm-dd), time (hh), language (= client area), breakdown area (= workshop area).

The selected variables regarding Staff dimensions are:

5. operators number: measured as daily mean of operators.

This variable has been segmented according to the dimensions of: data (yy-mm-dd), time (hh) and language (= client area).

The selected variables regarding Dossier are:

- time to assistance: measured as difference between the arrival time on breakdown area and the calling time;
- time to repair: measured as difference between the arrival time in the workshop and the vehicle delivery time;
- detected rate of repairs: measured as ratio between the reported repairs and the total number of calls to Customer Centre.

These variables have been segmented according to the dimensions of: data (yy-mm-dd).

- Number of calls: measured as the calls number needed to solve a dossier.

This variable has been segmented according to the dimensions of: data (yy-mm-dd), inbound calls number, outbound calls number, client code.

- Daily number of opened dossiers.

This variable has been segmented according to the dimensions of: data (yy-mm-dd), time (hh), language (= client area), breakdown area (= workshop area), breakdown market (= client market) and truck model.

The output of the quantitative analysis model, represented in Figure 7, defines which relations exist between the investment variables and the customer perceived value basing on the relations existing among the studied variables. Since value to customer is a latent variable the model provides its indicators too, even accounting the evaluation of the relation between the latent variable and each indicator.

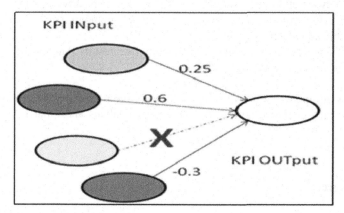

Fig. 7. An example of the Quantitative Model Output

In the end through the analysis Iveco can improve its awareness on how much value and importance customers associate to the supplied services. It is fundamental to know that piece of information in order to manage services development trying to reach customer satisfaction.

The whole analysis, according to the paradigm of CEM, is built around the customer need and expectation, both in terms of technology innovation and of the bid emotional aspects. Since our main scope has been to verify the concrete return on investments sustained to deliver to the customers services with the highest quality level.

4 Conclusions

The research of qualitative framework is highly beneficial for companies because it allows to explicit customer experience. Validation can be made by a variety of approaches that include test-groups, quantitative analysis on a sample of customers, extensive data mining. Our approach is to use a selective quantitative analysis to test and validate qualitative assumption and therefore to set a quantitative investment model in customer service. Further development might include a research project by which a panel of companies in a given industry (e.g. automotive) compare and benchmark their customer service practices. Such a panel allows to improve practice and engineer viable services identifying those services that meet customers needs and expectations. Actually, for management is critical to assess the return on investments, not to waste funds and time in campaigns that do not raise interest and loyalty from target customers.

Furthermore the analysis allows a deeper understanding of the customers which are the key asset for any service industry. Customers drive service economy : serving their attitudes is a must to improve competitiveness and reach a sustainable advantage.

Our research is now dealing with quantitative results that identify the actual value cluster represented by process variables.

Acknowledgments Authors will thank SAS for the financial and technical support that specially included software used for the analysis and that made research possible.

References

1. Addis M, Holbrook M (2001) On the Conceptual Link Between Mass Customisation and Experiential Consumption: An Explosion of Subjectivity. Journal of Consumer Behavior. An International Research Review, Vol.1, 50-66
2. Addis M (2005) L'esperienza di consumo. Analisi e prospettive di marketing, I ed. Pearson, Milano
3. Ashley R, Granger CWJ, Schmalensee R (Jul., 1980) Advertising and Aggregate Consumption: An Analysis of Causality. Econometrica, Vol. 48, No. 5, 1149-1167
4. Bracchi G, Francalanci C, Motta G (2005) Sistemi informativi per l'impresa digitale. MacGraw-Hill, Milano
5. Carbone LP, Haeckel SH (1994) Engineering Customer Experience. Marketing Management, Vol.3, Issue 3
6. Chesbrough H, Spohrer J (July, 2006) A Research for Services Science, Communication of the ACM, Vol.49, N.7, 35-40
7. De Nicolao G, Scattolini R (1997) Identificazione Parametrica. CUSL
8. Ferraresi M, Schmitt BH (2006) Marketing esperienziale. Come sviluppare l'esperienza di consumo, I ed. FrancoAngeli, Milano
9. Granger CWJ, Newbold P () Forecasting Economic Time Series. New York: Academic Press
10. Hamilton JD (1994) Econometria delle Serie Storiche. Monduzzi Editore
11. Hirschman EC (August, 1986) Humanistic Inquiry in Marketing Research: Philosophy, Method and Criteria. Journal of Marketing, Vol.23, No. 3, 237-249
12. Hirschman EC, Stern BB The Roles of Emotion in Consumer Research. In Advances in Consumer Research Volume 26, Eds. Arnould EJ and Scott LM, Provo, UT: Association for Consumer Research, 4-11

13. Hirschman EC, Holbrook MB (Summer, 1982) Hedonic Consumption: Emerging Concepts, Methods and Propositions. Journal of Marketing, Vol.46, N. 3, 92-101

14. Hirschman EC, Holbrook MB (1986) Expanding the Onthology and Methodology in Consumer Research on the Consumption Experience. In Brinberg D, Lutz RJ(Eds.), Perspectives on Methodology in Consumer Research, Springer-Verlag, New York, 213-251

15. Holbrook MB (June, 1987)What is Consumer Research?. The Journal of Consumer Research, Vol.14, No.1, 128-132

16. Holbrook MB (1999) Introduction to Customer Value. In Holbrook MB (Ed.), Consumer Value: A Framework For Analysis and Research, Routledge, London, 1-28

17. Holt DB (June, 1995) How Consumers Consume: A Typology of Consumption Practice. The Journal of Consumer Research, Vol. 22, No. 1, 1-16

18. Pine JBII, Gilmore JH (1999) The Experience Economy. Work Is Theatre & Every Business a Stage. Harvard Business School Press, Massachusetts, Boston

19. Schmitt BH (1999) Experiential Marketing. How to get consumers to SENSE, FEEL, THINK, ACT and RELATE to Your Company Brands. The Free Press (eds.), New York

20. Schmitt BH (2003) Customer Experience Management. A revolutionary Approach to Connecting with Your Customers. Hoboken NJ, John Wiley & Sons

21. Verbeek M (2006) Econometria, Zanichelli

22. Vercellis C (2006) Business Intelligence. Modelli matematici e sistemi per le decisioni. McGraw-Hill, Milano

23. SAS INSTITUTE INC. (2004) SAS/ETS_ 9.1 User's Guide. Cary, NC: SAS Institute Inc.

24. www.iveco.com

Explaining the Evolving Web - Mixing Technology with Pleasure

Robert I. Benjamin[1], Rolf T. Wigand[2], Johanna L. H. Birkland[3]

[1]Syracuse University

[2]University of Arkansas at Little Rock

[3] Syracuse University

1. Overview

This paper provides a framework for examining what services are and will be required for consumers participating in the vast electronic market that is the Internet. There are many profound changes taking place, somewhat different than could be envisioned when Electronic Market Theory was first developed, but in general quite consistent with the theory [1, 2]. From the perspective of the service provider the most important insights are that consumers have been empowered by the Web 2.0 technologies to provide or tailor the services that satisfy their needs, and that a key job of the service provider is to build the platforms that make the consumer's job as easy and transparent as possible. The chain of reasoning supporting this insight is summarized below and then elaborated on in the following sections:

- The technologies associated with Web 2.0 have been enabled by continued technology cost performance improvements and increased capabilities for coordination. This is observable since the 1970s and will continue possibly at higher rates of cost performance improvements in the coming decade [3]
- There have been several significant and related effects of the improved coordination capabilities that can be observed on the Internet as consumer electronic markets continue to evolve. They are described in more detail in the balance of this paper.
- Applications are now able to support a much wider range of human emotions/needs than in the past. Successful applications have become platforms that in effect assist the user in defining which needs are of interest to them and how they want them to be satisfied.
- Electronic consumer markets have evolved from simple and easy to describe, low asset specific, tangible products, to complex, higher asset specific, intangible products, therefore extending the size and nature of the electronic market quite dramatically.

Please use the following format when citing this chapter:

Benjamin, R.I., Wigand, R.T. and Birkland, J.L.H., 2008, in IFIP International Federation for Information Processing, Volume 280; *E-Government; ICT Professionalism and Competences; Service Science*; Antonino Mazzeo, Roberto Bellini, Gianmario Motta; (Boston: Springer), pp. 261–275.

- Everything the consumer does on the Internet is a market choice. Choosing Facebook or buying a book from Amazon are both market choices that must provide the revenue to enable the supplier to prosper.

The Internet has become a latent electronic market where the individual consumer creates the market space she is interested in by using facilitating software easily available on the Internet, including browsers, retrieval software and the like. Malone Yates and Benjamin [2] saw markets as moving from biased to unbiased to personalized. An example of the personalized market as the authors conceived it is typified by Amazon informing consumers that based on their last order they might be interested in a particular list of books. The concept of personalized markets has been greatly expanded by Web2.0 capabilities. To illustrate, many markets have become highly transparent (e.g., mortgages, interest rates, insurance) and many markets have become personalized by the consumer using the facilitating tools referred to above, as for example the markets to facilitate student loans [4].

2. Technology Cost/Performance and the Cost of Coordination

As technology cost performance driven by Moore's Law continues to unfold, it expands our capability to develop new and creative and often disruptive applications. Periodically such collections of technology through their ability to change coordination costs create vast new application potential and increase the ability of the technology to satisfy our human needs. Several examples illustrate this phenomenon:

- The increased capabilities in speed and storage capacity in the 1970s allowed PARC research to develop the Ethernet, the iconic desktop and other characteristics of today's workstation, thus precipitating the PC revolution [5].
- The improvements in computing power, telecommunications speed and reliability and large data bases made possible the emergence of electronic markets in the mid 1980s and subsequently the rapid exploitation of the Internet and Web browsers in the early to mid 1990s.
- The current bundle of Web 2.0 cost performance improvements have correspondingly enabled and made possible social networks, virtual worlds, and other Web 2.0 applications. It is the way in which these technologies are applied that allows us to satisfy a human need such as a sense of belonging in a social network. A fuller description of how human needs are satisfied through IT is developed later in the paper.

3. Web 2.0 and its Applications

Web 2.0 and the applications derived from it have typically been explained by its underlying technologies per se rather than the impacts of the applications (e.g., Wigand, 2007). From our perspective Web 2.0's importance is that it has enabled web sites to more fully express and manifest human needs, therefore enlarging the electronic commerce application space.

Web 2.0, a phrase coined by O'Reilly Media in 2004, refers to a perceived or proposed second generation of Internet-based services—such as social networking sites, wikis, communication tools, and folksonomies—that emphasize online collaboration and sharing among users. Smith (2007) states that "…Web 2.0 is not just a set of technologies, but also attributes that have a social dimension: new business models, user-contributed content and user-generated metadata, more open and transparent business processes, simplicity in design and features, and decentralized and participatory products and processes" [6].

Representative technologies offering discrete functionalities associated with Web 2.0 are:

- AJAX (Asynchronous Javascript and XML) – hybrid of Javascript and XML- provides dynamic, real-time, personalized services, increases speed, and flexibility.
- RSS (Really Simple Syndication) – provides live feeds from multiple sources, and personalized aggregation.
- Tagging – captures linkages, associate meanings/revealed family of interest structures, reveals untapped semantic structures associated with group interests. Sites such as Del.icio.us and Connotea allow users to organize information based upon user-generated tags.
- Wikis – collaborative authoring and editing, text-based, quick information sharing, as in the encyclopedia Wikipedia.
- Mashups – builds a composite integrated experience out of several related websites. Examples: Google Earth, ZIPskinny and comprehensive travel searches.

Two key attributes of these technologies are: 1) they are often used in different powerful compound applications such as tagging of wiki entries, social networking sites and the composite and integrated experience of mashups, and 2) users can easily add their content to the site using Web 2.0 technologies.

Figure 1 captures these interactions of technologies, and human needs in the context of electronic commerce from 1987 to today. It illustrates the progression of products amenable to electronic commerce from tangible commodity like products such as books to now highly intangible products such as information and social networks.

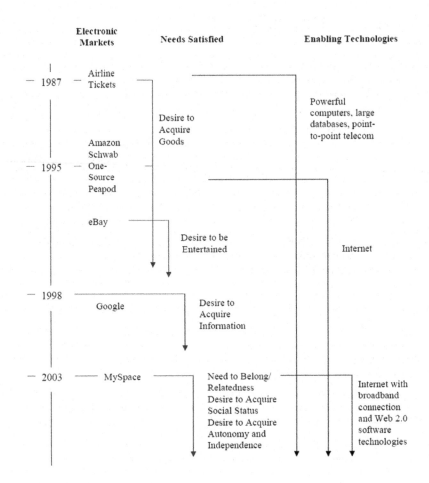

Fig. 1. Relationships between Technology Evolution, Ability To Express Human Needs and Forms of Consumer Electronic Commerce

The technology futurist or business strategist looking at this figure would be inclined to conclude that five years from now there will be sharper distinctions in human needs expressed and whole new classes of applications developed for the mass audience on the Internet.

4. Human Needs Satisfaction and the Internet

All behavior may be viewed as being motivated by basic human needs. Over the past century, several models of human needs have been proposed, including Maslow's Hierarchy of Needs [7, 8], Self Determination Theory [9-11], and Motivation Theory [12-15]. In the majority of these cases, one model of basic needs has built upon the previous model.

Underlying human needs can be used to describe the behavior we observe on the Internet, and these basic principles of human behavior can be used to explain current trends and predict future trends. As a foundation for our present examination of human behavior, we are using a set of human needs derived from Maslow's classical hierarchy of needs.

Maslow's hierarchy describes five fundamental needs that motivate human behavior:

1. Physiological Needs: the needs for food and shelter.
2. Safety Needs: the need to feel safe from harm.
3. Belongingness Needs: the need to feel affection and to belong
4. Esteem Needs: the need to have a stable high evaluation of oneself, including needs for achievement, adequacy, confidence, independence, strength and also the need for reputation, importance, attention, appreciation, and recognition.
5. Self-actualization: the need for self-fulfillment.

For the majority of modern Western society, we suggest that the most basic physiological and safety needs are met. Therefore, these needs should be reinterpreted in the context in which we live. It follows that it is more likely for such users to use the web to meet our needs for belongingness, esteem, and self-actualization. Individuals in developing nations oftentimes face severe restrictions on what sites may be accessed on the Internet, due to governmental control, cultural norms, or infrastructural constraints [16]. Due to these restrictions, individuals in developing nations may be more inclined to use the web to satisfy more basic needs as well.

In addition to Maslow's five needs, we have added an additional basic need, the need for entertainment. Entertainment or play has not been adequately addressed in Maslow's hierarchy of needs, despite being a vital aspect of human behavior. Aside from the obvious desire and need to play by children, play and forms of play as in entertainment are also an important component of adult life. Examples, physical or virtual, are games, participation in sports, solving puzzles, etc. Clearly, this is an essential element observable on the Internet: entire websites and applications have been developed to fulfill this particular need. Some popular online games are played by millions of users worldwide and for some a play cycle may be more than nine months. In terms of revenue, the gaming industry is larger than Hollywood. When viewing these basic needs in relation to the Internet, Maslow's basic need structure can be adapted to describe several needs observable on the Internet.

An example of human needs on the Internet applied to a social networking site follows below:

Table 1. MySpace as an Illustration Of Human Needs Satisfaction On The Internet

| MySpace | Need to Belong/Relatedness Desire to Acquire Social Status Desire to Acquire Autonomy and Independence | MySpace allows users to befriend other users, meet new people sharing common interests, and interacting with friends through blogs and guest books, fulfilling users' need for belongingness and relatedness. Through their social networks, users can also acquire social status by linking to more friends, with many users linking to hundreds of friends. Users can also identify their top friends (through the "top eight" feature), allowing a user to essentially sort their friends, indicating which friends users hold highest in esteem. Moreover, MySpace provides users with the ability to customize their profile page, including backgrounds, music, and pictures allowing users to fulfill their need of autonomy and independence. |

A more detailed description of human needs and the Internet in terms of popular sites is presented as an appendix to this paper. We understand that there are many ways of looking at human needs and the Internet, but we would like to suggest that what we present is a pointer to the kind of detailed analysis service providers will seek to satisfy, in order to achieve competitive positioning.

5. Surprises in the Evolution of Internet Consumer Markets

Electronic market theory describes the attributes of tangible products that with increasing IT cost performance will be more and more conducive to market transactions rather than controlled through traditional hierarchical models of management. As evidence, e-commerce sales now account for a significant portion of overall retail spending, and are growing at a rate faster than retail sales in general. Sales of $108 billion in 2006 topped those at electronics and appliance stores. And in the final quarter of 2006, online shopping accounted for 3% of total retail sales; nearly double the share at the end of 2002 [17]. According to the research firm Cowen & Co., e-commerce retail sales are said to have climbed another 20%, to $129 billion, in 2007. All of the above demonstrates a basic agreement with the principles of electronic market theory.

However a number of surprises have occurred in the consumer market evolution:

- As Figure 1 reveals there has been a shift from tangible products such as books to intangible products such as information and social networks.
- Personalized consumer specific markets on the Internet are for the most part formed not by market makers, but by the consumer using the facilitating tools of the Internet, browsers and retrieval programs such as Google to create the desired market space to search in. Thus a Google search on hearing aids produces a list of such devices and a product code sent to a specialized retrieval site such as Price Grabber provides a list of sites and prices for the hearing aid product. Market maker profits (as theory predicted) have been hard to find but much of their profits have gone to the owners of the facilitating tools such as Google. We note that there have been some very successful market makers, notably E-Bay who provides a market for a vast array of consumer products, and the brokerage firm Charles Schwab [1] who created the first and most successful market in mutual funds.

- Although the market for tangible products can be very large as exemplified by Amazon's current volume. They are tiny in size compared to the markets in intangible products such Google, MySpace and FaceBook. Creating the revenue base to provide the technical and administrative support these volumes require provides a significant level of risk to the newer class of intangible market choices. For example, how sticky will Facebook be as other and trendier social networks arrive, and will the social network users buy into the type of advertising model developed so successfully by Google.

6. Conclusions and Reflections for Service Providers

In concluding this brief overview of how consumer electronic markets are changing let us first consider the key areas of immediate concern for those in the business of providing services.

- First and probably most significantly, service providers must realize that the consumer has been freed from the vendor as pusher of information. She can now use the Web2.0 technologies and be quite specific about what services are desired, as she creates her personalized market. Thus rather than providing a set of options, a platform that allows the consumer to develop her market of choice and its attributes becomes of primary importance.

- Second, understanding consumers and being able to help consumers differentiate the various human needs they want to satisfy becomes an important aspect of service.

- Third, the ability to create and maintain sticky sites that can deliver the advertising able to yield the revenues necessary for sustaining the volumes of consumer interactions we are now discovering on the information and social network sites becomes a major consideration.

- Finally, the service providers must recognize that technology cost performance will create new technology capabilities. We refer to them as Web 3.0 for convenience and suggest that these will allow more sophisticated expression of needs The challenge to keep up with the empowered consumer will get more and more challenging.

To summarize, services offered within the Web 2.0 framework are now part of the Internet's evolutionary history. In the short term, a firm that today wants to be active on the Internet, has no choice but to find its appropriate role via Web 2.0. Most major firms, including BMW, Google, IBM, and many others are aware of the issues presented above, and, are positioning themselves to find their strategic place, position and fit within these developments. They are also looking at the longer-term consequences.

- Providers of services on the Internet must recognize what may well be described as a shift in how we view the web. This shift forces service providers to take a new look at recognizing innovative opportunities and challenges that cross a number of dimensions, including media, the Web, organizations, economics, society and culture.

- Providers of services on the Internet must recognize the increased participation of the users on the web, who tend to interact to the content produced by other users, leading to increased participation in social networks. Users are able to debate on Weblogs and distribute information faster and more personalized via the RSS (Real Simple Syndication) format than via the classical media. Users leave MySpace and Facebook windows open all day to receive alerts: the average stay for MySpace users is 29 minutes and the average number of pages viewed is 75.6.

- Providers of services on the Internet must recognize that the trends we have examined are just one more iteration of capabilities. As the waves of IT cost performance inexorably continue, they will create new business opportunities. Thus user personalized applications can be expected in the living room and in the office alike, and will find parallel manifestations in the mobile communications area
- Providers of services on the Internet must recognize that these advances strongly suggest that firms have no choice but to keep in step with these developments. The challenges for firms and users will be to blend, merge and consolidate these into an integrated and comprehensive concept such that users enjoy a best possible experience while satisfying the widest range of human needs.
- Finally, providers of services on the Internet must find their way in dealing with several interrelated forces: 1) the rapid and enormous growth of social network products whose longevity and stickiness in the marketplace has yet to be proved as sustainable business models, 2) determining which pricing structures work best, and 3) and what users are willing to pay to fulfill their needs. These, as well as many other questions will have to be addressed by future research.

We hope that these contributions shed some light on how management and the academic world may view and understand these developments.

Appendix

Derivations of Human Needs Satisfaction on the Internet
Tables 2, 3 and 4 depict our perspectives, explanations and examples of human needs satisfaction on the Internet. The framework and examples chosen are to be seen as illustrative of our needs satisfaction perspective.

Table 2. Hierarchy of Needs Reflected on the WWW

Maslow's Hierarchy of Needs	Corresponding Website Hierarchy
1. Physiological Needs	a. Desire to Acquire Goods
	b. Desire to Acquire Information
2. Safety Needs	a. Desire to Acquire Goods
	b. Desire to Acquire Information
3. Belongingness Needs	c. Need to Belong/Relatedness
4. Play/Entertainment Needs	d. Desire to be entertained, to be playful
5. Esteem Needs	e. Desire to Acquire Social Status
	f. Desire to Acquire Power and Authority
	g. Desire to Acquire Autonomy and Independence
6. Self-actualization Needs	f. Desire to Acquire Power and Authority
	g. Desire to Acquire Autonomy and Independence

Using a selection of human needs including those above, we can categorize popular websites and web services by the needs they meet and fulfill. For example, certain websites may help humans to fulfill their need to belong and relate to others, provide a means for their need to communicate within their chosen community, or help an individual to acquire forms of power and authority. Many webservices meet several such needs.

Here we choose to categorize several popular websites, including five social networking sites. The social networking websites included in our analysis were chosen based upon their relatively large number of users, i.e. MySpace, Hi5, Xanga, Classmates.com, and Orkut [18]. Several sites were chosen because they are representative examples of Web 2.0 functionalities. Others were chosen because they were historically interesting sites that were developed before Web 2.0 emerged (but have since developed Web 2.0 capabilities), while other sites were chosen because of their uniqueness and the possibility that they are indicators of future functionalities. As described, these sites were chosen to provide an interesting, illustrating and partially representative popular mix. Within this specific context they may be seen as representative, yet the authors openly admit that their choice represents a convenience sample.

We envision the WWW as a mirror-like reflection of real-life human (dyadic, group, organizational and societal) activities, in which these sites' respective functionalities appeal to basic needs of human nature. By examining that subset of activities on the WWW that entail business transactions, we realize that it is the challenge for business to find out how to best use the web while realizing that these developments must be embraced and incorporated judiciously and sensitively.

Table 3 depicts a representative sample of websites from our list with a detailed explanation of the needs met by that site's functionality. For clarity and simplicity, we have chosen to only assign a maximum of three needs to each website/web service listed below. Table 4 categorizes all websites by need and highlights characteristics of sites that help users to fulfill these needs.

Table 3. Salient Examples of Websites Fulfilling Different Human Needs

Website	Human Behavior Attribute(s)	Explanation of reasoning
Amazon	Desire to Acquire Goods Desire to Acquire Information Desire to Acquire Power and Authority	Amazon allows users to acquire goods (e.g., books, videos, and other items) and acquire information about these goods, including previews and recommended titles (based upon other users buying patterns). Additionally, users can also obtain peer-created information about the book through others' reviews and ratings before purchasing an item. By submitting reviews, individuals can exert power and authority that may influence users' purchasing decisions.
Del.icio.us	Desire to Acquire Information Desire to Acquire Power and Authority	Del.icio.us allows users to tag and use tags created by others in order to facilitate finding and organizing information on the web. Users can also use tags to express themselves and assert their knowledge for the purpose of classifying a website.
MySpace	Need to Belong/Relatedness Desire to Acquire Social Status Desire to Acquire Autonomy and Independence	MySpace allows users to befriend other users, meet new people sharing common interests, and interacting with friends through blogs and guest books, fulfilling users' need for belongingness and relatedness. Through their social networks, users can also acquire social status by linking to more friends, with many users linking to hundreds of friends. Users can also identify their top friends (through the "top eight" feature), allowing a user to essentially sort their friends, indicating which friends users hold highest in esteem. Moreover, MySpace provides users with the ability to customize their profile page, including using backgrounds, music, and pictures allowing users to fulfill their need of autonomy and independence.

Website	Human Behavior Attribute(s)	Explanation of reasoning
SecondLife	Need to Belong/ Relatedness Desire to Acquire Goods Desire to Acquire Social Status Desire to Acquire Autonomy and Independence Desire to be Entertained	SecondLife is unique as it serves as a platform for many different activities. SecondLife has been used as a place where users can meet others with similar interests, can acquire goods using Linden dollars (which relate to USD exchange rates), and can express themselves through things they build, create, or buy for their avatar. Additionally, goods acquired or built in SecondLife can help users to improve their social status, such as a user building a large mansion on his/her island. Users also often use SecondLife as a form of entertainment, much like a game.
YouTube	Desire to Acquire Information Desire to be Entertained Desire to Acquire Autonomy and Independence	YouTube allows users to view clips of videos for entertainment purposes or view informative videos (such as how-to videos). YouTube allows users to post their own self-created videos, facilitating self-expression.

Table 4. Human Needs and Corresponding Exemplary Websites

Human Need	Websites	Explanation
a. Desire to Acquire Goods	Amazon.com Clipsyndicate.com Craigslist Ebay Freecycle Google Napster SecondLife	These websites allow users to acquire goods. E.g., amazon.com allows users to acquire goods including books, movies, and music, while Google's advertising allows users to acquire goods related to users' searches.
b. Desire to Acquire Information	Amazon.com Craigslist Del.icio.us Freecycle Google Smallworld.net Wikipedia YouTube	These websites allow users to find or to organize information. E.g., Amazon.com allows users to read reviews and view metadata on books and other products; Del.icio.us allows users to organize and search information through tagging, while Google allows users to search information.

Human Need	Websites	Explanation
c. Need to Belong/ Relatedness	MySpace Hi5 Xanga Classmates.com Orkut SecondLife Craigslist	These websites allow users to connect and link to others, meet new people based upon shared interests, and interact through various features. E.g., MySpace allows users to link their profiles to other users' profiles, Xanga allows users to create blogrings of blogs on related topics, and SecondLife allows users to interact through real-time chat and meeting spaces.
d. Desire to Acquire Social Status	MySpace Hi5 Xanga Classmates.com Orkut SecondLife	These websites allow a user to acquire social status through the number of connections to others (such as the number of friends their respective profile is connected to) and the status of the individuals they are connected to, through ranking or rating of others, or through displays of virtual goods. E.g., MySpace indicates how many profiles/friends a person is linked to and allows users to indicate their top friends, Orkut allows users to rate others on "trust", "coolness" and "sexiness," and SecondLife allows users to acquire virtual goods (such as clothing for users' avatars) which may increase users' social status.
e. Desire to Acquire Power and Authority	Amazon Clipsyndicate.com Del.icio.us Smallworld.net Wikipedia Youtube	These websites allow users to exert their power, opinion, influence, control and authority by serving as reviewers, rating materials, or creating or organizing information. E.g., Wikipedia allows users to create and review entries/information, Del.icio.us allows the tagging and organizing of information, and Smallworld.net allows users to rate restaurants and destinations.

Human Need	Websites	Explanation
f. Desire to Acquire Autonomy and Independence	SecondLife SimCity MySpace Hi5 Xanga Classmates.com Youtube Facebook	These websites allow users to express themselves through website features, such as through designing or building items or customizing features. E.g., SecondLife allows uses to express themselves through their choice of avatar and through building virtual objects, while SimCity allows uses to build and maintain a city.
g. Desire to be entertained	Ebay Google Napster SecondLife SimCity YouTube	These websites allow users to be entertained. They provide goods, information, or services which users find entertaining. E.g., SecondLife can be used as an escape or game for entertainment, YouTube allows users to watch a wide array of videos, Ebay allows users to watch the excitement of an online auction, and Google allows users to surf the web and be "entertained" by the list of search results they find.

References

1. R. Benjamin and R. Wigand, "Electronic Markets and Virtual Value Chains on the Information Superhighway," Sloan Management Review, vol. 36, pp. 62-72, 1995.
2. T. W. Malone, J. Yates, and R. I. Benjamin, "Electronic markets an electronic hierarchies," Communications of the ACM, vol. 30, pp. 484-497, 1987.
3. R. Kurzweil, Fine Living in Virtual Reality, in The Invisible Future: The Seamless Integration Of Technology Into Every Day Life: McGraw Hill, 2002.
4. E. Levenson, "How to Shop For Student Loans," in Fortune, 2008.
5. M. A. Hiltzik, Dealers of Lightning: Xerox PARC and the Dawn of the Computer Age. New York: Harper Collins, 1999.
6. D. M. Smith, "Web 2.0: Structuring the Discussion," Gartner Research October 31, 2007.
7. A. H. Maslow, Motivation and Personality. New York: Harper & Row, 1970.
8. A. H. Maslow, "A Theory of Human Motivation," Psychological Review, vol. 50, pp. 370-396, 1943.

9. E. L. Deci and R. M. Ryan, "The "what" and "why" of goal pursuits: Human needs and the self-determination of behavior," Psychological Inquiry, vol. 11, pp. 227-268, 2000.

10. R. M. Ryan and E. L. Deci, "Self-determination theory and the facilitation of intrinsic motivation, social development, and well-being," American Psychologist, vol. 55, pp. 68-78, 2000.

11. E. L. Deci, H. Eghrari, B. C. Patrick, and D. R. Leone, "Facilitating internalization: the self-determination theory perspective," Journal of Personality, vol. 62, pp. 119-142, March, 1994.

12. D. C. McClelland, Human motivation. New York: Cambridge University Press, 1987.

13. D. C. McClelland, Power: the inner experience. New York: Halstead, 1975.

14. D. C. McClelland, "Toward a theory of motive acquisition," American Psychologist, vol. 23, pp. 321-333, 1965.

15. D. C. McClelland, The achieving society. Princeton, N.J.: Van Nostrand, 1961.

16. M. L. Kaarst-Brown and J. R. Evaristo, "The Role of Culture in Global Electronic Commerce," in Global Information Technology and Electronic Commerce: Issues for the New Millennium Marietta, Georgia: Ivy League Publishing, 2002.

17. J. Mehring, "Cash Registers Are Ringing Online," in Business Week. vol. 24, 2007.

18. Wikipedia, "List of Social Networking Sites," 2007.

Value-Aware Service Model Driven Architecture and Methodology

Xiaofei Xu[1] and Zhongjie Wang[2]

[1]School of Computer Science and Technology, Harbin Institute of Technology, China. xiaofei@hit.edu.cn

[2]School of Computer Science and Technology, Harbin Institute of Technology, China. rainy@hit.edu.cn

Abstract: Fully realizing proposed "value" for both customers and providers is considered as an ultimate goal of developing a good service system. In this paper, based on the mechanism of "value co-production" in services we propose a value-aware service methodology based on Service Model Driven Architecture and Service Quality Function Deployment. Such methodology integrates top-down service model transformation and bottom-up service component reuse together, to help service designers be fully aware of service values, i.e., how "value" is defined, decomposed, transferred and transformed in the lifecycle of a service system. Aiming at some key decision-making points that have great influences on the delivery of service values, we also present some general ideas.

Keywords: service, value-aware, methodology, transformation

1. Introduction

Innovations on service business patterns have been a key force to accelerate GDP growth. By importing new information technologies, new management techniques, new resource configuration patterns and new specialized social division of labors, the invented service patterns are expected to produce new added-values. Specific service pattern describes how customers and providers co-produce value and share risk [1], whose innovations are that it could provide some new values that other service patterns cannot provide.

However, service patterns just make value proposition in high level. These innovative values should be elaborately defined and refined in detailed service models (e.g., service process, configuration of resource and people, etc) during service de-sign, then step-by-step transformed into the infrastructural IT-based service systems. During the execution of service systems, these values are delivered to customers and providers, respectively.

Please use the following format when citing this chapter:

Xu, X. and Wang, Z., 2008, in IFIP International Federation for Information Processing, Volume 280; *E-Government; ICT Professionalism and Competences; Service Science*; Antonino Mazzeo, Roberto Bellini, Gianmario Motta; (Boston: Springer), pp. 277–286.

It is easily to see that, whether and to which degree the proposed values are to be effectively realized and delivered to customers and providers as expected, depend on the design quality of service models and IT-based service systems to a great ex-tent. In practical services, because there might be some thinking gaps between service innovators, service designers and service system developers, the proposed values might not be fully top-down transformed and implemented [2], i.e., "good ideas cannot become good reality", just as shown in Figure 1.

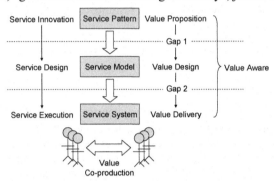

Fig. 1. Gaps between three phases of service lifecycle

In order to reduce or eliminate Gap 1, there should be a systematic service de-sign method to transform service patterns into service models which have the ability of describing innovative service values [3]. By evaluating and optimizing such service models, we reach the objective of "be aware of values during service de-sign, and make service models fully express service values".

To reduce or eliminate Gap 2, there should be some service system design method to transform service models into IT-supporting service systems, i.e., selecting proper service elements (or called "service component", "service asset", including service behaviors, resources, people, technology, etc [4]) and compose them together according to some specific architectural styles. By evaluating and optimizing such service systems, we reach the objective of "be aware of values during service system development, and make service systems support value delivery as far as possible".

In conclusion, initial proposed service values should be materialized in each phase of service lifecycles, e.g., modeling, design and implementation. In traditional service methodologies, they focus most of attentions on service functionalities while ignore "value". For this issue, we do some research on value-aware methodologies for service innovation, modeling, implementation and optimization, i.e., "be aware of service values every when and everywhere".

This paper is organized as follows. Section 2 explains some primary concepts relating to services. In section 3 we briefly introduce the framework of value-aware methodology containing five horizontal layers and three vertical threads. Section 4 and 5 introduces top-down and bottom-up approaches of the methodology, respec-tively. Finally is the conclusion.

2. Basic Concepts on Services

In recent years, "service" becomes more and more a hot topic in both industry and academia. In broad sense, a service is defined as the application of compe-tences for the benefit of another, meaning that service is a kind of action, perform-ance, or promise that's exchanged for value between provider and customers [1].

Different with manufacturing in which values are transferred thoroughly from providers to customers, values in services are co-produced and shared between service provider and customers.

Each party of a service has his own expectations on values [5], which are further classified into more detailed types, e.g., (1) economic values; (2) improvement on knowledge or skills; (3) improvement on experiences; (4) improvement on market competitiveness; (5) physical values; etc. Some of them are tangible values while others are intangible ones. Based on a well-designed service system, these values would be delivered to related parties by co-production, and the degree of value de-livery lies on the design and development quality of service models and service systems to a great extent.

To support the implementation of services, there must be corresponding service systems to compose various service elements together. A service system is considered as a complex socio-technological systems and is defined as "a value co-production configuration of people, technology, other internal and external service systems connected by value propositions, and shared information (such as language, processes, metrics, prices, policies, and laws)" [1]. Generally speaking, a typical service system is composed of the following service elements:

- People: service customers, service providers, including their organizations, roles, human resources, professional skills and capabilities.
- Resource: including technological resources and physical material resources, e.g., software, equipment, physical environment and IT infrastructure, etc.

- Shared information: files, data and documents that are created, transacted by and exchanged between service customers and providers.
- Behavior: physical, mental or social behaviors of people doing work in service systems. Such behaviors are usually stochastic and can't be easily modeled and simulated.

Service methodology is defined as the method for systematical planning, developing and managing full lifecycle of service systems, to support service providers build well-designed services and service systems [6].

Strictly speaking, service methodology is such a technological way to describe, define, design, build, implement, provision, and dynamic evolution services and service systems, by importing and applying related theories and methods of ser-vices science, management and engineering, and providing enabling tools and platforms, thereby validating whether customer requirements would be satisfied on demand, and whether value would be properly co-produced.

3 A framework for value-aware service methodology

In this section we will give a brief introduction to the value-aware service methodology, which forms a two-dimensional framework shown in Figure 2.

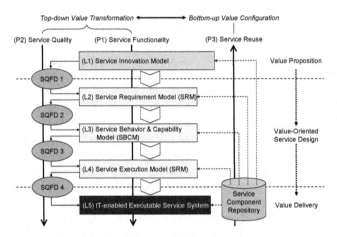

Fig. 2. Framework for value-aware service methodology

In horizontal dimension, multi-layered service models are developed for describing customer requirements of services, detailed behaviors of services, etc. There are five layers, i.e.,

(L1) Service Innovation Model (SIM);
(L2) Service Requirement Model (SRM);
(L3) Service Behavior and Capability Model (SBCM);
(L4) Service Execution Model (SEM);
(L5) IT-enabled Executable Service Systems (SES);

L1 declares the objectives of services, especially what kinds of innovative value-added would be provided to customers and providers. Purposes of L2, L3 and L4 are design of the services, showing details of service behaviors and processes, service parties and people, service resources and their capability, and shared information. How proposed values are realized step by step in services is emphasized, too. L5 is actually not models but real executable systems in reality under the support of information technologies. It delivers values to each related party. Detailed specifications of these models could be found in our previous works, e.g., [7][8].

Above models describe contents of service in different phases of its lifecycle, and there are close associations between neighboring layers. Therefore in vertical dimension we design three inter-related paths to connect these models, i.e.,

(P1) Top-down transformation of service functionality;
(P2) Top-down transformation of service quality;
(P3) Bottom-up service component based reuse.

P1 is the most fundamental transformation in our methodology. After SIM is gradually made clear, service designers begin to collect customer requirements and model SRM, which are then gradually transformed to SBCM and SEM, then to SES. In such procedure, each proposed value is allocated to one or more specific service functionalities and refined along with the top-down transformation.

However, P1 only concerns about how values are embedded in and supported by various layers of service models, it does not mention to which degree each value is to be implemented. In fact, every layer of service models is attached with a set of quality parameters (e.g., time, cost, price, etc) to quantitatively measure such degree, and such quality parameters should also be fully considered during functionality transformation. We use P2 for this purpose.

In P2, Quality Function Deployment (QFD) technique is imported to transform quality parameters of upper layer to the neighboring lower layer. P1 and P2 are interrelated closely.

From another point of view, most of services need not be completely developed from scratch, and there might be some existing service elements (e.g., people, service behaviors, resources, etc) that could be reused. In our methodology we import the third path P3, which is a bottom-up transformation. After a specific layer is modeled, service designers may pick out service components that most match with service models in both functional and quality aspects, then select a proper service architecture style to compose them together to implement service system. Objective of P3 is to find the best reuse solution to maximize the degree of implementing proposed values.

In conclusion, the ultimate goal of value-aware service methodology is to "be aware of values in each phase of service lifecycles and maximize them". By means of such methodology, a service system can be developed on demand of customers, be implemented efficiently and run with good service performance. We will discuss detailed P1, P2 and P3 in Section 4 and 5.

4. Top-down: SQFD-based model transformation

Concerning P1 and P2, for arbitrary neighboring models there are three types of top-down transformation policies, i.e.,

- Direct mapping, i.e., a service element in upper-layer model is directly mapped and referenced in lower-layer model;
- Refinement, i.e., after one service elements in upper-layer model is mapped to lower-layer model, it should be manually refined to describe more details of services;

- Instantiation, i.e., an abstract service element in upper-layer model is instantiated to one or multiple concrete service elements.
- No matter what types of transformation, the following two aspects should be elaborately considered, i.e.,

- Service semantics driven transformation. Semantic information (e.g., re-source availability, customer preferences, skills of providers, etc) attached to upper-level models should be fully utilized and transformed to lower-level models to make the models more feasible and close to reality. Ontology-based rules for semantics mapping are adopted for this purpose;

- Service quality based transformation. Quality requirements consisting of a set of quality parameters (e.g., SLA) are elaborately transformed between layers. QFD-based method is imported here [9].

The main reason we consider quality transformation along with functionality transformation is to lessen the gap between customer perceived service from the service system and their expectations. As core of QFD, the House of Quality is adopted as the tool for quality transformation. There are three-level HoQs to transform VOC to SRM, SBCM and SEM, respectively, as shown in Figure 3. Figure 4 shows an example of the first HoQ in Figure 3.

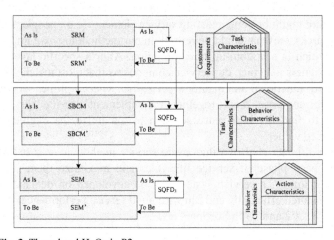

Fig. 3. Three-level HoQs in P2

However, even the designed service models and systems fully reflects customers' quality requirements, during the execution of service systems, there might still exist some gaps. Therefore run-time quality performance evaluation is necessary for future optimization. In run-time quality/performance evaluation phase, monitoring tools will be imported to automatically send queries and receive reports from different service component environments periodically. The system run-time Key Performance Indicators (KPIs) will be evaluated based on collected data. The results from run-time quality/performance evaluation are analyzed for further ser-vice system optimization.

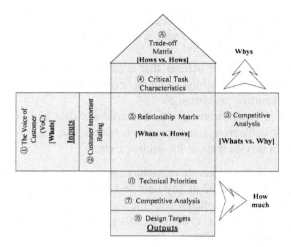

Fig. 4. Service House of Quality

Service quality/performance optimization is the third phase of P2. The gaps between customer expected service quality from SRM and customer perceived ser-vice quality from service system are identified, analyzed, and traced backward to early phase for reasoning the causes. In order to improve the quality of service system efforts are made to optimization by considering re-design, re-configuration, and or re-negotiation. This closes the loop of quality assurance for lifecycle.

5. Bottom-up: reuse-based service system development

Besides top-down transformation (P1 and P2), a bottom-up service reuse (P3) are important likewise. Basic idea of P3 is to fully make use of existing service elements to develop service systems instead of doing from scratch, so as to improve development efficiency, quality and to decrease cost.

Since service system is a complex socio-technological system which is com-posed of various elements, we classify service elements as the following five types, i.e.:

- People-ware SC: a service person with specific professional skills to provide specific behaviors during services.
- Software SC: a software entity with specific transaction or computation capabilities to provide specific behaviors in services, e.g., a web services with WSDL-based interfaces, an encapsulated legacy system, etc.
- Hardware SC: a hardware or equipment with specific capabilities, e.g., a computer server for residing software, an instrument for measuring and checking, a GPS for indicating directions, etc.

- Environment SC: a location with specific facilities as a container where ser-vice behaviors will take place, e.g., a meeting room with tables, chairs, projectors and whiteboards for training activity, etc.
- Behavior SC: processes, activities or actions that a person could behave to accomplish a service task, e.g., consulting, training, manipulating a machine, using a software system, reporting problems, etc.
- Information SC: a physical or electronic entity that contains data and is ex-changed and shared among software systems, people, hardware, etc, e.g., a sales order, a log of call center, a service manual for guidance, etc.

If there has been a large service component repository, service modelers could leave the top-down process of P1 and P2 at any time and shift to the bottom-up P3, i.e., selecting proper SCs that most match with the service models and compose them together to form the service system. In this process, there are two decision-making issues that should be addressed, i.e.,

(DP1) Selection of service architecture styles (SAS)
As there have reached a consensus that there are some similarities between service system and software system, it is possible to use some software design principles and methods for reference in service system design, e.g., firstly dealing with architecture design by considering what (types of) service elements are required and how they are connected together, then carrying out detailed behavioral design for each service element. Here, architecture design is the most important step, where a high-level design solution is achieved by continuous decision-makings on some functional and non-functional dimensions aiming at specific features of ser-vice business.

Until now we have summarized tens of service architecture styles (SAS) already by investigating different service domains, including creational, structural and behavioral styles, e.g., Call-Return, Service Desk, Service Grid, Service Outsourcing, etc, and a comparison has been made to find that different SAS have different non-functional performance to support value delivery (detailed information could be found at [8]). Aiming at the features of a specific service system, an evaluation method is developed to prioritize various SAS to find the best one.

(DP2 & DP3) Selection of service components.
There might exist multiple service components which could provide the same service functionality that contains in specific layer of service models, however there would be difference on their non-functional performance (or, degree of value delivery). During SC selection, the first step is to identify each independent service elements from service models, then select a set of candidate SCs which would provide optimal values for each element (DP2). Because there would be some dependencies between different service components, it is necessary to look for a global optimized solution for the composition of above candidate SCs for

optimization of service value delivery (DP3). General process is shown in Figure 5.

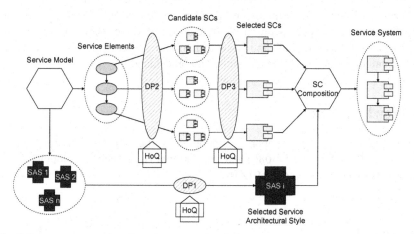

Fig. 5. Bottom-up: reuse-based service system development

During above process, the following matching and selection policies are considered to evaluate and prioritize SCs, i.e.,

- Whether and to which degree could the functionality of a SC satisfy requirements described in service models;
- Whether and to which degree could the non-functional performance (SLA) of a SC satisfy requirements described in service models;
- Whether is a SC usable, e.g., whether it satisfies time constraints, physical environment constraints, or connectivity constraints, etc;
- Whether and to which degree could a SC deliver the values that have been declared in service models;
- Whether and to which degree could multiple candidate SCs match with each other on functionalities, SLA, various constraints and value delivery.

We develop a QFD based decision-making algorithm to support above process. In this algorithm, input of House of Quality (HoQ) is a set of functional, non-functional, value and constraint parameters picked up from service models, and a set of candidate SCs. By specific decision making process, optimal SCs are selected as output of the HoQ.

6. Conclusions

Target users of such value-aware methodologies are large numbers of service providers or service designers. After they have formed some innovative ideas on services, such methodologies would provide them a systematic approach to define and refine such services, until to build an executable service system.

Compared with existing methodologies on service system development, ours help service designers focus on "how to be aware of values (both customers and providers) as far as possible" and "how to improve service system's capability to deliver values to each party right, rapidly and on demand".

Acknowledgments

Research works in this paper is supported by the National Natural Science Foundation (Grant No. 60573086) and the National High-Tech Development Plan Foundation (Grant No. 2006AA01Z167).

References

1. J. Spohrer, P. Maglio, J. Bailey J and D. Gruhl. Steps towards a Science of Service Systems, IEEE Computer, vol. 40(1), pp. 71-77, 2007.
2. H. Cai. A Two Steps Method for Analyzing Dependency of Business Services on IT Services within a Service Life Cycle, Proceedings of International Conference on Web Service, pp. 877-884, 2006.
3. [M. Henkel, E. Perjons, J. Zdravkovic. A Value-based Foundation for Service Modelling, Proceedings of the European Conference on Web Services, pp. 129-137, 2006.
4. H. Akkermans, Z. Baida, J. Gordijn, et al. Value Webs: Using Ontologies to Bundle Real-World Services, IEEE Intelligent Systems, vol. 19(4), pp. 57-66, 2004.
5. C.B. Stabell and Ø.D. Fjellstad. Configuring value for competitive advantage: On chains, shops, and networks, Strategic Management Journal, vol. 19(5), pp. 413-437, 1998.
6. X.F. Xu, Z.J. Wang and T. Mo. An Introduction to Methodology for Service Engineering, Computer Integrated Manufacturing Systems, vol. 13(8), pp. 1457- 1464, 2007.
7. X.F. Xu, T. Mo and Z.J. Wang. SMDA: A Service Model Driven Architecture, Proceedings of the 3rd International Conference on Interoperability for Enterprise Software and Applications, pp. 291-302, 2007.
8. Z.J. Wang, X.F. Xu and T. Mo. Service Architecture: High Level Descriptions of Service System, Journal of Harbin Institute of Technology (New Series), vol. 15(Sup.1), pp. 7-12, 2008.
9. S. Liu, X.F. Xu and Z.J. Wang. SQFD: QFD based Service Quality Assurance for the Lifecycle of Services, Proceedings of the Fourth International Conference on Interoperability for Enterprise Software and Applications, 2008.

Strategic Modelling of Enterprise Information Requirements

A normative model of information domains and information types

Gianmario Motta, Giovanni Pignatelli

Department of Informatics and Systems, University of Pavia, Pavia, Italy

gianmario.motta@unipv.it , giovamni.pignatelli@unipv.it

Abstract: We illustrate a model to define information requirements for the whole Enterprise. The key novelty is that the model is a normative one. Actually it assists the analyst in defining the contents data bases should have. The approach is founded on some key ideas. First, an enterprise processes information on domain families, that include stakeholders, products, process and contexts. By specializing these domain families the analyst identifies domains specific to an individual enterprise. Second, information of a given domain includes different information types, namely master information, that defines structural properties, transaction information, performance / analytical indicators. By crossing information domains and information types the analyst identifies normative entities, that can be used to assess effectiveness and coverage of actual data bases and other IT strategy issues and, of course, to design a top-down design of the data base. The model develops and generalizes the Aggregate Business Entity incorporated the e-TOM framework, a reference model developed for telecommunications, and it has been tested in a pilot project in health care.

1 Introduction

Defining information domains for an enterprise is an issue from the heydays of Information Technology and it implies questions as "are we processing the information we should?", "which is the coverage of our data bases?", "are we buying software that fits our information needs?"... Of course, these issues are critical for the quality of the IT strategic plan.

To deal with such issues in a very simplistic way, an enterprise can look on data schemas of its computerized databases. This can be practical but never will realize the gap between what the enterprise should have and what actually has. Furthermore, distilling into a compact strategic design hundreds of relations of actual databases can result into a hard if not useless task.

Please use the following format when citing this chapter:

Motta, G. and Pignatelli, G., 2008, in IFIP International Federation for Information Processing, Volume 280; *E-Government; ICT Professionalism and Competences; Service Science*; Antonino Mazzeo, Roberto Bellini, Gianmario Motta; (Boston: Springer), pp. 287–297.

The need of a structured top-down approach to identify high level information requirements emerged already in Seventies, with first really large information systems. A champion of this early methods is Business Systems Planning (BSP), very popular in Eighties. BSP [5] associates data classes and processes in a grid, that shows which data are used by which process. BSP is a robust, structured, comprehensive but time consuming methodology, and, specifically, it does not indicate the information classes a system should process. Nor the subsequent champion, Information Strategy Planning (ISP) in the comprehensive Information Engineering framework [9], that integrates different information models, such as BSP, Entity Relationships and Data Flow Diagrams (DFD), gave a normative framework. The flood of methods started in the early days [2] but it still continues. However, all of them only structure information requirements. To define "what information do we need?" you depend on interviews and on a costly process you cannot always afford.

In recent times, normative industry models are emerging. Some model provides reference frameworks of business processes, as SCOR (Supply Chain Organization and Reference Model) that has been developed for the manufacturing industry [1, 13]. In telecommunications industry, the Shared Information Data Model (SID) of eTOM (Enhanced Telecom Operations Map®) proposes a normative framework for shared information / data. SID uses, based on the concepts of Business Entities and Attributes [14, 15]. A Business Entity is a thing of interest to the business, while Attributes are facts that describe the entity. SID is a real normative model but it lacks universality, since it is solely oriented on telecommunications, and it does not provide an axiomatic approach to identify Entities.

Also some management theories have addressed the issue of information needs for management. In the Nineties and in New Century, Balanced Score Card (BSC) [7, 8] and 6Sigma [4] had a great success not only as models for overall strategic and management control but also as frameworks for identifying management information needs. Actually BSC proposes a list of indicators for strategic control, that includes data on various domains (financial performance, performance of internal processes, performance on learning and growth). However, these models are normative but not universal, since they consider management and not the operational aspects.

To summarize the positions of the existing approaches we have used three axes (Figure 1). The axis of generality represents the universality of an approach in front of industries: the wider the range the higher the universality. The axis of normative capacity measures the ability to suggest the "right" information requirements. The axis of completeness of domains represents the capacity of considering all information uses, namely management, analytic, operational. Different approaches excel on different axis, but no one of them offers a comprehensive coverage. BSP is universal but it is not normative at all. BSC is general and normative but not complete. Finally, SID is normative, but not general nor complete.

Our purpose is a normative model that fills the three axes of normative capacity, generality and completeness. With such model, the analyst will get a list of the potential contents of the data base of the enterprise, that can be further validated and expanded.

Of course, our analysis considers aggregated information requirements. The output of the analysis are schemas of aggregated information. However, these schemas nay be a first deliverable of a top down design process or be used in IT strategic planning to assess the coverage of information needs by existing databases or the impact of business and technological discontinuities on information domains.

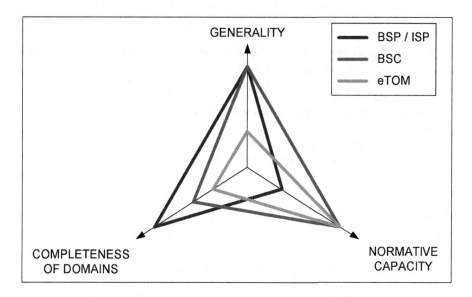

Fig. 1. Comparison of frameworks for enterprise information analysis

2. The information catalogue

"An Aggregate Business Entity (ABE) is a well-defined set of information and operations that characterize a highly cohesive, loosely coupled set of business entities" [14]. However, the key point is to identify are candidate ABEs of enterprises. As we have said at the very beginning of our paper, the catalogue of candidate ABEs result from crossing two main categories, information domains and information types.

2.1 Information domains

The concept of information domain is already used in the SID model. We assume an enterprise process information on the domains where it operates. Our first level is nothing else but a generalization of the SID semantics and it includes stakeholders, resources, context, output. Let us consider each of these domain.

Our vision of stakeholders reflect Freeman's concept [3], where "a stakeholder in an organization is (by definition) any group or individual who can affect or is affected by the achievement of the organization's objectives". In our catalogue stakeholders include Law, Competitor, Customer, Supplier, Broker, Shareholder. In short, stakeholders are the who's of the enterprise.

The domain of output reflect the operations of the enterprise and include Process, Product and Service information.

Resource domains reflect classic economics and includes Personnel (= Human Resources), Plants and equipments (= Technological Assets), Materials, Cash (= Monetary Resources). In short, resources are input used by enterprise to produce its outputs.

Finally, the domains of context reflect the environment where the enterprise operate and include and its structure and include Structure, Project, Region.

2.2 Information types

From countless years, analysts classify information in database in three classes, namely master data, transactions data, analytical / calculated data. This intuitive taxonomy is very valuable when generalized.

Master Data represents structural entity properties and are typically "strong entities". Transaction Data describe the properties of events a given strong entity is generating or receiving, as orders, state changes and alike, and are typically weak entities. Finally Analysis Data are indicators that are calculated from Transaction and Master data, and provide information for management and governance e.g. profitability of a plant, a customer or quality of a supplier.

2.3 The structure of the catalogue of ABEs

The result of the combination of information types and information domain is a grid that contains the ABEs of "level zero" (Table 1). Each cell represents an ABE that could be seen as a couple (D,E) where D is the domain and E is the information type.

Table 1. The first level of Aggregated Business Entities

			INFORMATION TYPE		
			Master Data	Transaction Data	Analysis Data
INFORMSTION DOMAIN	Stakeholders	Law	LAM	LAT	LAA
		Competitor	COM	COT	COA
		Customer	CUM	CUT	CUA
		Supplier	SUM	SUT	SUA
		Broker	BRM	BRT	BRA
		Shareholder	SHM	SHT	SHA
	Resources	Personnel	PEM	PET	PEA
		Plants	PLM	PLT	PLA
		Raw materials	RAM	RAT	RAA
		Cash	CAM	CAT	CAA
	Context	Structure	STM	STT	STA
		Project	PJM	PJT	PJA
		Region	REM	RET	REA
	Output	Process	PRM	PRT	PRA
		Product	PDM	PDT	PDA
		Service	SEM	SET	SEA

2.4 Customization, refinement and validation of the catalogue of ABEs

The simple grid is of course useless. To get real data the analyst customizes ABEs that are specific to the individual enterprise within the analysis scope. An example of such customization is Table 2 where the aggregate domain "customer" is specialized in the sub-domains "private" and "enterprise". Similarly, master data are specialized into "Identification and "Social" and the same happens with Transaction data.

In short the customization is obtained by well known primitives of Creation, Specialization, Decomposition used on aggregate information domains and information types. Actually, the customization is iterative, with refinement and validation sessions with key business representatives. In this process, the analyst will also identify attributes, e.g. key and attributes of customer identification information.

Of course the information requirements can be also expressed by using standard ER notation. In this case, you can track the process of specialization and decomposition, but you loose the double dimension of information types and domains.

Table 2. An example of specialization of "Customer"

		INFORMATION TYPES				
		Master Data		Transaction Data		Analysis Data
		Identification	Social	Man-Machine transaction	Machine-Machine transaction	
Customer	Private					
	Enterprise					

3 Aggregated Entities and IT Strategic Planning

The main use of strategic information requirements is in IT strategic planning. An IT strategic plan will summarize (a) the architecture of applications, data and infrastructure and (b) assess the impact of technology and business discontinuities [10, 11].

The architecture of data is obtained by customizing the general catalogue of ABEs. Also, by crossing the catalogue and the actual database the analyst can assess the current information support.

In a similar way, the analyst can do some form of sensitivity analysis of technology and business discontinuities. Technology discontinuities, e.g. Service Oriented Architecture, may impact on a wide span of elements of the enterprise architecture. Business discontinuities are strategic business moves of the enterprise, e.g. the convergence between telecom and media business, or change of the whole business, e.g. the switch from analogical to digital TV.

3. 1 Assessment of information support

To assess to what extent ABEs are supported and / or used, ABEs are crossed with business processes, organizational structures, IT applications and IT architecture. The grids describe relations G information classes I to information users U (business processes, organizational structures, IT applications and IT architectural elements): $G = \{U,I,A\}$.

The ABE meta-model (Figure 2) may be used to assess both as-is and to-be scenarios from a variety of perspectives:

1. Information and Databases grid: assesses the databases coverage by qualitative metrics

2. Information and Application grid: assesses the use of information by applications in terms of information lifecycle and/or qualitative metrics

3. Information and Organizational structure grid: it identifies information ownership;

4. Information and processing levels: it identifies how information is distributed on and used by the processing architecture (client, server, mobile devices)

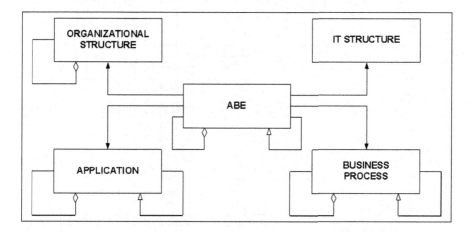

Fig. 2. Relationships between Aggregated Business Entities and other ABE Relations of IT Strategic Planning

In Table 3 the coverage given by actual databases (Laboratory, Financial, Reservation) of a healthcare institution is assessed. The coverage looks poor and no integrated of patient and service data are possible. Of course assessment metrics is qualitative and reflects a joint evaluation by analysts and user, but, management know where gaps are.

Table 3. Assessment of ABE coverage (absent, poor, average and good) in a generic Healthcare Institution by using qualitative evaluation scale (**M** = Master information; **T** = Transaction Information; **I** = Indicators information)

					LAB			FINANCIAL			RESERV		
					Completeness	Correctness	Timeliness	Completeness	Correctness	Timeliness	Completeness	Correctness	Timeliness
Regulation		M	Regulation ID	Privacy Laws Healthcare regulations				■	■	■			
		T	Certification Events	List of Certifications				■	▨	▨			
		I	Certification KPIs	Certification levels				▨	▨	▨			
Customer	*Emergency*	M	ID	Master data	▨	▨							
			Properties	Patient Record	■	■					■		
		T	Emergency events	Reception	■	■							
				Prescriptions	■	■							
				Treatments	■	■							
				Other	■								
			Release	Referral & payments	■	■							
		I	Process KPIs	Quality - Service - Cost	■	■							
	Hospital	M	ID	Master data	▨	▨					▨		
			Properties	Patient Record	■								
			Care process events	Reservation	▨	□							
				Check-in	▨	■							
				Prescriptions	■	▨							
				Treatments	■	■							
				Patient management	■	■							
			Release	Referral & payments	■	■							
		I	Process KPIs	Quality - Service - Cost	■	■							
Commis-sioner	*authorities Healthcare*	M	ID	Master Data				■	▨				
			Properties	Financial data				■	■				
		T	Events	Advance payments				■	■	■			
				Reimbursements				■	■	■			
		I	Process KPIs	Quality - Service - Cost				▨	▨	▨			
	Medical Technical &	M	ID	Master data	▨			■					
			Properties	Job data	■	▨		■	▨				
				Skill and education	■			■					
		T	Events	Presences & Payroll				■					
				Career				■	▨				
			Certifications	Skill certificates				▨	■				
		I	KPIS	Performance & potential				■	■	■			

3.2 Sensitivity Analysis

Sensitivity analysis identifies information domains impacted by strategic discontinuities, e.g.:

1. Business Discontinuity: the impact of enterprise strategies e.g. mergers, acquisitions, new products, new services is assessed (which ABEs will be affected and how much?)

2. Technology Discontinuity: the impact of technology changes on information is considered (which ABEs will be affected by emerging technologies e.g. Service Oriented Architecture and how much?)

3. Normative Discontinuity: the impact of regulations e.g. privacy, security etc. is identified and possibly described (which ABEs will be affected by privacy restrictions etc?)

3. 3 Position of the ABE method in Zachman's Framework

The method as described here has a rather good coverage in the Zachman's framework [6], a popular reference to position what really a method does (Table 4).

Table 4. Coverage of the ABE method in Zachman's Framework

Layer	What (Data)	How (Function)	Where (Network)	Who (People)	When (Time)	Why (Motivation)
Scope (Contextual) Planner	List of things important to the business	List of processes the business performs	List of locations in which the business operates	List of organizations important to the business	List of events significant to the business	List of business goals/strategies
Business Model (Conceptual) Owner	Semantic or ER Model	Business Process Model	Business Logistics System	Work Flow Model	Master Schedule	Business Plan
System Model (Logical) Designer	Logical Data Model	Application Architecture	Distributed System Architecture	Human Interface Architecture	Processing Structure	Business Rule Model

Layer	What (Data)	How (Function)	Where (Network)	Who (People)	When (Time)	Why (Motivation)
Technology Model (Physical) Builder	Physical Data Model	System Design	Technology Architecture	Presentation Architecture	Control Structure	Rule Design
Component Configuration Implementer	Data Definition	Program	Network Architecture	Architecture	Timing Definition	Rule Specification
Functioning Enterprise Worker	Data	Function	Network	Organization	Schedule	Strategy

4. Conclusions

We have illustrated a strategic information model, based on a normative framework with numerous advantages:

1. It assists the analyst in identifying "right" information requirements

2. It is cross-industry and can be specialized as needed

3. It is strategic and it can stop at the detail levels defined by the planning process, by zooming critical areas and summarizing non critical ones

4. It easy to understand for management and supports a what-if analysis of business strategic alternatives

5. It can be linked to detailed information requirements analysis.

The framework has been partially used in a strategic planning of a very large telecom corporation and has been successfully tested in healthcare to identify the information strategy. On going work includes the development of a web application to customize the overall catalogue and of a knowledge base where the analyst can find and modify predefined information models.

References

1. Bolstorff P., Rosenbaum R., 2007, Supply Chain Excellence: A Handbook for Dramatic Improvement Using the SCOR Model, 2nd edition, AMACOM, New York

2. Colter, M.A. 1984, A comparative analysis of systems analysis techniques, MIS Quarterly, Vol. 8, N.1, March

3. Freeman R.E., 1984, Strategic management: A stakeholder approach , Pitman (Boston)

4. Gupta, P., 2006, Six Sigma Business Card, McGraw Hill, New York

5. IBM, 1975, Business Systems Planning, GE 20-0257-1

6. Inmon W.H., Zachman J.A., Geiger J.G., 1997 Data Stores, Data Warehousing, and the Zachman Framework: Managing Enterprise Knowledge, Mcgraw-Hill, New York

7. Kaplan R. S., Norton D. P., 1996, The Balanced Scorecard: Translating Strategy into Action, Harvard Business School Press, Boston;

8. Kaplan R. S., Norton D. P., 2006, Alignment: Using the Balanced Scorecard to Create Corporate Synergies Harvard Business School Press, Boston

9. Martin J., 1990, Information engineering, Prentice Hall, New York

10.Motta G., Roveri P., 2007, Best practices for the innovative Chief Information Officer, ITAis

11.Nolan R.L., McFarlan W.F., 2005 Information Technology and the Board of Directors, Harvard Business Review, October 2005

12.Scheer, W. 2000 ARIS – Business Process Modelling, 3d edition, Springer, Berlin

13.SCOR, 2001, Supply Chain Operations Reference Model version 5.0, www.supply-chain.org

14.TMForum, 2003, Shared Information/Data(SID) Model - Concepts, Principles, and Domains- GB922, July 2003

15.TMForum, 2005, Enhanced Telecom Operations Map (eTOM), The Business Process Framework – GB921, November.

ICT Portfolio: Mapping Business and ICT Services

Giovanni Pignatelli[1], Gianmario Motta[1], Giovanni Umberto Germani[2]

[1] Department of Computer Engineering and Systems Science, University of Pavia, Italy
gianmario.motta@unipv.it, giovanni.pignatelli@unipv.it

[2] Business Integration Partners, Milan, Italy
giovanni.germani@mail-bip.com

Abstract: This paper presents a research project of University of Pavia that has been implemented by Business Integration Partners (BIP). The project concerns a Knowledge Base on Business and IT Processes. The Knowledge Base maps Business and related IT Processes and stores knowledge structures in different forms, such as diagrams, text, multimedia. The analyst can navigate stored information and create new processes by using a design methodology, that includes the definition of process structure, the association of performances to process structures and the design of a individual process performances by using inheritance methods. The Knowledge Base was successfully implemented in a large telecommunication organization.

1. Introduction

The portfolio of IT applications of a typical large organization can account hundreds of titles. Additionally, individual Business Process uses multiple applications – e.g. mortgage delivery process uses front end applications, credit check and credit delivery applications. Furthermore, organizations operate hundreds of Business Processes. Most Business Processes are service chains that cross multiple functions in one organization or several organizations [1] [2]. Finally service organizations offer hundreds of services to their customers and, last not least, other hundreds of services to their internal employees - such as information. In short, current organizations have an intensive and extensive use of Information Technology (IT). The knowledge on IT application portfolio, Business Processes, information technology map and their relations is, therefore, a key element for an informed and effective innovation.

Please use the following format when citing this chapter:

Pignatelli, G., Motta, G. and Germani, G.U., 2008, in IFIP International Federation for Information Processing, Volume 280; *E-Government; ICT Professionalism and Competences; Service Science;* Antonino Mazzeo, Roberto Bellini, Gianmario Motta; (Boston: Springer), pp. 299–307.

2. From Business Process Knowledge to ICT Management

Our project moves from an initial research that led University of Pavia to design a Knowledge Base on Business Process. Our ancestors are Business Processes Reference Models such as MIT Process Handbook [3] that defines a universal taxonomy (including SCOR model) and uses Software Engineering principles (aggregation, specialization and reuse).

Other frameworks propose a structured approach to information strategy, such as the Shared Information Data (SID) Model [4] that is included in eTOM framework [5]. The model is based on the concepts of Business Entities (a generic logic entity of interest for the business) and Attributes (facts that describe the logic entities).

From an extension and generalization of the SID method, we have developed a more general framework called Aggregated Business Entity (ABE) [6], which models relationships between Business Processes and IT Application/Structures with the aim of correlate the application portfolio (ERP, CRM, BI etc.) with processes and their structure in order to evaluate the distribution of the information on the technological infrastructures.

ABE and the work on the Business Process Knowledge Base provide the foundations of the ICT Governance model we discuss here. The model considers and links three logical levels:

1. *Service*, i.e. the end-to-end service provided to the customer (for instance order fulfilment)
2. *Business Process*, i.e. the company activities performed by the organizational functions to supply the service.
3. *IT Process*, i.e. the activities performed by the IT Systems to support Business Processes.

Each level is described by two kinds of elements, namely the structure of the elements that make the layers and their respective performance measures. We here focus on the structural elements, particularly Business Processes (Business Processes mapping) and IT Processes (analysis of the Company's IT Architecture), as shown in figure 1.

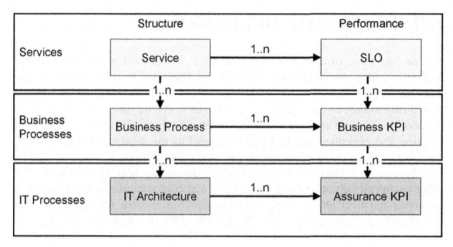

Fig. 1. The proposed framework

Elements of the models are in a many to many relations. A service supply involves a collection of Business Processes and Business Process uses many IT Architecture   elements.

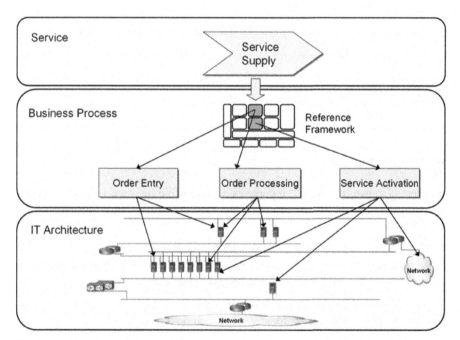

Fig. 2. Relations between the elements of the model

3. The Meta-Model of the ICT Knowledge Base

The starting point of the meta-model of the ICT Knowledge Base is a simple framework that associates the concepts of Business Process, Systems and Infrastructure.

A Business Process is a sequence of activities. As we have seen, a Business Process involves one or more Systems. On the other hand, the self-relationship of Business Process entity indicates that Business Process structure is alike a bill of materials, with decomposition and specialization relationships.

A System is a platform, functionally and technologically homogenous, that relies on Infrastructures, namely processing and communications resources such as servers and other physical devices. Of course, Systems are grouped in Clusters (for example a Cluster can group the Systems used for Business Intelligence).

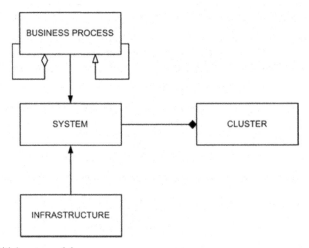

Fig. 3. The initial meta-model

A schema (shown in figure 3) represents a relationship between Business Process and Systems that shows the usage of the Systems in corporate processes. This usage can be:

1. A System performs a Functionality within a Business Process.
2. A System exchanges information flows. Such Macro-flow is described by a source System, a target System and an exchanged entity.

These entities represent aggregation of data at a logic level with variable granularity (i.e. "Customer Master Data" and "Order Code" can be both considered logical entities).

The concept of Macro-flow allows information tracking within the ICT Systems without complications, but may result too aggregated for users who want a higher detail (developers are interested in the detailed flows). Therefore we use other additional meta-entities, such as Detailed Flows and Sequence Diagram.

Finally, we have introduced the meta-entity "Initiative", that represents projects affecting IT Architecture (i.e. creation of new information flows, development of new Systems) or involving a new Business Process. An Initiative is described by a set of Requirements. By the framework we intend to map the impact of these Requirements on the Business Process or IT Architecture. In short the knowledge base allows to visualize:

- the coverage of an individual Requirement
- all data of a new System under development
- new Macro-flows and related Detailed Flows
- new Business Processes affected by an Initiative

The overall meta-model is shown in figure 4.

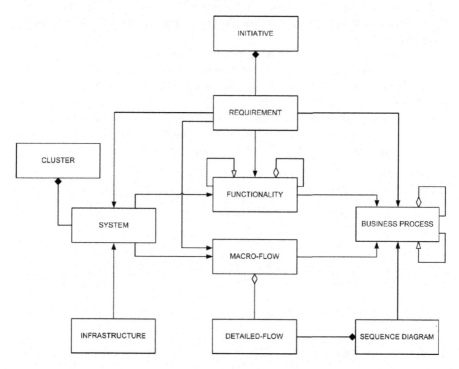

Fig. 4. The overall meta-model

4. The Model in the Real World: a Case Study

ADSL is a telecommunications company that delivers a wide range of services, such as wireline and wireless, internet and television. As it happens in telecommunication industry, ICT is playing a critical role in product innovation and overall competitiveness. No new product is feasible without IT support and, moreover, a new product implies a new Business Process. Therefore the equation *new service = new business process = new IT process* is dramatically actual; foreseeing and evaluating the impact of new or modified Requirements is not a wishful thinking but a survival need.

Phase 1 – Design and Implementation
The project was intended to design a governance map and was carried on with the cooperation of Business Integration Partners. The first step was to gather architectural information (Systems, Infrastructures, Flows and Functionalities). The subsequent step mapped Business Processes and particularly the role of IT Architecture.

The implementation of the knowledge base has followed these steps:

The first step defined the perimeter of Architecture and information relevant for the classes of users. We also decided to use the eTOM framework, since it is a reference model in TELCO.

The subsequent step was dedicated to interviews, where we collected the information for the construction of the Functional Framework, obtained from the standard eTOM model and shown in Figure 5.

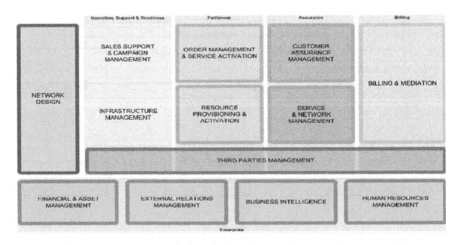

Fig. 5. Functional Framework of ADSL case study

Each Cluster was detailed by mapping the Functionalities of the company IT Architecture. The Functionalities were structured in a three levels grid, following the subdivision proposed in the eTOM framework. Level 1 and 2 Functionalities are the same as in the standard framework, while Level 3 has been added or modified to reflect the specific context of ADSL. Thanks to data collected, we determined the features of Level 3 provided by individual Systems, and completed the Application Framework (figure 6).

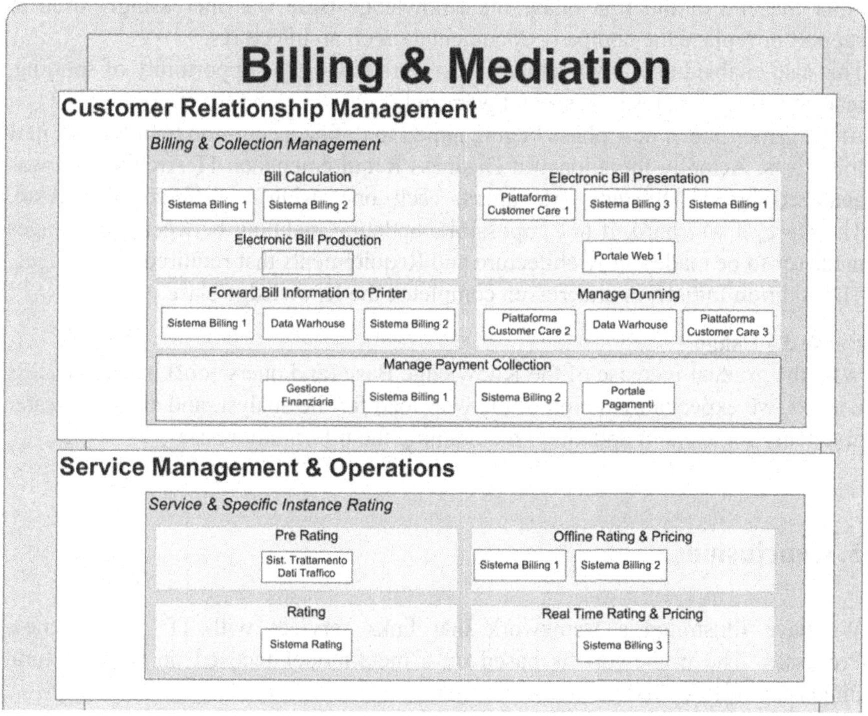

Fig. 6. Example of Billing Area Application Framework

From an analysis of the Application Framework, you can have a first idea on the role played by IT Systems in Business Processes. The remaining information on Business Processes were taken from company documents (e.g. feasibility analysis) The data on Systems and Infrastructure, the Functionalities provided and the main logical Macro-flows were validated by the leaders of the Systems and incorporated in the database. At this point we had to deal with some new issues:

- Leaders of IT Systems and managers of Infrastructure technology use different taxonomies. Different names are part of corporate culture, and a common standard didn't look feasible. It was therefore agreed to have two entries in the Knowledge Base.
- Interviewees gave a different interpretation of "Functionality" and logical "Macro-flow". Therefore we reworked the data obtained by the leaders of Systems before populating the Knowledge Base.

- Process Owner did not exist for some core processes and in these cases gathering information on Business Processes was rather hardier.
- Documentation was often incomplete and not updated.

Phase 2 – Information Refinement and Updating
After the end of the first phase the Knowledge Base was increasingly used to support or replace the company documentation on architectures.
This also enabled user involvement, who were having the opportunity of spotting, inaccuracies / outdates by a special web-tool.
At the same time, a new phase begun, aimed to define a common template for new Initiatives. Actually the impact of Business Requirements on IT Architecture was analyzed by the Systems Managers, each one using a different formalism. Therefore, it was hard, if not impossible, updating mapping between the changes made (or to be made) on Architecture and Requirements that required the changes. The addition Initiatives undertaken completed the Knowledge Base.

Phase 3 - Usage
With the gradual increase of the Knowledge Base (and query tool) in the business context, we expect a reduction of the workload for the analyst, and an ever greater autonomy for users in updating / maintaining the information base.

5. Conclusions

We have illustrated a framework that links services with IT and Business Processes. The framework is based on a meta-model focused on the structural dimension of ICT, that includes:

- IT Systems;
- Functional Framework and Application Framework;
- Business Processes.

The use in a real company (ADSL) has been a success. The project has not only validated the concepts but also developed a tool for the navigation of the models. Without a structured Knowledge Base:

- a structured control over the development of the ICT Systems is almost impossible;
- allocating investments is very hard since it is almost impossible to visualize easily the different coverage of services.

With the Architecture mapped, it is easy to assess the impact of the Requirements of projects on the Architecture itself; furthermore, with the analysis of the Application Framework, you can highlight the Business Processes not adequately supported, and hence where to invest.

References

1. Maglio P, Spohrer J (2005) Emergence of Service Science: Services Sciences, Management, Engineering as the Next Frontier in Innovation. Presentation at IBM Almaden Research Center.
2. Maglio P et al (2006) Service Systems, Service Scientists, SSME, and Innovation. Service Science. doi: 10.1145/1139922.1139955
3. Malone T W et al (1999) Tools for Inventing Organizations: Toward a Handbook of Organizational Processes. Management Science 45:425-443
4. TeleManagement Forum (2005) Shared Information/Data (SID) Model. Concepts, Principles, and Domains. NGOSS Release 6.0, GB922
5. TeleManagement Forum (2005) Enhanced Telecom Operation Model (eTOM) The Business Process Framework for the Information and Communication Service Industry. NGOSS Release 6.0, GB921
6. Motta G, Pignatelli G (2008) Strategic Modelling of Enterprise Information Requirements. Paper accepted to ICEIS 2008